Becoming Babasaheb

Celebrating
30 Years of Publishing
in India

Praise for *Becoming Babasaheb*

'Rathore's earlier books had shed new light on Dr Ambedkar's source materials for his innovative interpretation of Buddhism, as well as his previously unknown direct authorship of the Preamble to the Indian Constitution. In *Becoming Babasaheb*, Rathore once again uncovers totally new facts about Babasaheb's extraordinary life and times.'
— Prakash Ambedkar, lawyer, president of the Vanchit Bahujan Aaghadi party and grandson of Dr B.R. Ambedkar

'Rathore's first volume is a meticulously researched account of Ambedkar's early life as a student in Bombay, New York and London, his struggles against poverty and caste discrimination, and his emergence as a scholar, barrister and leader of the Dalits. Rathore's signal achievement is to present Ambedkar in flesh and blood, and not allow his admiration for the man to slip into hagiography.'
— Partha Chatterjee, Professor Emeritus of anthropology, Columbia University

'Aakash Singh Rathore's biography is outstanding for the way in which he interweaves the personal and the political to reveal the making of one of India's greatest leaders. He, thus, gives the reader a far richer and more vivid understanding of the man and the events that unfolded around him. By his rigorous checking of sources and aligning of chronologies, Rathore also clears up many prevalent misconceptions. His book is essential reading for anyone seeking to understand some of the central developments of the twentieth century that shaped India as it has come to exist today.'
— Tony Joseph, journalist and author of *Early Indians: The Story of Our Ancestors and Where We Came From*

'Scholarly biographies based on archival sources are rare in India. Rathore's first of a two-volume account of Dr Ambedkar's life is a

notable exception. He deserves huge appreciation for this endeavour, which sheds fascinating new light on arguably the most highly educated and intellectually gifted of our founding fathers' generation.'
— Jairam Ramesh, member of Parliament (Rajya Sabha), and author of *The Light of Asia: The Poem That Defined the Buddha*

'*Becoming Babasaheb* is essential reading for anyone interested in joining the global movement for caste abolition. Accessible and finely researched, it humanizes Dr Ambedkar while providing new detail to the incredible hurdles he faced as he worked tirelessly to end caste. The empathy of Aakash Singh Rathore's biography is unparalleled and enriches our understanding of Ambedkar as a giant of history—but also as a very human leader, who became larger than life through his courage, brilliance, integrity and persistence. It is credit to Rathore that he holds all of the complex strands of Ambedkar's intellectual and political life so deftly that the book can offer new insights for both the expert and the new reader of Ambedkar's legacy alike. Buy *Becoming Babasaheb* for yourself and for a young person you care about, for it introduces Ambedkar to a new generation at a time when his lessons are more important than ever.'
— Thenmozhi Soundararajan, executive director of Equality Labs, and author of *The Trauma of Caste: A Dalit Feminist Meditation on Survivorship, Healing, and Abolition*

'Rooted in extensive archival research, *Becoming Babasaheb* follows Ambedkar's personal and intellectual development on his path to becoming one of India's greatest statesmen. In clear and wonderfully descriptive writing, Aakash Singh Rathore's first volume brings Ambedkar—the subjugated village child, the brilliant student, the rising leader—to life.'
— Shashi Tharoor, member of Parliament for Thiruvananthapuram (Lok Sabha) and author of *Ambedkar: A Life*

Becoming Babasaheb

*The Life and Times of
Bhimrao Ramji Ambedkar
Volume 1: Birth to Mahad
(1891–1929)*

Aakash Singh Rathore

HarperCollins *Publishers* India

First published in India by HarperCollins *Publishers* in 2023
4th Floor, Tower A, Building No. 10, DLF Cyber City,
DLF Phase II, Gurugram, Haryana – 122002
www.harpercollins.co.in

2 4 6 8 10 9 7 5 3 1

Copyright © Aakash Singh Rathore 2023

P-ISBN: 978-93-5699-121-7
E-ISBN: 978-93-5699-122-4

The views and opinions expressed in this book are the author's own and the facts are as reported by him, and the publishers are not in any way liable for the same.

Aakash Singh Rathore asserts the moral right
to be identified as the author of this work.

All rights reserved. No part of this publication may be reproduced, stored in a retrieval system, or transmitted, in any form or by any means, electronic, mechanical, photocopying, recording or otherwise, without the prior permission of the publishers.

Typeset in 11.5/15.5 Bembo Std at
Manipal Technologies Limited, Manipal

Printed and bound at
Replika Press Pvt. Ltd.

This book is produced from independently certified FSC® paper to ensure responsible forest management.

For the Khobragades

Contents

Preface	*There Will Be Blood*	xi
Chapter One	From Bhiva Ambadawekar to Bhimrao Ambedkar (1891–1912)	1
Chapter Two	The Alma Mater (1913–16)	10
Chapter Three	An Indian in New York	22
Chapter Four	London Calling (1916–17)	32
Chapter Five	Sleepless in Baroda (1917–20)	41
Chapter Six	Struggle, Sydenham, Southborough and Shahu Maharaj	49
Chapter Seven	A Loud Voice for the Voiceless (1920)	59
Chapter Eight	Lunchless in London (1920–22)	69
Chapter Nine	Mr Ambedkar, to Ambedkar Bar-at-Law, to Dr Ambedkar (1922–23)	81
Chapter Ten	A Barrister in Bombay (1924–26)	92

Chapter Eleven	'Educate, Agitate, Organize'	107
Chapter Twelve	From Bhima Koregaon to the Mahad Conference (1927)	117
Chapter Thirteen	From Doctorsaheb to Babasaheb	131
Chapter Fourteen	Mahad Reloaded: The Satyagraha	147
Chapter Fifteen	Between Mahad and the Round Table Conference (1928–29)	162
Bibliography		183
Appendix 1:	*Table of Contents of* Dr Bhimrao Ramji Ambedkar Charitra *(in twelve volumes) by Changdev Bhavanrao Khairmoday*	195
Appendix 2:	*The Resolutions of the Mahad Conference (20 March 1927)*	203
Appendix 3:	*First editorial by Dr Ambedkar for* Bahishkrut Bharat *(3 April 1927)*	207
Appendix 4:	*Final Order of the Bombay High Court Re: Mahad Tank (17 March 1937)*	213
Notes		229
Index		261

Preface
There Will Be Blood

Primrose Hill in northernish London is pretty bougie now, but with the railway line that has run through it for nearly two centuries—its tracks crossing the back garden of 10 King Henry's Road, aka the Ambedkar House Museum, London—in the early 1920s, when young Ambedkar lived there, the neighbourhood would have been chronically caked in soot from the black smoke and dirt pouring out of every passing steam locomotive. Ambedkar's small, square-shaped single room was at the back of the house, grimly overlooking the railway tracks through a solitary window. The walk from that small bedroom down to the massive and ornate reading room of the British Museum and Library would have taken him around fifty minutes on a fair day. I have myself plodded it several times.

What is now the French consulate, at 21 Cromwell Road, just south of London's Hyde Park, used to lodge the National Indian Association as well as the Northbrook Indian Society. It also lodged a very young Ambedkar in 1916. It is about an hour's walk from there to Gray's Inn, where Ambedkar sat in on law classes for passing the bar exam, and only forty-five minutes to the London School of Economics' Passmore Edwards Hall on Clare Market, where he had enrolled for his second master's degree in economics. I've ambled through these routes too.

Whether it's the King's Crown Hotel on West 116th Street in New York, an old brownstone at 554 West 114th Street in New York, or 95 Brook Green in Hammersmith, London; whether it's rooms 50 and 51 of the Number 1 BIT Chawl in Parel, Damodar Hall in Parel, or Rajgruha in Dadar, Mumbai; whether it's 26 Alipur Road in Delhi; Gaekwad Wada (now known as Kesari Wada) in Narayan Peth, Pune; or the site of the old Dak Bungalow in Mahad—I have spent time at every known address where Ambedkar may have experienced a moment of personal significance, trying to recreate it in my mind, imagining how it all must have played out, trying to feel it somehow.

This technique has served me well in a decade-long effort at capturing something of his clearly manifest yet elusive personality. This personality—complex, charismatic, kind, conflicted—has never really seemed to me to come through at all in any biography of Ambedkar that I have read. Many of them are lifeless lives. After all the time that I have spent attempting to walk in Ambedkar's footsteps, I am hopeful that his pulse will reverberate in this one.

When I speak to anyone who knows anything about the life of Dr Ambedkar, the first thing that they want to know from me is how my biography will be different from those that have come earlier—and there have been quite a few. I have given a variety of replies, but my answer really boils down to two main things. The first is what I have just mentioned, that I have sought to foreground Ambedkar as an individual, rather than produce a bloodless political or intellectual biography; and the second is that I have sought to be more consistent with historical accuracy than the other biographies now available.

The former point being less audacious, I'll expand a bit more upon it first.

What really intrigues me about Dr Ambedkar, perhaps even more than his historic accomplishments, is his personality—more accurately, how elusive it has been for biographers. Because he meant so many different things to so many different people, it is genuinely difficult to try to make objective sense of what he was really like. This difficulty is compounded by the fact that Ambedkar was actually a complex, multidimensional person.

In this book, I have sought to capture something of Ambedkar as a person—his personality, especially in how this helps us understand how Ambedkar became Ambedkar. This is not an intellectual biography that delves into his vast output, summarizing and analysing his books and speeches, as several biographers—especially Dalit intellectuals—have previously done, and have often done well. Nor is this merely a political biography, with a set focus on chronicling the rise of this towering statesman as he negotiated the politics of his era—which is what the anglophone biographies (and non-Indian biographers) have tended to do, and have also often done well. A full-length, personality-driven narrative has not yet been attempted by anyone.[1] I do not just want to recount what Ambedkar did—I am trying to understand who he was as he was doing all of it.

This is the opposite of Shashi Tharoor's approach in his recent biography, *Ambedkar: A Life*. He states at the outset,

> The biography of a man who is principally noted for his words rather than his actions inevitably suffers from a deficiency of incidents and a surfeit of ideas. There is undoubtedly drama and suffering in Ambedkar's life, *but far more consequential* is the weight of his writings, speeches, and interventions in the public debates of his time. In opting to reflect this reality, the biographer is obliged to acknowledge that this sometimes makes for a curiously bloodless tale.[2]

We don't want to follow that formula. It is the same as has been done so often in the past by all of the anglophone biographers (Eleanor Zelliot, Christophe Jaffrelot, Gail Omvedt and so on). So no more lifeless lives of Dr Ambedkar. In the pages that follow, there will be blood.

Quite in contrast to the 'bloodless' narrative of anglophone biographers, Dr Ambedkar's widow, Savita Ambedkar, in her own autobiography had focused almost exclusively on Ambedkar as a man, a husband and a person. Her book, we might say by reversing Shashi Tharoor's expression, suffers from a surfeit of incidents and a deficiency of ideas. But importantly, she made a point that should here be noted:

> Dr Ambedkar possessed an impressive personality. His grand forehead, his bright, piercing eyes, his sharp look, his ultra-modern, tip-top attire, the lustre that rested upon his visage—the very first sight of him gave assurance of an utterly exceptional personality.[3]

In such a case, why pass up the opportunity to feature the man along with his work? In foregrounding Ambedkar as a person, I have steered clear of the Scylla and Charybdis that have doomed so many prior Ambedkar biographies. One danger is hagiography, as we frequently find, especially but not exclusively in vernacular biographies, making them almost unreadable and inevitably inaccurate;[4] and the opposing danger is character assassination, such as that exemplified by Arun Shourie's *Worshipping False Gods*,[5] which, to anyone who actually knows something about the life and times of Ambedkar, reeks so much of bullshit that it waters the eyes.

Speaking of bullshit transitions us rather nicely to the more contentious point I make about historical accuracy. It is an obvious generalization—but I still believe it's a valid one—to observe that all of the published biographies of Ambedkar currently available rely primarily on one of two sources. The first, relied upon exclusively by Marathi speakers, is C.B. Khairmoday's twelve-volume *Dr Bhimrao Ramji Ambedkar Charitra*, yet to be translated into English[6] (for which reason I have included a complete translation of the table of contents of all twelve volumes in Appendix 1).[7] The second source, relied upon by non-Marathi speakers, and one of the most cited books in the entirety

Preface   xv

of Ambedkar studies, is Dhananjay Keer's *Dr Babasaheb Ambedkar: Life & Mission*.[8]

I do not know how to sugar-coat this, so I am just going to come out and say it: Both of these hugely influential, classic, standard and even 'authoritative' biographies of Ambedkar are riddled with inaccuracies. And for that very reason, so are all of the subsequent biographies that have relied upon them—and that is, to a greater or lesser extent, all of them.[9]

The audacity of this claim may seem even more egregious when we note that the book cover of Keer's biography carries a starburst reading, 'The one and only authentic biography read and approved by Dr Ambedkar himself!' Or otherwise, when we note that Khairmoday—the person who first referred to Ambedkar as 'Babasaheb'—himself worked as an archivist for Ambedkar, gathering innumerable documents to form one of the largest collections of Ambedkar-related source materials available, originally housed at Ambedkar's own Siddharth College. And yet, despite the odds, I have to assert that the claim is sadly true.

We may begin to understand how and why these authors personally familiar with Dr Ambedkar and ostensibly penning 'authentic' biographies made as many errors as they did if we pay some attention to the context and circumstances under which they were working. For one thing, Ambedkar himself was uniquely absent-minded about dates and accurate chronology when it came to his own life. He could recall mountains of information about books, legal codes and clauses, economic data, historical and social-scientific facts, and yet he was hopeless when it came to mundane things about himself. Indeed, Ambedkar's own autobiographical fragments, titled *Waiting for a Visa*,[10] are replete with erroneous dates for events that Ambedkar himself experienced and even regarded as important enough to take the time and trouble to describe. For example, he mentions the wrong years for his own period of study in New York and London. He also misdates his sojourn in Baroda (now Vadodara). It is hardly surprising, then, that if

Ambedkar's biographers relied only upon his own recollections during interviews, that errors did very often creep in.

Keer did not seem to try to authenticate his information with any other sources at all. Khairmoday, however, was more punctilious. The problems arose for Khairmoday when the other sources that he was relying upon themselves misinformed him. This happened, for example, when seeking information from the London School of Economics about Ambedkar's period of study in England. Khairmoday was fed inaccurate information by the registrar of the University of London, as well as by the secretary of LSE. A brief reply by the latter, J. Mair, to a letter of inquiry asking about Ambedkar is a perfect example of the kind and quantity of misinformation that London universities have consistently been disseminating about him over the past 100 years:

> 3rd May, 1922
>
> Dear Sir,
> *With reference to your letter ..., Mr. B.R. Ambedkar was a student ... from October, 1919, to June, 1921 ... He was successful in obtaining the Degree of M.Sc. (Econ.) in July last, and I believe, then returned to India.*
>
> *Yours faithfully,*
>
> *[signed]*
> *Secretary.*[11]

This entire letter in its original comprises only two sentences and yet contains three errors: Ambedkar joined LSE in 1920, not 1919; Mrs Mair, who only became school secretary in 1920, had herself enrolled him. Ambedkar obtained the MSc in June 1921, not in July; and he did not return to India after receiving the MSc but stayed on in pursuit of the doctorate. Unbelievably, this letter was issued while Ambedkar was still right there in London!

Preface   xvii

To make matters worse, when, in the early 1950s, LSE itself requested updated information from Khairmoday about their now-renowned alumnus Dr Ambedkar, the eager Khairmoday sent LSE a two-page note titled 'Brief Information of the Career of Dr. Bhimrao R. Ambedkar, M.A., Ph.D., D.Sc., Barrister-at-Law', which contained several errors of dates and facts. Somewhat surprisingly, these errors continue to be reflected in the LSE archives, right up to LSE's present-day 'online living exhibition' about Ambedkar. Even today the LSE archivists and librarians are unaware of their persistent errors surrounding Ambedkar's education. Similarly, Columbia University has long publicized erroneous information about their distinguished alumnus. Their misleading source has more often been Keer than Khairmoday.[12]

A further peculiarity with Keer is his simultaneous devotion both to B.R. Ambedkar and to V.D. Savarkar. Indeed, in addition to his Ambedkar biography, Keer authored a much-referenced, full-length biography of Savarkar. Astoundingly, an endorsement by 'Veer Savarkar' sits prominently upon the back cover of Keer's Ambedkar biography. It reads in part, 'note that the life and career of a great man in our generation should have found a great biographer'. This 'authentic' biography of Ambedkar mentions Savarkar no fewer than fifty times, referring to him as a 'great man', a 'great leader' and as fully dedicated to the uplift of the untouchables. Not only is Savarkar's name superfluously brought up throughout the biography, but Keer also seems to have inserted fictitious meetings and conversations between Savarkar and Ambedkar that cannot be corroborated through any other source—Keer was intent on uniting his two heroes, seemingly filling in with fantasy what failed to realize in historical fact.

The following passage from Keer can illustrate how he constantly crafted the most arbitrary occasions to attempt to bring Ambedkar closer to Savarkar:

> Ambedkar, who was the symbol of a suppressed people who suffered throughout ages, smashed and hammered the scriptures

with the violence of Voltaire … What Ambedkar did to these scriptures, Savarkar would have done with equal violence, and what Savarkar wrote, Ambedkar would have asserted with equal force had they been born in the opposite communities.[13]

There is absolutely no objective reason to bring in the comparison with Savarkar, but Keer brought him in over and over again. Dozens of other examples can be cited. What *cannot* be cited from Keer's biography, however, are any of the number of criticisms that Ambedkar made against Savarkar over the years, both in public speeches and in published writings. Keer suppressed them all. A talk that Ambedkar gave to an overflowing crowd at Nare park in Parel, Bombay, gives a taste of his true attitude: 'One should not place much trust in such irresponsible people. Some people say that Savarkar spit venom, but I say that he spewed out the hell that resides in his stomach.'[14]

Through his gratuitous additions and strategic omissions, Keer has not only managed to create confusion among Ambedkar biographers, but among Savarkar biographers as well. Vaibhav Purandare, for instance, stated in the preface of his 2019 Savarkar biography that he had made a 'deep dive' into Marathi literature, both by and about Savarkar, which included 'trawling through Marathi newspaper archives' and mining 'the audio archives of Cambridge University's Centre of South Asian Studies', not to mention the Maharashtra State Archives, the India Office collection and so on. Despite all of this, when it was time for Purandare to mention a 1933 letter that Keer quotes from, written by Dr Ambedkar to Savarkar supposedly praising the latter's commitment to destroying *chaturvarna* (the caste system), Purandare cites Keer rather than any of the thousands of authentic records that he had deep-dived into.[15] The reason is obvious: The contents of this letter are not corroborated by any other source but Keer. The problem, however, is that Keer cited very selectively from the letter, quoting only Ambedkar's pleasant opening remarks and none of the forceful criticism that he actually closed the letter with: 'You still use the jargon of chaturvarna …

I hope that in the course of time you will have courage enough to drop this needless and mischievous jargon'![16] Hence Purandare too, relying on Keer, completely misrepresents Ambedkar's words in his Savarkar biography.

The anti-Muslim bias of Keer is also sadly worth noting, and his prejudice on this point also seems to have led him to weave fictional events into his Ambedkar biography in an effort to bring Savarkar and Ambedkar closer together. All of this misinformation is now doing the rounds among revisionist right-wing historians and appropriators of Ambedkar, who claim—following Keer's fantasies—that Ambedkar's ideas were often close to those of the author of *Hindutva*.

So how could this biography have been 'read and approved by Dr Ambedkar', as the starburst on the front cover of Keer's book exclaims? Well, it actually wasn't. Ambedkar had met with Keer on two or three occasions to discuss certain queries about his life that Keer had posed, but beyond that, there was no personal interaction.[17] As for having actually read the biography, the story that Ambedkar's secretary and typist Nanak Chand Rattu tells explains a good deal:

> I stammered, 'Sir, here is your biography written by Dhananjay Keer.' He held the book in his hand, made a quick glance at its contents, pored over a few pages hurriedly and smiled. 'The author,' he said, 'did meet me twice or thrice for clearing some points in relation to certain events, but this is not everything, what he has written [here].' 'It is a long, very long story'. 'No one,' he said with a sigh, 'could write it.' 'Anyhow', he said further, 'he has made an attempt.'[18]

And that was the extent of Ambedkar 'reading' and 'approving' Keer's biography. At most, Ambedkar perused the table of contents and glanced through a few pages. After glancing at it for a moment, he put it aside and went back to work.

Keer's biography of Ambedkar is not 'authoritative'. It is packed with misinformation. Much of it because of speculation and shoddy fact-checking, and some of it in a conscious effort to align Ambedkar with Savarkar.

Khairmoday, on the other hand, had made many good-faith efforts towards sourcing and fact-checking, but a number of errors crept into his massive work despite this. It is also worth noting that only the first four volumes of the twelve-volume biography were published by Khairmoday himself, who died in 1971 from a heart attack before being able to complete the rest. All of the remaining volumes, though published under Khairmoday's name, were edited and published by other persons or organizations, including his wife, Dwarkabai, the publisher Sugava Prakashan and later the Maharashtra Rajya Sahitya Ani Sanskruti Mandal. It is safe to assume that no fact-checking was done prior to the publication of Volume 5 onwards. Even with respect to the volumes that Khairmoday himself produced, he unfortunately would often rely upon Keer to confirm his own information. And then, alas, there is also the problem of hagiography. To illustrate, a brief excerpt from one of Khairmoday's early volumes should suffice:

> Ambedkar's fingers were just like a baby's—beautiful and endearing. But when he overworked, they became like wilted flowers. He took great care over his hair ... often running his hand through it as he sat chatting with someone. It almost looked like he was being coquettish. Other times, like when he was engaged in physical labour, or when he was despondent, he would not take any care of his hair at all. It was long and curly, and would dance freely in the wind. Even with his hair loose like that Ambedkar's face looked charming.[19]

When it comes to saccharine devotion, Khairmoday's work remains unrivalled even by the standards of more recent Marathi biographies.

Having already admitted to the audacity of my claim, I might as well compound it and mention that it is not only Keer, Khairmoday and the LSE and Columbia University archivists and librarians who have so many of their facts mixed up. The same errors regarding dates, meetings, degrees and so on are repeated and perpetuated in the most important collection of Ambedkar's oeuvre till date—*Dr Babasaheb Ambedkar Writings and Speeches* (*BAWS*), published in multiple volumes by the Maharashtra government. As valuable as this collection is for the work it contains, it is nevertheless also a mess of misinformation. The same is true for the material on display at the otherwise splendid Dr Babasaheb Ambedkar Museum and Memorial at Symbiosis in Pune, and reprinted and displayed at the Ambedkar House Museum in London. The government of India's own Ministry of Law and Justice, which Dr Ambedkar once led, offers an erroneous biography of independent India's first law minister on its website—with mistakes about his legal education, no less! And because all of these authors, collections and institutions have been relied upon by Dr Ambedkar's numerous subsequent biographers, we find that the factual errors originating in these writings from the 1950s have persisted in the most widely read and cited biographies of recent times, including those by Eleanor Zelliot (2004), Christophe Jaffrelot (2005), Gail Omvedt (2004) and Shashi Tharoor (2022).[20]

It has been around twenty years since the just-mentioned slew of influential biographies came out, and around seventy years since the two by Keer and Khairmoday were published. Today's readers continue to rely on these, as do—rather unfortunately—today's biographers (the biographical section of Tharoor's 2022 biography relies almost exclusively on Keer and Jaffrelot; its more significant and insightful analytical section, however, is of course all original). All of this suggests that, irrespective of my other remarks about historical accuracy, a fresh and current biography of Ambedkar is long overdue.[21]

As for the biography now before you, I have spent some ten years engaged in original research for it, assembling the narrative as though the earlier biographies did not exist at all. Starting from scratch, I scoured newspapers, magazines and journals from the 1890s to the 1950s, and ransacked the India Office in London, as well as other archives in New York, New Delhi, Mumbai and elsewhere. I re-examined the oft-referenced files, microfiches and other material at the Nehru Memorial Museum and Library, the National Archives, Siddharth College, Mumbai University, Columbia University, LSE and so on. I even made some important new discoveries at the Senate House Library in London. I interviewed living family members of Ambedkar, as well as knowledgeable private collectors, early activists and Panthers, and anyone relevant who was willing to meet me over the years. I've also taken great advantage of any original research (discoveries not sourced back to the Keer or Khairmoday biographies) appearing in other secondary sources, articles and biographies. These are the reasons why I believe that this biography will be more consistent when it comes to historical accuracy than all of the others. Besides, I have no axe to grind with anyone. I am just endlessly fascinated with trying to discover who Ambedkar was and how he came to be that inimitable person.

Although Dr Ambedkar had said, while placing Keer's book aside with a sigh, that his biography would be a very, very long story that no one would be able to write, I have nevertheless made a fresh attempt at it. After all, on another occasion, Ambedkar had also stated how particularly fond he was of biographies. He avidly read many and often spoke of writing two of them himself, one on a false Mahatma (Gandhi) and one on a true one (Phule). Moreover, in a letter justifying his suggestion to his future second wife to read the biography of Leo Tolstoy, Ambedkar noted how important biographies were for exposure to the unique experiences of others, as well as to their virtues, affording the reader the opportunity to assimilate those qualities into themselves:

> I am very fond of literature, particularly biography. Every man's and woman's life is short—and the channel in which it runs is always very narrow. Consequently the experience of every

individual is always very limited. A limited experience gives a narrow range of sympathies ... [U]nless one is aware of experiences undergone by other people there is no ennoblement and enrichment in the values of life ... I choose what is worth choosing from any author worthy of perusal—and assimilate into myself and build my own personality, which if you will allow one to say is not an imitation of anybody howsoever high. It is my own original self.[22]

I have not been able to capture everything in this biography. Dr Ambedkar was sceptical that such a thing could even be done, and anyway it was not my aim. What I do hope is that this work will serve to bring the reader closer to Ambedkar's experiences and personality, to his life and times. What follows endeavours to convey the awe-inspiring passion that went into Ambedkar building, as he put it, his 'own original self' over time—or what I call *becoming Babasaheb*.

Chapter One

From Bhiva Ambadawekar to Bhimrao Ambedkar (1891–1912)

Ever since 1928, the birthday of Dr Bhimrao Ramji Ambedkar has been joyously celebrated every 14 April. But this is not really his precise date of birth. And Bhimrao Ambedkar was also not really the name he was given at birth. As he says,

> My father did not keep records and my exact date of birth is not known. I was born about midnight and my mother had great pains at the time of my delivery. An astrologer said on the occasion of my birth that my mother would die soon, and consequently I was resented by my brothers and sisters.[1]

In a later exchange of letters with his fiancée regarding the fixing of their matrimonial date, Ambedkar noted,

> You asked me why the 15th and not the 14th ... The only thing in favour of the 14th is that it is my official date of birth, but no

one can say that it is my real date of birth. Different astrologers have given different dates as my birth dates. Some have given 14th April, others 17th April, others 15th May.[2]

In the same exchange of letters, dated 1948, Ambedkar claimed that although he was officially fifty-four years old, he was more likely to be only fifty-two. The statement in this letter was not the first time that Ambedkar had attempted to correct the record. In 1927, shortly after his appointment to the Bombay Legislative Council (BLC), Ambedkar submitted to the council a brief biographical note about himself, in which he gave 1893 as the year of his birth. We also have Ambedkar's original passport from 1932, for which Ambedkar provided 1892 as his birth year. Perhaps most interesting among these many anomalies, the Dr Ambedkar Diamond Jubilee Celebration Committee was formed by the Scheduled Castes Federation to celebrate Ambedkar's sixtieth birthday in a massive function at Purandare stadium in Dadar, Bombay, with tens of thousands of people. The date that Ambedkar's diamond jubilee was celebrated? 14 April 1954![3] That is, what we today would have thought of as his sixty-third birthday, had he been born in 1891.

Indeed, I have found several signed documents in Ambedkar's own handwriting giving variously 1891, 1892 and 1893 as the year of his birth! We should point out that nearly all of the other historical records appear to corroborate that Ambedkar's birth year was actually 1891, even if the exact day of his birth might forever remain shrouded in mystery.

Ambedkar mentioned that an astrologer had said that his mother would die soon after his birth. That tragic prophecy foretold, Ambedkar's mother, Bhimabai Murbadkar, did die within a few years of his birth. She had borne fourteen children in all, the youngest being Bhima—or Bhiva, as she called him—named after herself. Of these fourteen children, seven died during childbirth or soon thereafter. Four of Bhiva's six surviving elder siblings, whether they indeed resented him or not, played significant roles in Ambedkar's life, from the early years and well into his adulthood. We will again encounter the eldest brother, Balaram, and the younger (but still elder to Bhiva), Anandrao, as well as Bhiva's slightly older sisters, Manjula and Tulsa. About the two eldest sisters, Ganga and Ramabai, however, very little is known, and it seems that they also died very young.[4]

Bhiva's father was Ramji Maloji Sakpal (occasionally rendered as Sankpal in other biographies), who hailed from the village of Ambadawe—and *not* Ambawade, as is falsely written in nearly every English-language biography—in the Ratnagiri district of present-day Maharashtra. Ramji occasionally used the name Ambadawekar in place of, or in supplement to, Sakpal.[5] By 1900, as a school registry attests, Ramji Sakpal Ambadawekar's youngest son had begun calling himself 'Bhiva Ramji Ambedkar'—scrawling next to this neatly recorded name a nine-year-old's signature, reading 'Shri Ramji Abedkar' (he had neglected to write the *anusvara* representing the '*m*' sound). It is believed that a teacher in the school where young Bhiva was registering, a good-natured but not-very-hard-working Brahman by the name of Krishna Keshav Ambedkar, encouraged the boy to use the name Ambedkar in place of Ambadawekar.

The story, of course, suffers from a fundamental anachronism—Ambedkar signed his name as 'Ambedkar' (rather, 'Abedkar') in the register of the very school where the teacher Ambedkar, presumably later than on that registration day, taught him. Despite this, and despite contention from some researchers, the story does seem credible.[6] This is because of what Ambedkar himself later recounted, including that decades later, when Dr Ambedkar met his former teacher K.K. Ambedkar, he showed him reverence and referred to him as his guru. K.K. Ambedkar also wrote Dr Ambedkar a warm letter in 1930, congratulating him for the distinction of being invited to the Round Table Conference in London. But this and so many other distinctions of Dr Ambedkar are all a matter for much later. His early childhood, quite to the contrary, did not bud in the sort of social environment that routinely cultivates greatness.

Young Bhiva did have several things going for him, despite the hardship and humiliation that he would face throughout his early years. For one thing, both Ambedkar's maternal and paternal relations were army men, many of them achieving the highest ranks possible in the British Army for enlisted Indians. Several were also literate and educated. By the time Ambedkar was born in 1891—was it 1891?—his father was the headmaster of an army school in a town called Mhow, believed to stand for 'Military Headquarters of War', although this seems to be a backronym.[7] With a diploma from the Army Normal School in Pune, Ramji Sakpal had a sound command of English, which played no small role in fostering young Bhiva's own eloquence in the language. Ambedkar's early years were thus spent in the presence of educated elders, steeped in certain virtues typical of the army, such as bravery, pride and fortitude.

Ambedkar reminisced not only on the recognized importance of education within his family, but also on that of religion:

> Ours was a poor family but its atmosphere was like that of a progressive educated family. That we should take interest in our studies and our future be bright was the ardent desire of our father and he took all possible steps in this respect. Before allowing us to take our morning meals he made us say prayers in the family shrine … At eight o'clock in the night my two sisters, elder brothers and myself, all of us had to be present in the family shrine … when our father recited the devotional songs of Kabir and other saints. The atmosphere was filled with holiness and seriousness. Following him, when my sisters began singing bhajans in their sweet voice, I felt convinced that religion and religious instruction were essential in life.[8]

After retirement from the army, Ramji Sakpal landed a post-retirement position as keeper of the stores for the army barracks at Satara, a sixteenth-century Maratha stronghold about 100 km from Pune.

Here, in 1896, Ambedkar's mother Bhimabai would die, leaving him and Anandrao in the care of his paternal aunt, Meerabai. Balaram was already a working man with a family of his own, residing in another town. Ambedkar's two sisters, Manjula and Tulsa, were also married and living elsewhere. Though loving, Meerabai had severe kyphosis—what is ordinarily referred to as a hunchback—and was unable to manage the household or help much in the rearing of Bhiva and Anandrao. Ramji Sakpal thus thought it fit to remarry, and, in 1898, wed a widow named Jijabai. Young Bhiva was not fond of his stepmother, and the ill feeling lingered. A half-century later, when Dr Ambedkar would himself contemplate remarriage, one of his greatest concerns would be about how his own son, Yashwant, would tolerate having a stepmother. As we shall see later, that relationship turned out to be even more strained than the one between Bhiva and Jijabai.

It's said that in Satara, young Bhiva amused himself by planting saplings, nurturing them and watching them grow.[9] But that he was also unhappy and restless is apparent from several of his antics. Annoyed that his stepmother had begun wearing his mother's jewellery, Bhiva plotted to purloin money from his aunt Meerabai's purse so he could purchase a train ticket to Bombay to go find work as a labourer in the mills. Again to try to earn some money, and much to the chagrin of Meerabai, Bhiva snuck out to the Satara railway station and freelanced as a porter.

The chief reason for Ambedkar's early restlessness was the stinging casteism that he suffered. At school in Satara, Bhiva and his brother Anandrao were forced to sit apart from the other students in the class, all caste Hindus, lest they pollute them. In his autobiographical fragments, *Waiting for a Visa*, Ambedkar described the circumstances of his early schooling thus:

> I knew that I was an untouchable, and that untouchables were subjected to certain indignities and discriminations. For instance, I knew that in the school I could not sit in the midst of my

classmates according to my rank, but that I was to sit in a corner by myself. I knew that in the school I was to have a separate piece of gunny cloth for me to squat on in the classroom, and the servant employed to clean the school would not touch the gunny cloth used by me.[10]

Ambedkar and Anandrao were also forbidden from drinking from any common water source and not permitted to touch any water tap. Ambedkar recalls a time in school when he was terribly thirsty due to the heat, but there was no attendant to open the water tap for him. He decided to open it himself, as he had watched other students routinely do. When the other children saw that he had 'polluted' the drinking water, a few of them beat him black and blue.[11]

In an effort to provide Bhiva and Anandrao better educational opportunities and to get them away from the heavy burden of caste discrimination and humiliation, Ramji moved the family to Bombay in 1904. The family of five squeezed into one room in Dabak Chawl, Lower Parel. The year 1905 started with Bhiva and Anandrao gaining admission to the well-regarded Elphinstone High School. Here, although still vulnerable to frequent stings of casteism, Ambedkar had a far wider world available to his imagination. The Manuvaadi faculty of the school refused to allow Bhiva or Anandrao into the Sanskrit course, so they took Persian instead. In later years, Ambedkar made up for the loss by studying Sanskrit and authoring numerous books and pieces of legislation, such as the Hindu Code Bill, that challenged several basic principles taken as gospel by the orthodoxy versed in Sanskrit.[12] But for the time being, Ambedkar settled for Persian, and demonstrated his knack for languages by earning his highest marks in that course. He played cricket in the evenings, and in the day, though not quite applying himself to the prescribed schoolwork, slowly developed the habit of immersing himself in books. This lifelong obsession with books thus began on Elphinstone Road. And people took notice.

While no written record exists, during high school, Bhiva—who had been nicknamed Raja by his Elphinstone classmates, though we do not know why[13]—apparently also penned a short play called *A Wise Girl*, which was based on Shakespeare's *King Lear*. He even managed to get his play staged. Fond of Shakespeare, Ambedkar would later cite apt lines from various plays to fit the circumstances. One he was especially attracted to was Brutus's words in *Julius Caesar*: 'There is a tide in the affairs of men. Which, taken at the flood, leads on to fortune.' For young Bhiva, that tide was about to show a steady rise.

Ambedkar's habit of reading all sorts of books was growing, thanks to his father's support and encouragement. Ramji even asked Bhiva's sisters, Manjula and Tulsa, to pawn some of the jewellery from their wedding so he could feed Ambedkar's growing appetite for books. Ramji instructed his son to sleep as early as he could in the evening, so that he could awaken him at 2 a.m. to study for his exams. Only at this early hour would the crowd and chaos of their living quarters permit the quiet and tranquillity required for study. The method bore fruit, because, in 1907, Bhiva matriculated—he was only the second from among the Mahar caste known to have done so. For want of money, Anandrao was withdrawn from school before he was able to matriculate. Ramji was now pinning all of the family's hopes on Bhiva alone.

There was a celebration held to recognize young Bhivarao's accomplishments. Several prominent persons were in attendance, including S.K. Bole, a member of the Bombay Legislative Council. Also present was a certain man who had often observed Bhiva reading near Elphinstone and had befriended the boy. This was Krishnaji Arjun Keluskar (later widely known as Dada Keluskar). He gifted the increasingly voracious reader a book that he himself had authored— *Life of the Buddha*. Keluskar's book had been published in Maharajah Sayajirao Gaekwad of Baroda's Oriental Series, and within a few years, Keluskar would be instrumental in bringing young Ambedkar to the notice of the Maharajah.

In the meantime, Ramji had secured slightly better living quarters. He shifted the family to the Number 1 Chawl (there were six *chawls*, or tenement buildings, in all) of the Bombay Improvement Trust (BIT) in Parel, where they were allotted rooms 50 and 51 (out of a total of eighty in the tenement building) on the second floor. The BIT had been established in 1898 by an Act of the British Parliament in response to the bubonic plague epidemic that ravaged Bombay in 1896. Modelled on the Glasgow Trust of 1866, the BIT augmented the activities of the municipality and was responsible for planning and public work, including road widening, suburban layout, slum clearance and rehousing. The rehousing was out of crowded and unsanitary bustees and into chawls, which were equipped with plumbing within, and proper drains and footpaths without.[14] Ambedkar lived in this chawl for nearly twenty-two years. Even as barrister Ambedkar, even as Dr Ambedkar, even as member of Bombay Legislative Council, B.R. Ambedkar, MLC. He and his family continued to live in these two rooms in what he would later colourfully describe as 'the underworld of Bombay'.[15]

His family had also added one more significant member. True to hoary tradition, Bhiva's father had arranged his son's marriage with Ramabai Walangkar, a child herself, also from an army family.[16]

On 3 January 1908, Ambedkar entered Elphinstone College, listed on the roll-call sheet as 'B.R. Ambedkar'. That the B still stood for Bhiva and not for Bhimrao can be inferred from a letter—the first extant letter in Ambedkar's hand—addressed to the principal of Elphinstone College, dated 11 September 1908. In it, Ambedkar requests opting out of the year's politics and economics examinations to be held in November, as he had not been able to prepare for the maths segment. He signs off as 'Ambedkar Bhivram Ramji'.

It appears that illness lasting the better part of a year prevented Bhivram from attending classes and adequately preparing. But there was an even deeper problem about to force Ambedkar out of college and into the labouring life of his brothers. The family was broke. Let alone the books, Ramji could not manage to scrape together even the tuition fees. At this point, Dada Keluskar mobilized his access to the Maharajah of Baroda, and, in April 1911, managed to secure Ambedkar a scholarship paying Rs 25 per month until the completion of his BA degree.[17] The award of the scholarship came with conditions of service to the state of Baroda, but they all agreed that that issue could be dealt with at a later date. For now, given that Ramji Sakpal's entire army pension amounted to only Rs 50 per month, the prospect of this new income covering all of Bhiva's tuition fees, books and possibly even a little bit more was a windfall.

A year later, B.R. Ambedkar emerged as the first Mahar to have earned a Bachelor of Arts degree from Bombay University. A plaque now commemorates this historic moment at Mumbai University's beautiful convocation hall in Fort. But that was not the only joy that 1912 brought for the family. That same year, Bhivrao and Ramabai's first child, Yashwant, was born. Although the couple had four more children between 1913 and 1924, their firstborn was the only one to survive beyond infancy and into adulthood.

B.R. Ambedkar, then twenty-one years old, a graduate and a father, decided to be known as Bhimrao—his late mother's pet name of 'Bhiva' was finally put aside.

Chapter Two

The Alma Mater (1913–16)

What next? A difference arose between young Bhimrao and his father Ramji on the response to that question. Bhimrao thought it fit to fulfil his part of the agreement with Baroda state, his BA now completed, and head there to join the administrative services. Ramji was greatly concerned about Baroda's reputation for casteism, and felt that his son would suffer fewer caste-based obstacles and enjoy greater opportunities if he stayed on in Bombay.

Bhimrao finally opted for Baroda in early January 1913, but quickly learnt that his father had been quite right. Although appointed by the Maharajah with the distinguished rank of lieutenant (probationary) of the 1st infantry, Ambedkar was unable to find accommodation, all doors shut to him the moment his caste was disclosed. He ended up sleeping in the office of the Arya Samaj, the well-known Hindu reformist organization working towards mainstreaming untouchables and bringing them into the Hindu fold.[1] As for meals, those he could only find if he travelled to the untouchable quarters on the outskirts of the city, and the constant need to travel back and forth from the city centre to the outskirts for each of his meals was extremely tedious.[2] But he did have time on his hands, because none of the administrative departments wanted to employ a Mahar in their office. To be more precise, his caste at this time was officially recorded not as Mahar but as Parwari, a nineteenth-century designation for military Mahars. Being an army man must have thrilled young Ambedkar, a lifelong admirer of the army. Others were far less pleased. As the assistant resident in Baroda noted in an office file, with obvious annoyance: 'Bhimrao Ramji Ambedkar is a Parwari, a resident of Bombay, who ... figures in the Baroda Service List as a Military Probationer, but has done no military training and was apparently appointed in order to draw pay.'[3] Mahar or Parwari, army man or no, he was unwanted. Within his first two weeks in Baroda, he was shuffled from department to department several times.

His first two weeks turned out to be his last two weeks, for, towards the end of the month, Ambedkar received a telegram informing him that his father had fallen seriously ill. Bhimrao rushed back to Bombay, but his presence was of no help. Ramji Sakpal died on 2 February 1913, leaving his youngest son, Bhimrao, forlorn. To compound the tragedy, later in the same year, another son only just born to Ramabai and Bhimrao, named Ramesh, died in his infancy.[4]

Ambedkar's father had had a huge impact on his young self, and some of this, as well as a glimpse into the nature of their relationship, can be discerned from a charming story that Ambedkar recounted towards the very end of his own life:

> My father was a military officer, but at the same time a very religious person. He brought me up under strict discipline. From an early age I found certain contradictions in my father's religious way of life ... He compelled me and my elder brother to read every evening a portion of the Mahabharata and Ramayana to my sisters and to others who assembled at our house. This went on for years ...

One day I asked my father why he insisted upon our reading the Mahabharata and Ramayana, which recounted the greatness of the Brahmans and the Kshatriyas and repeated the stories of the degradation of the Shudras and the Untouchables. My father did not like the question, merely replying, 'You must not ask such silly questions. You are only boys. You must do as you are told.' He was a Roman Patriarch exercising *Patria Potestas* over his children. I alone could take a little liberty with him, and that was because my mother had died in my childhood, leaving me to the care of my aunt.

After several days I asked the same question. My father had evidently prepared a reply in the meantime. 'The reason I ask you to read the Mahabharata and Ramayana is this: we belong to the Untouchables, and you are likely to develop an inferiority complex, which is natural. The value of the Mahabharata and Ramayana lies in removing this inferiority complex. Witness Drona and Karna, they were low-born, but to what heights they rose! Look at Valmiki, he was a Koli but authored the Ramayana. It is for removing this inferiority complex that I ask you to read the Mahabharata and Ramayana.'

There was some force in my father's argument, but I was not satisfied. I responded, 'I do not like Bhishma and Drona, or Krishna. Bhishma and Drona were hypocrites. They said one thing and did quite the opposite. Krishna believed in fraud. His life is nothing but a series of frauds. I also dislike Rama. Just examine how he behaved in the Shurpanakha episode and in the Vali Sugriva episode, and his monstrous behaviour towards Sita.'

My father was silent, and made no reply. He knew that this was a revolt.[5]

When back in Bombay attending to his father's funeral arrangements, Ambedkar went to call on Maharajah Sayajirao Gaekwad, impressing

The Alma Mater (1913–16)

upon him in his eloquent English all of the difficulties that he had been facing while trying to satisfy his obligation to serve the state of Baroda. The results of the encounter were historic and life-changing: Excusing Ambedkar from the previous debt of service, the Maharajah would soon sanction a scholarship of £230 per annum for Ambedkar to study at Columbia University in New York City.

The Maharajah was a firm believer in the demands of social justice, and also knew from personal experience how much an education abroad could contribute towards inculcating this ideal. He already had a programme in place to send bright students abroad. As he had written in an article titled 'The Depressed Classes' just a few years before:

> In the political world a struggle has commenced for wider self-government and greater racial equality. The same principles which impel us to ask for political justice for ourselves should actuate us to show social justice to each other ... [W]ider ideals derived from our foreign education and contacts with Western thought have opened our eyes to our own shortcomings.[6]

The order supporting Ambedkar's foreign education was issued on 5 April 1913, and by the summer of that year, Ambedkar set off for the United States. What is interesting is the specificity of Gaekwad's order. It mandated that Ambedkar earn his degree in economics, finance and sociology, and that he *not* pursue pedagogy as a subject. This specificity resulted from a series of back-and-forth discussions between the Maharajah and his bureaucracy over the prior two months.

The Baroda state scholarship had ordinarily been given for Indian students to study in London, and in the beginning, the path-dependent bureaucracy was planning on sending Ambedkar to London as well. It was the cheaper option at the time. When Ambedkar and Gaekwad decided upon New York instead, the bureaucracy accepted it by deciding on pedagogy as the field of study. This was simply because the only information that they had with respect to the costs of studying in

New York was from another student who had studied at Columbia's Teachers College. Once again, Ambedkar and the Maharajah prevailed upon the bureaucrats to stop simply making everything easier for themselves and to permit Ambedkar to study what he himself was actually interested in—economics and finance. The Maharajah was happy with Ambedkar's choice, as he fully expected to appoint Ambedkar as the finance minister for the state of Baroda upon his return from New York, as he later disclosed to others was his true intention. As a condition of the stipend, Ambedkar was bound to serve Baroda state in an administrative capacity for a period of ten years.

The order for the scholarship also assumed that a period of two years would be sufficient for Ambedkar to earn the MA degree, but as it turned out, Ambedkar would eventually manage to get the period extended to four years, allowing him to enrol for much more than just an MA degree in the US.

That the Maharajah had such ambitions for Ambedkar is made even more evident by another order appearing in April 1913. The death of a certain Shivlal Jeram left a vacancy in the legislative council of Baroda. On 24 April, an order was issued, reading: 'His Highness the Maharajah Saheb has been pleased to nominate Mr B.R. Ambedkar, B.A., as an additional member of the local Legislative Council.'[7] It appears that this order never came into effect, as within six weeks of its issuance, Ambedkar was signing an altogether different agreement with Baroda state authorities, which finalized the conditions of his extended study and stay abroad.

This agreement, too, was remarkably detailed. For one thing, it itemized every single expense that would be covered by the stipend, for how much and for how long. There was an outfit allowance permitting Ambedkar to purchase finely tailored European suits—this moment in 1913 thus marked the beginning of Ambedkar's lifelong preference for the formal suit jacket, necktie and trousers. All of his statuary still appears outfitted like this today. Another specific mandated by the agreement was the national origin of the steamer by which he was permitted to cross, and, of course, the class of travel.

On 15 June 1913, Bhimrao set off for New York City on the SS *Sardinia*, leaving wife and family in Bombay. The SS *Sardinia* was a British ship heading to England, but it halted at Naples in Italy. From Naples, Ambedkar boarded the SS *Ancona*, an emigrant ship on a regular route between Italy and the United States, which arrived at New York City on Monday, 21 July 1913, around noon. Although he had arrived too late to join the summer session, Ambedkar enrolled in Columbia University that same month simply for the convenience of it. His studies, however, began only in September.

Ambedkar's first lodging upon arrival was at Hartley Hall, a campus student dormitory. Though a meat eater, Ambedkar was not accustomed to the insipid, undercooked beef dishes served up at the Hartley canteen and quickly looked for another arrangement. In August, Ambedkar shifted to the Cosmopolitan Club at 554 West 114th Street, an international housing club early on organized by Indian students and then later financed by the business tycoon John D. Rockefeller Jr and administered by the YMCA. The tycoon-backed iteration of the club was conceived to give foreign students of Columbia University more cultural freedom, as it had been noted that 'colonies' were beginning to be formed in the student dormitories, the Chinese colony of Hartley Hall being the most notorious. *The New York Times* reported:

> As for the foreign students, they will be able to burn incense, eat Turkish food, debate international problems in twenty-six different languages, and then get up and worship the sun—if they please. They will not be hindered by the peculiar American people, who never object to anybody staying up making noise until 5 o'clock in the morning, but who have come to think that it is unhealthy and in bad judgement for anybody to get up

and make noise at that hour—which is what Chinese students do sometimes.[8]

Despite that foreign students were clearly at liberty to maintain their own cultural and social practices within the Cosmopolitan Club, Bhimrao found that none of the Indians with whom he was lodging, dining and socializing had any of the usual caste hang-ups that he would routinely encounter while living anywhere in India. In New York City, they were all simply Indians, and Ambedkar got along very well with his peers. By coincidence, an old classmate of Ambedkar's from his school in Satara a decade earlier was also residing at the Cosmopolitan Club, and Ambedkar became re-acquainted with him. But Ambedkar became closest to a Parsee student from Bombay named Nowrosji M. Bhathena, but who went by the name Naval, with whom he eventually doubled in another of the Columbia University dormitories, at that time called Livingston Hall and now known as Wallach Hall. Naval, a year junior to Bhimrao in the economics programme but never managing to graduate from Columbia, became a lifelong friend for him.[9] Other than Naval, Ambedkar most often remembered his faculty rather than his peers. In a small piece featuring in the *Columbia Alumni News* some two decades later, Ambedkar was quoted as saying, 'The best friends I have had in life were some of my classmates at Columbia and my great professors, John Dewey, James Shotwell, Edwin Seligman, and James Harvey Robinson.'[10]

Who were these four 'best friends' and 'great professors'? The first mentioned, the eminent American pragmatist philosopher John Dewey, would prove to be a major and lifelong influence on Ambedkar, the enormous extent of which is only now becoming clear as Deweyans begin deeper comparative studies of the writings of Dewey and Ambedkar.[11] In later years, Ambedkar would boast that he could reproduce every lecture of John Dewey's verbatim. His second wife, Savita Ambedkar, once remarked that Ambedkar would imitate Dewey's lecturing style and voice intonations for her.[12]

The Alma Mater (1913–16)

It seems that Bhimrao did not encounter Dewey until as late as 1915, when he enrolled on the course Philosophy 231, titled 'Psychological Ethics, and Moral & Political Philosophy'. The course evaluated individual moral conduct and character from the vantage point of social psychology. Here Ambedkar was introduced to the moral philosophies of Plato, Aristotle, Kant, the Utilitarians and others. Falling just as much for the brilliance and erudition of the professor as for the inherent fascination of the subject, Ambedkar then enrolled on four more philosophy courses throughout the academic year 1915–16. Two of these courses were on the naturalist and materialist philosophers and their nemeses, the idealist philosophers such as Schopenhauer, and the post-Hegelians such as F.H. Bradley and Josiah Royce. These classes would get deeply into the weeds of esoteric metaphysical minutiae and may have helped push Ambedkar further into his more natural inclination towards less baroque, more pragmatic ways of thinking about the world.

The other two philosophy courses were again with John Dewey, and more in line with Ambedkar's natural interests—a full year of Moral and Political Philosophy. This pair of courses focused on the relationship of the individual with the nation state, as well as on that of the individual with other social relations and associations. Caste would *not* have been among the associations that Dewey would have covered, but as Ambedkar's later writings showed, Dewey's perspective could incisively be applied to the relationship between the individual and caste, as well as caste, or castes, and the nation state.

What Ambedkar studied in these philosophy courses would be implicitly relied upon or explicitly called back in his later writings, speeches and debates. This was true not only for philosophy, but also for many of his other subjects. He was enjoying an academic education of great breadth, depth and distinction.

Regarding the other three professors mentioned by Ambedkar as his closest friends, James Shotwell, Edwin Seligman and James Harvey Robinson, two were well-known historians and one a renowned economist. James Robinson—who had himself been educated at

Harvard and Freiburg—was earlier the professor of James Shotwell (who had earned his PhD at Columbia), and Bhimrao had enrolled on a surprising number of courses by both of them throughout his years of study at Columbia. With Robinson, Ambedkar took History 226, on the Protestant revolt. Then he signed up for a year-long pair of philosophical, history-of-ideas-type courses on 'The History of the Intellectual Class in Europe'—both part I (covering the Greek sophists, the wider Greek speculative philosophy and its transmission to Europe by the Romans, the rise of the Christian conception of man and the world, the origin of medieval universities, and the revival of Aristotle and the range of university teaching in the thirteenth century) as well as part II (covering the decline of scholasticism from the fourteenth century on, the intellectual aspects of the Renaissance and the Protestant revolt, the birth of the modern scientific spirit with Bacon and Descartes, deism, French philosophy and some new, contemporaneous European thinkers).

One can only imagine the confidence boost that such courses would have provided a budding young intellectual from a marginalized community, previously accustomed to being talked down to, but now having mastered the entire intellectual history of Europe, from the ancient Greeks to contemporary times.

After three semesters with Robinson, Ambedkar enrolled on another set of history courses with Shotwell, these more anthropological, beginning with a course on 'The Origins of European Society' (with a survey of prehistoric man, the stone, bronze and early iron ages, the rise of agriculture, ancient city states, commerce and slavery, moving on to feudalism, the rise of European cities, the emergence of capital and the origins of the nation state) and then another course on the 'Social and Industrial History of Modern England' (covering the Commercial Revolution, the influx of gold and silver into Europe from the Americas, the rise of factories and the formation of the industrial proletariat, movements towards reform, social legislation, trade unions, Chartism and the historical setting of socialism).

Curiously, Ambedkar also enrolled on a narrowly focused research course on 'Europe in the Twelfth and Thirteenth Centuries', which Shotwell only permitted specially qualified students to take. Given that the developments in Europe during that period were so arcane and obscure, it must have been Ambedkar's desire to study closely with Shotwell rather than any keen interest in the subject that prompted him to enrol on that course. We see this again the following year. Ambedkar enrolled on one of the very same courses that he had already completed the previous year, 'The Origins of European Society'. He re-enrolled not because he had not done well in the course the first time round, but because he was intent upon taking even more courses with James Shotwell. Specifically, Shotwell was teaching a specialized course, 'Primitive Institutions in European History', that was only open to students who were concurrently enrolled on 'The Origins of European Society' course; hence, Ambedkar re-enrolled on the course that he had already completed, just so he could qualify for the new, advanced course that ran concurrent with it. Ambedkar clearly loved James Shotwell.

Out of all of these excellent teachers whom young Ambedkar studied under, he was probably personally closest to Edwin Seligman, with whom he maintained correspondence for many years. Professor Seligman was the head of the economics department, strangely referred to in those days as the 'executive officer'. He was not only Ambedkar's supervisor, but also supported Ambedkar in other ways. For example, after the completion of his studies in New York, when Ambedkar decided to pursue further studies in London, Seligman wrote kind letters of reference and introduction for him, enabling him to meet important professors in England and enrol at the London School of Economics. In these letters, Seligman described Ambedkar as 'an excellent student and a nice fellow, moderate, broad, and able'.[13] Years later, upon Ambedkar's second voyage to England to complete his post-graduate studies, Seligman again wrote reference letters for Ambedkar, in one of which he wrote that Ambedkar was 'not only a very able, but also an exceedingly pleasant fellow'.[14] And when the fruits of Ambedkar's time spent in studies in London manifested through the 1925 publication of his research, *The Evolution of Provincial Finance in British India*, it was Seligman who wrote the foreword to the book.

It was from Seligman that Bhimrao learnt economics 101—literally! In Economics 101, Ambedkar's first and earliest course on economics at Columbia, named 'The Science of Finance', he was introduced to finance from a historical as well as a comparative and critical perspective. He continued this course, as Economics 102, for the rest of his first year, moving from the history of finance to the study of actual finance, taxation, budget and so on, in existing federal states such as the US. He also enrolled on Seligman's theory course, the 'History of Economics since Adam Smith', which delved first-hand into the writings of the English classical school, the early British socialists, continental economic theories, early American writers, the German historical school, socialists and the Austrian school, ending with the leading contemporary economists, within which John Maynard Keynes was not yet to appear. The latter had, just the year before, published his first major book, *Indian Currency and Finance* (London, 1913), which Ambedkar himself closely wrestled with in the years to come.

Ambedkar also took a specialized course in the economic, social and legal problems of railroad systems, which scrutinized railways and railway policies in the US and Europe from the four-fold aspect of their relation to investors, employees, the public and the state. This way of viewing a specific issue from multiple points of view would later become quite characteristic of Ambedkar's own approach, well exemplified in writings such as *Thoughts on Pakistan*, in which he looks at the idea of Pakistan from the perspective of Indian Muslims, then from the perspective of Hindus then in terms of the abstract idea of the nation, and then in terms of the concrete idea of the state. This ability to examine an issue from multifarious viewpoints was unusual amongst Ambedkar's contemporaries. Indeed, even today, readers are often confused by this technique as it appears in Ambedkar's writings, attributing certain ideas to Ambedkar as his own, which he had in fact simply presented as possible points of view on the matter under investigation.

Finally, Ambedkar also enrolled on the advanced 'Seminar in Political Economy & Finance' course with Seligman, and it was here that his own thesis in economics and finance was given its final shape and focus.

Beyond the confines of the varsity, Seligman was on friendly terms with Lala Lajpat Rai, and made the latter aware of Ambedkar's talents. In November 1914, Lala Lajpat Rai's mission to spread the ideology of the nationalist movement brought him to New York. Having established the Indian Home Rule League of America, he was eager to get Bhimrao actively involved. Lala remained in the US from 1914 until 1919, launching the inaugural issue of *Young India* from New York in January 1918. As often as he came across Ambedkar in this period, he sought to bring him into the movement. But Ambedkar's rebuffs were pointed. On one occasion, he is reported to have responded to Lala, 'You have enslaved untouchables in your struggle—but now you seek to do away with your own political enslavement!'[15]

Not only this remark, but also some of Ambedkar's academic work bears witness to his emerging consciousness of caste and untouchability as objective, systemic problems, over and above being merely subjective, painful personal experiences. The numerous courses that Ambedkar was taking at Columbia that traced social, political or economic structures and patterns of the current world back to the ancient world, and indeed further back into prehistory, took hold of Ambedkar's imagination, and he began to develop a more organic consciousness of caste and untouchability through the academic aperture. He was, in brief, in the process of discovering, and partly even inventing, the sociology of caste.

Chapter Three
An Indian in New York

Young Ambedkar's emerging academic understanding of caste was helping him give systematic expression to his many prior years of the lived experience of systemic caste prejudice. Alongside and as an impetus to this were also his widening experiences on issues of race, class and gender. To some extent, this new exposure was a result of his coursework at Columbia. But much of this exposure came more experientially, from treading the streets of Upper Manhattan and Harlem.

Describing his usual New York day, Ambedkar emphasized that the vast majority of his time, some eighteen hours daily, was spent on campus, either attending lectures and seminars, or otherwise working in Columbia University's magnificent and exceptionally stocked Low Library. But he often ate off campus, opting to eat only one meal per day to save both time and money. For food he spent, on average, $1.10 daily, which would buy him a cup of coffee, two muffins and either a meat or a fish dish. He was on a tight budget. New York City living was not cheap, and he had to send money home to his family as well. But that was not all. His voracious reading habit, cultivated earlier in his life under the shadow of the Bombay-Gothic tower of Elphinstone, had only grown stronger atop the grand staircase of the Roman–neoclassical library of Columbia. Ambedkar was now in the first stage of what would turn out to be a lifelong obsession with collecting books. He spent all the leisure time that he had browsing Manhattan's numerous second-hand bookshops and sidewalk stalls, amassing a personal library of some 2,000 volumes over his three-year stay.

The quest for books led young Ambedkar out of Upper Manhattan down to 42nd Street on Fifth Avenue, where the imposing Beaux-Arts-style New York Public Library had recently opened its doors, and opened them to all, including black people and women. So impressed was Ambedkar with the public library that upon learning of the death of Sir Pherozeshah Mehta in Bombay, and the Bombay municipality's plan to prominently erect his statue, Ambedkar shot off a provocative letter from New York to *The Bombay Chronicle*, the English-language weekly that Mehta had himself launched in 1910. Ambedkar, fresh from another inspiring visit to the New York Public Library, argued in his letter that erecting a public library in Bombay instead of a 'trivial and unbecoming' statue would be a far better tribute to the memory of this great man:

> It is unfortunate that we have not as yet realized the value of the library as an institution in the growth and advancement of a society. But this is not the place to dilate upon its virtues. That an enlightened public as that of Bombay should have suffered so long to be without an up-to-date public library is nothing short of disgrace and the earlier we make amends for it the better. There are some private libraries in Bombay operating independently by themselves. If these ill-managed concerns be mobilized into one building, built out of the Sir P.M. Mehta memorial fund and called after him, the city of Bombay shall have achieved both these purposes.[1]

The week following Pherozeshah Mehta's death in Bombay, Booker T. Washington died in Tuskegee, Alabama. Washington, who had been born into slavery, was the most prominent southern black activist of his day. As the principal of the Tuskegee Institute and author of a bestselling autobiography, *Up from Slavery*, Washington's work and writings would have been well known to Ambedkar. Indeed, he would have heard his name prior to reaching America, given that his patron, Maharajah Sayajirao Gaekwad, had long before taken to referring to the great social reformer Jyotirao Phule, author of *Gulamgiri* (or 'Slavery') as 'India's Booker T. Washington'.

The streets of Upper Manhattan were beginning to buzz with a new black consciousness that expressed itself not only sociopolitically—for example with the writings and activism of W.E.B. Du Bois and the National Negro Committee (which would soon become the NAACP, National Association for the Advancement of Colored People)—but also aesthetically, with emerging literary, theatrical and musical innovations that would set the stage for the later Harlem Renaissance.

Besides his letter to the *Bombay Chronicle*, Ambedkar sent off numerous letters to family and friends in India during his stay in New York. The letters show that Ambedkar was as attuned to issues regarding gender as he was to those regarding race. One worth mentioning was addressed to a friend of his father, a retired jamadar of the Indian Army, also from the Mahar caste. In it, he implored the recipient—who was the father of a young girl gaining notoriety for having made it all the way to the fourth standard in school, unheard of for a Mahar girl— to preach the idea of education to anyone from their community who was willing to listen. Ambedkar wrote that he should continue the education of his daughter and that the entire community would progress more quickly if boys and girls were educated side by side, with no difference between them.

This letter, too, can be seen to reflect the environment Ambedkar now found himself in. For, alongside the emergence of a new black consciousness, New York City was also buzzing with the tireless activism of suffragists demanding the enfranchisement of women in America. And some of the most dynamic of these suffragists were young Ambedkar's fellow Columbia classmates—and some, as luck would have it, turned out to be his favourite professors.

The summer just prior to Ambedkar's arrival at Columbia, his soon-to-be classmate, Chinese-born Mabel Ping-Hua Lee, was one of the fifty suffragettes on horseback leading a procession of 10,000 people up Fifth Avenue to Carnegie Hall. Among those marching were Ambedkar's future philosophy professor John Dewey and his future economics professor Vladimir Simkhovitch. In the spring of 1914, Lee published an article in a campus paper, titled 'The Meaning of Woman Suffrage', advocating equality of educational opportunities and the economic liberation of women. In terms identical to those Ambedkar would himself utter frequently in his later speeches, Lee referred to 'equality of opportunity' as the essence of 'democracy'. To her, feminism meant 'nothing more than the extension of democracy or social justice and equality of opportunities to women'.[2]

Lee, supervised by Simkhovitch, and Ambedkar, supervised by Seligman, were together enrolled on the course leading towards the PhD in economics at Columbia's Graduate School of Arts and Sciences. Later, Mabel Lee would become the first Chinese woman to earn a doctorate in economics in the United States, just as Ambedkar was one of the first Indians (and certainly the first Dalit) to do so.[3]

Vladimir Simkhovitch, apart from being Lee's doctoral supervisor, was the husband of Mary Kingsbury Simkhovitch, the well-known social worker who could often be heard giving public talks on issues of women's suffrage and social reform. But he was also one of the world's leading experts in socialist economics and Marxist thought. Ambedkar enrolled on his Econ 114 ('Marx and Post-Marxian Socialism'), Econ 303 ('Seminar on Political Economy'), Econ 109 ('History of Socialism'), Econ 242 ('Radicalism and Social Reform') and Econ 119 ('Economic History')—five full courses on Marxism and socialism! At least for some of these courses, if not out of wider interest, Ambedkar would have had to have purchased some of Marx's original writings; books by Marx must have been among the 2,000 volumes he acquired while in New York. As we will later learn, the vast majority of these books never made it back with Ambedkar to India. Several of them, such as the writings of John Dewey, Ambedkar subsequently repurchased elsewhere. But curiously, we can find none of Marx's books among Ambedkar's extant library. It seems that his later experience with Brahmanical Indian Marxists so soured Ambedkar's view of Marx that he never even bothered to replace his lost books.[4]

One book that Ambedkar purchased in New York that clearly made it with him to India, as apparent from his inscription, was Mrs Rhys Davids's *Buddhism: A Study of the Buddhist Norm* (first published in New York in 1912). This book focused on the most ancient Pali sources of the Buddhist tradition. Ambedkar inscribed the first page in his hand, 'Columbia Varsity, New York', and then later on the right-hand side adjacent to it, 'Bombay, India'. The book and its inscription both show a continuity of his interest in Buddhism, initiated by Dada Keluskar years ago.

Of course, Ambedkar's main focus of study, and the degree towards which he was working, was economics. The study of ancient Buddhism proved useful towards the first iteration of his master's thesis, titled 'Ancient Indian Commerce', which may have first been written as an original research paper for submission as a component of the MA examination.[5] Only about seventy-five pages of this manuscript are extant, and the rest lost. Columbia University has no record of this work in its archives, and the incomplete version that we have is found among the Ambedkar papers in the possession of the Maharashtra government.

This text at first deals with the trade and commercial relations of ancient India with ancient Egypt, west and east Asia, and then the Greeks and the Romans. Throughout, Ambedkar strikes a proud, nationalist tone in the work, citing sources to emphasize the superior science, technology and splendours of ancient India over ancient Europe:

> It is in the orient, especially in these countries of old civilization, that we must look for industry and riches, for technical ability and artistic productions, as well as for intelligence and science, even before Constantine made [the Roman empire] the centre of political power. Nay, all branches of learning were affected by the spirit of the orient, which was her superior in the extent and precision of its technical knowledge, as well as in the inventive genius and ability of its workman.[6]

Remember that Ambedkar was by now thoroughly familiar with the political, economic and intellectual history of classical Europe and ancient Rome, so his claims regarding ancient India's technical superiority were not merely rhetorical.

'Ancient Indian Commerce' then goes on to cover India's commercial relations in the Middle Ages, covering industry, trade and commerce throughout the rise of Islam and the expansion of western Europe. The next couple of chapters are missing, and the extant thesis ends with a chapter titled 'India on the Eve of the Crown Government'. In this chapter too, Ambedkar exhibits a fierce nationalism, excoriating British imperialism and taking to task historians of British India who misrepresent the achievements of India prior to the arrival of the British: 'Not only have they been loud in their denunciation of the Moghul and the Maratha rulers as despots and brigands, they cast slur on the morale of the entire population and their civilization.'[7] What follows are twenty pages of argument and evidence, replete with tables, graphs and charts, of how India systematically contributed to the prosperity of Britain while itself being consistently degenerated, beaten down and sucked dry.

This tour de force of Indian nationalist commercial and economic history then concludes with these damning words:

> The supplanters of the Moghuls and the Marathas were persons with no better moral fiber, and the economic condition of

India under the so-called native despots was better than what it was under the rule of those who boasted being of superior culture. It is with industries ruined, agriculture overstocked and overtaxed, with productivity too low to bear the high taxes, and with few avenues for display of native capacities, the people of India passed from the rule of the Company to the rule of the Crown.[8]

American academia was far more accommodating of this magnitude of critique of British imperialism than either British or Indian universities were. Nevertheless, for reasons still unknown to us, Ambedkar abandoned the topic of ancient Indian commerce as his MA thesis and, instead, drafted and submitted a much more technical, scope-limited and positivist text, titled 'Administration and Finance of the East India Company'. The most likely explanation is that Professor Edwin Seligman had been assigned as Ambedkar's supervisor, and Seligman was a no-nonsense, technical economist, who viewed the subject of economics as a fact-based, impartial 'science'. Seligman taught Ambedkar 'The Science of Finance' and was averse to the introduction of subjective viewpoints. As Seligman would write ten years later in the preface to Ambedkar's published PhD, 'The value of Mr. Ambedkar's contribution to this discussion lies in the *objective recitation of the facts* and the impartial analysis ...'[9]

The officially submitted thesis, at only forty-five pages in length, avoided speaking of history at all (the opening line reads: 'Without going into the historical development of it ...') and was more restrained in claims regarding the systematic cultural destruction and impoverishment of India by the British. Nevertheless, in the end, Ambedkar exhibits the irrepressibility of his innate need to call out injustice, and closes the thesis with these reproaching words:

It remains, however, to estimate the contribution of England to India. Apparently the immenseness of India's contribution to England is as astounding as the nothingness of England's contribution to India ... England has added nothing to the stock of gold and silver in India; on the contrary, she has depleted India—'the sink of the world'.[10]

The thesis was accepted by Seligman and passed, and on 2 June 1915 Ambedkar was awarded the degree of Master of Arts in economics. He had completed the requisite thirty credit hours for the MA, but sixty credit hours were required for a doctorate. He thus continued in his coursework and in his research and writing, and from that point on, all the credits were counted towards the completion of his PhD.[11]

Ambedkar continued working on 'the science of finance' as the subject of his doctoral dissertation under Seligman at Columbia. The tentative title for his PhD thesis was 'The National Dividend of India', a historical and analytical study of Indian finance.[12] But, interestingly, following the award of his MA in economics, nearly every course that Ambedkar enrolled on as credit towards his PhD in economics was a non-econ one. After the summer of 1915, Ambedkar took only one economics course (Econ 183, on railways)—all of the rest were in languages (French and German), history (four courses), philosophy (four courses), politics (one course) and anthropology (four courses).

All four of these anthro courses were taught by Alexander Goldenweiser, actually an instructor and not a professor (having just earned his PhD from Columbia in 1910), who was himself a student of Franz Boas, the 'father of American anthropology'. Boas was then head, or rather executive officer, of the anthropology department at Columbia, and he co-taught a course with his friend John Dewey during the same semester that Ambedkar was attending Dewey's philosophy course. In short, there is no doubt that young Ambedkar was exposed to the modern anthropological method of Boas. One of the primary features of Boas's approach was his flat rejection of the racial typologies that were so popular in late-nineteenth-century anthropology. These racialist theories attributed fixed mental and physical characteristics to specific races.[13] Boas (and indeed Dewey and Goldenweiser) rejected race as the dominant characteristic of a people and emphasized far more malleable and conditional characteristics, such as culture, history and psychology instead.

In May 1916, Ambedkar wrote an extensive and innovative research paper for one of Goldenweiser's general ethnology courses, where the influence of Boas's ideas against racial fixity is clear. In addition to opposing a basic Marxist tenet about class antagonism that Ambedkar learnt from Simkhovitch's courses, also discernable within the paper are many echoes of Ambedkar's everyday experiences regarding race and gender from his wanderings away from campus. In the paper, titled 'Castes in India: Their Mechanism, Genesis and Development', Ambedkar argued that caste was a distinct social category that could not be accounted for either by theories of race or by class antagonism. Rejecting the standard explanation of the racial origins of caste popular in colonial ethnography (i.e., a consequence of Aryan invasions, wherein the darker-skinned earlier inhabitants were subjugated) and also the dominant sociological claim that caste was maintained through a hierarchy of purity and pollution, Ambedkar boldly asserted that the essence of caste was the control of women's sexuality—foremost, the practice of endogamy.

Ambedkar was exceptionally proud of the work. A year later, it became his first scholarly publication, appearing in the professional journal *The Indian Antiquary*. Later, when publishing his PhD dissertation as a book, he is described on the title page as the 'author of "Castes in India"'. Years later, in 1944, when he was publishing a third edition of his explosive essay 'Annihilation of Caste', he revealed that the third edition had been delayed for so long after the print run of the 1937 second edition was exhausted because he had been trying to find the time to recast 'Annihilation of Caste' 'so as to incorporate into it another essay of mine called "Castes in India"'.[14] Indeed, even Ambedkar's latest writings from the 1950s, when he was nearing the end of his life, referenced assertions that he had first posited as a young doctoral candidate at Columbia.

In many ways, Ambedkar's 'Caste' paper captured everything other than 'the science of finance' that Ambedkar had learnt and discovered, both on and off campus, during his three formative years in New York. The formal structure of this rich education was giving shape to his profound lived experiences being Dalit—all of those childhood experiences that he had written about in his autobiographical fragments, *Waiting for a Visa*—forging an uncommon and unprecedented concatenation of events that helped make Ambedkar the person that he was.

Chapter Four
London Calling (1916–17)

By the summer of 1916, Ambedkar had completed all of the requisite coursework and other requirements for the PhD, other than the doctoral dissertation. He was, as it's commonly called, ABD—all but dissertation. After exhausting his initial two-year scholarship, Ambedkar had secured an extension for another year. After three years in New York, he received one more extension.[1] However, as an ABD doctoral candidate, Ambedkar was under no further obligation to remain at Columbia University, or indeed even in the United States. All that was required of him was to submit a completed dissertation vetted and approved by his supervisor, and that he could do from anywhere. Moreover, to complete his dissertation, which was on the topic of imperial finance in India and once again under the supervision of Professor Seligman, Ambedkar needed access to documents that were only available at the centre of the empire. With nothing keeping him in New York, with a year of scholarship remaining and with a need for resources only London could offer, Ambedkar immediately set his sights on the UK.

London Calling (1916–17)

This decision faced two major setbacks. First, he did not have a passport valid for travel to England; and second, even if he could manage the travel documents, he had no research institution to affiliate with to permit him to enter limited-access venues such as the India Office library. The latter problem his Columbia University professors readily solved. Ambedkar's doctoral supervisor, Professor Seligman, wrote a kind letter of introduction that would allow Ambedkar to gain access to Sidney Webb, who, along with his wife Beatrice, was the main founder of a well-respected institution in the heart of London dedicated solely to the study of economics and political science from a Fabian (or democratic socialist) angle—the London School of Economics and Political Science, or LSE. In his letter dated 23 May 1916, Seligman wrote:

> Will you permit me to introduce to you one of my graduate students, Mr. Bhim Rao Ramji Ambedkar? Ambedkar came to us on a State Scholarship from Baroda and has been with us for three years. He is now spending a year in London to finish up his dissertation, on the financial history of India. He is an excellent student and a nice fellow, moderate, broad and able, and I know that you will be glad to be of service to him in the prosecution of his researches.[2]

Another economics faculty member from Columbia, Professor Henry Rogers Seager, with whom Ambedkar had taken three courses, as well as a year-long seminar in political economy that Seager co-taught with Seligman, wrote a letter introducing—and 'highly recommending'[3]— Ambedkar to Edwin Cannan, professor of political economy at the University of London. It appears that Ambedkar was able to meet Sidney Webb only for a brief moment (just long enough to get a letter of access to the India Office library, but not long enough to make a lasting impression), but Seager's letter to Cannan was enough to do the trick. Immediately after reviewing Ambedkar's Columbia University records, Cannan offered to attach Ambedkar to LSE and paved his way to accessing all of the material that LSE and other University of London libraries, as well as the British Museum, had to offer.

But there was still the setback of travel documents. During Ambedkar's stay in New York, the First World War had erupted across much of the globe. While the US was yet to enter the war by 1916, the UK was deep in the middle of it. War-time regulations were thus in effect, and a passport for travel to the UK could not be issued by the British consulate in New York without prior clearance from the India Office in London. On 17 May 1916, Ambedkar addressed two letters to the British consulate from his Livingston Hall accommodation at Columbia.[4] He asked for a passport urgently, indicating that he intended to leave for England by steamer on 3 June 1916. He said he was in a hurry because he needed 'to meet certain professors of the English Universities before they disperse for the summer vacation'.[5]

The British consul general first took clearance from the British embassy in Washington, and then, on 22 May, forwarded Ambedkar's application to the Foreign Office in London. He attached a copy of Ambedkar's certificate of identity, which had been issued to him by the British Resident in Baroda on 4 June 1913, just prior to his departure for the US. This certificate mentioned his name as 'Bhimrao alias Brimvran Ambedkar', the first 'r' in 'Brimvran' clearly a careless typo by the British. Although Ambedkar had indicated that he wished to depart on 3 June, it was not until 8 June that the undersecretary of state of the Foreign Office even forwarded Ambedkar's application to the India Office in London. The India Office, as bureaucratic as could possibly be, then began moving the file around, with superfluous deliberations about whether there was 'any objection to the Consul giving him a passport endorsed for the journey to England',[6] or whether instead they should issue him an emergency certificate.

Young Ambedkar grew impatient with the bureaucrats needlessly forcing him to waste time waiting in New York when he could be getting busy at work in London. On 11 June, Ambedkar boarded the

SS *New York* bound for Liverpool without a passport! Several biographers have claimed (without corroborating evidence) that Ambedkar was closely interrogated by the secret police when he reached the UK on suspicion of being a revolutionary.[7] If Ambedkar had been held up at immigration, it would have been because he had arrived without a passport. When the bureaucrats at the India Office found out Ambedkar had arrived, they were livid. One wrote on the file: 'Keep these papers pending till I find out from him how he got his passport.'[8] As late as July, the India Office staff were still puzzled over how Ambedkar had arrived in the UK 'when his case was still under discussion here'. Finally resigned to it, an officer of the India Office took the bold step of seeing the file closed, noting, 'I am directed to inform you that the Indian in question has since arrived in England and no action in the matter appears now to be called for.'[9]

The 'Indian in question' had indeed reached England and was putting up at 21 Cromwell Road, South Kensington, London. This is now the address of the French consulate in London, but in the early twentieth century, it was a major focal point for Indian students in the UK. The detached corner house opposite the Natural History Museum was rented by the India Office to facilitate the arrival of new students reaching England. Starting from 1910, the National Indian Association (NIA) (of which Sarojini Naidu was a prominent member), the Northbrook Indian Society and a newly created Bureau of Information for Indian Students were all accommodated in the building, in addition to the guest rooms providing lodging. The NIA held regular lectures, meetings and soirées at the house, while the Northbrook Society provided newspapers and recreational activities, such as billiards. The India Office would send an educational advisor there to greet new Indian students and advise them on courses, degree requirements and how to find more permanent lodging in the UK.[10] The Bureau of Information also did its fair share of spying on the Indian students, but there is no extant file on Ambedkar from that period.[11]

As he had been so eager to do, Ambedkar had managed to meet some key professors before the summer holidays. One meeting—with Seager's contact Professor Cannan—would completely alter the course of Ambedkar's educational destiny. Cannan, though something of a racist and averse to Indians, was quite fond of Ambedkar, and greatly impressed by him. In a letter from a friend of Cannan's to Percy Anstey, a former LSE graduate and future boss of Ambedkar at Sydenham College, Bombay, we find some gossip about Cannan's atypical like for Ambedkar: 'Professor Cannan, who saw him several times, judged him to be capable and well-instructed with no lack of self-appreciation.'[12]

Either Cannan or the educational advisor apprised Ambedkar of the fact that simply being a Columbia University doctoral candidate in the middle of London would not grant him full access to the bounty of resources that England had to offer, but enrolling as a full-fledged student at LSE would. And certainly, as Ambedkar would have quickly grasped from any of the NIA soirées, making connections with people in England and earning British academic credentials would be of far greater utility back in Bombay. It was British India, after all, and Britain's supersession by America as the dominant global power was still decades in the future.

On 11 October 1916, on the basis of his Elphinstone BA and Columbia MA degrees, Ambedkar enrolled as a master's student at LSE (in the University of London system to which LSE belonged, this degree was designated as an MSc and doctorates were designated as DSc). While it was customary to allow foreign students to skip the bachelor's if they possessed its equivalent from elsewhere,[13] the MSc remained a prerequisite for enrolling for the doctorate. Sure enough, the admit card—which had cost Ambedkar a bit over £10—served as a crucial gate pass into guarded spaces of knowledge and endless shelves of books. At the bottom, the card read, 'Must be shown to the Doorkeeper'!

There are four points worth noting about what Ambedkar filled into his LSE application for admission. He wrote his surname as Ambedkar, and his 'Christian name', as the form refers to the primary name, as 'Bhimrao R.'; he wrote his London address as '21 Cromwell Rd, SW, London', confirming that he lived there; under permanent address he simply wrote 'Bombay, India', instead of specific details; and, under degree of standing, he wrote 'MA', as he was ABD and had not yet actually earned the PhD degree. All this will be of interest when we compare the same responses to the same form the next time he had the occasion to fill it.[14]

Although the MSc was not a diploma that Ambedkar in later life would list on his stationery or stamps—we will explain why in Chapter Ten—being an MSc student in London afforded him the efficient and attractive opportunity of continuing his doctoral research at Columbia on imperial finance, a portion of which could be submitted to LSE as the master's thesis, and later the full version to Columbia as the doctoral dissertation. This was the strategy that was ultimately executed—only, it took a great deal longer than anticipated, since, as we shall soon see, Ambedkar's initial stay in London was cut short by the expiry of his Baroda scholarship. It also granted Ambedkar the opportunity to attend an entirely fresh offering of courses from a set of faculty members completely new to him.

The attendance sheet for 1916–17 offers some insight into Ambedkar's chosen courses at LSE. He enrolled on geography, which was taught by Sir Halford Mackinder, previously a permanent professor of geography at LSE, but who had earlier resigned to contest elections as a member of Parliament. He was, in fact, an MP during the time he taught Ambedkar, and thus only a part-time lecturer. This was no matter, as Ambedkar behaved like a part-time attendee—out of eleven sessions in the course, Ambedkar was marked as present for only six.

A course Ambedkar skipped even more often was called 'Political Ideas' taught by the classicist Goldsworthy Lowes Dickinson, a lover of all things Hellenic—which, of course, India was not. After a first book on the ideal political life of the ancient Greeks, Dickinson had then published his thoughts on India—'supernatural, uncanny, terrifying, sublime, horrible, monotonous, incomprehensible'—in a 1914 book titled *An Essay on the Civilisations of India, China and Japan*.[15] Dickinson was clearly not favourably moved by Indian civilization, and Ambedkar was obviously not favourably moved by Dickinson, having been marked present for only two out of his eleven sessions.

The UK's very first permanent professor of sociology, Leonard Hobhouse, taught Ambedkar two courses—one called 'Social Evolution' and another called 'Social Theory'. These obviously captured Ambedkar's imagination, as he attended every one of Hobhouse's classes, save one. Beyond a mere lack of interest, there was another reason to explain why Ambedkar missed so many of his LSE classes. For, just a month after enrolling at LSE, Ambedkar paid out a substantial deposit of £50 (nearly a quarter of his entire scholarship) to the Honourable Society of Gray's Inn, to begin terms of study to be qualified as a barrister. Gray's Inn was one of the four Inns of Court in London (another was Lincoln's Inn, with which Gray's was temporarily merged during the time that Ambedkar was there).[16] Basically a professional association for barristers and judges, membership with one of the Inns of Court was required to be called to the bar, the condition for practising law as a barrister in England—and at that time, also in British India.

This was an added advantage of studying in London over New York, as a law degree from the United States would not have allowed Ambedkar to practise law in India. Ambedkar needed to complete twelve semesters (called 'terms') at Gray's Inn to qualify for the bar. The first term (autumn/winter) had started on 11 November 1916, with his £50 deposit, and the twelfth term (spring/summer) ended six years later when, on 28 June 1922, Ambedkar was finally called to the bar. All those years of study and preparation took time away from Ambedkar's other endeavours, and help to explain why he was often not in attendance for his LSE classes.

Although busy juggling three separate highly advanced educational and professional qualifications at the same time—the PhD dissertation for Columbia, the MSc coursework at LSE and legal studies at

Gray's Inn—Ambedkar did take out time in London for book collecting, his favourite hobby. He acquired in that period a couple of books that would turn out to be very significant towards his later thought and writing. One was *Democracy and Education* by his Columbia University professor John Dewey. The book was inscribed by Ambedkar on 6 January 1917 and remains one of the most marked-up books in his personal library, with innumerable underlines and margin scribbles.[17]

Another book Ambedkar bought in London at that time was Bertrand Russell's *Principles of Social Reconstruction*,[18] which he seems to have bought in 1917 and about which he published a review the following year. Several biographers of Ambedkar claim that he actually met Russell in 1920,[19] but Scott Stroud and Landon Elkind have established that this is probably false. Their time in London hardly overlapped for ten days in 1920, and there is no mention of such a meeting in Russell's meticulously kept diary for that year.[20] But Ambedkar certainly was out and about meeting other significant people.

One of them was Baron George Sydenham Clarke, who had been governor of Bombay from 1907–13, and then in 1913 was raised to the peerage and took the title of Lord Sydenham. Although Lord Sydenham has been described as 'an insensitive, clumsy, uncouth and infinitely boring man',[21] and spent his later years promoting racist, anti-Semitic and fascist propaganda, one of his only redeeming features was that in 1918 he proved helpful in securing Ambedkar a position at the eponymous Sydenham College in Bombay.

Why Ambedkar should need such a position in 1918 must be explained. By the summer of 1917, a year after reaching London, Ambedkar's Baroda scholarship extension expired and the state administration refused to grant him any further extensions, forcing his return to India. Although he had completed all of the required coursework for the MSc at LSE, he still had his master's thesis to write and submit before his degree could be granted. Not only that, he still had not finished writing his doctoral dissertation for the Columbia PhD. Add to this enormous pile of pending London work the fact that he had only just completed his second of twelve terms at Gray's Inn. A much lengthier commitment to his legal training in London was necessary before he qualified to be called to the bar.

For all these reasons, he was resolved eventually to return to London to complete all of this work that he had so ambitiously undertaken. Fortunately, his supervisor at LSE, Professor Cannan, went to bat for him and convinced the university authorities to grant him an 'excused interruption of his course of study for a period not exceeding four years from October 1917 and further that on resuming his course he be exempted ... for one term provided that his teachers certify that he has made use, adequate for such exemption, of the material for his thesis available in India'.[22]

Seeking solace in the display of trust exhibited by his LSE supervisor and this four-year-plus-one-term official reprieve that he had secured, Ambedkar prepared for his voyage back to India.

Chapter Five
Sleepless in Baroda (1917–20)

In late July 1917, Ambedkar packed his personal belongings and booked his voyage back home. Securing passage on the stylish and comfortable SS *Kaisar-i-Hind*, Ambedkar was unable to take his enormous collection of books in tow. The *Kaisar-i-Hind* was purpose-built as a passenger liner and was short on cargo space. Ambedkar thus entrusted his book collection to Thomas Cook & Son, which would send the cargo directly to Bombay on another liner, the SS *Salsette*.

Ambedkar left London and made the routine Dover-Calais crossing, then boarded a train there for the south of France and finally embarked on the SS *Kaisar-i-Hind* at Marseille. It was a remarkably fast ship, and everyone also thought of it as a lucky one. During the First World War, it had been fired upon by German submarines on five separate occasions (once in 1916 with the Viceroy of India, Lord Chelmsford, on board), and on four of these occasions it had sailed at its top speed and outrun the torpedoes. The one time a torpedo actually struck, in March 1917, the warhead failed to explode and no damage was done.[1] This time, with Ambedkar on board, the *Kaisar* was lucky once again and sailed safely to Colombo, then onward to Bombay. Ambedkar disembarked on 21 August 1917.

Not as lucky as the *Kaisar-i-Hind*, however, was the other steamer carrying Ambedkar's enormous book collection. On 19 July 1917, the SS *Salsette* set sail from London bound for Bombay, with passengers, general cargo and pay for the British troops serving in Egypt on board. The very next day, just after rounding Portland Bill in the English Channel, the ship was struck by a torpedo fired by the infamous German submarine *UB-40*. The *Salsette* was the fiftieth ship that the UB-40 had sunk, and it would go on to sink another fifty within its two short years of operation. Although all of the *Salsette*'s passengers had got off safely, fifteen crew members lost their lives.[2] The SS *Salsette* sank forty-five minutes after the torpedo hit, taking the vast majority of Ambedkar's books and papers, including the first draft of his Columbia University doctoral dissertation ('The National Dividend'), to the bottom of the sea.

Upon Ambedkar's own safe return to Bombay, prominent members of the Mahar community held a function, where he was to be felicitated for his academic achievements. At that time, among their population of some sixteen lakh people in the Bombay Province, only six untouchables were known to have completed high school and only one other to have earned a BA.[3] Surprisingly—at least it was surprising from their point of view—Ambedkar was a no-show. But this was not surprising at all from Ambedkar's point of view. He had spent a full four years abroad, leaving his wife and family in circumstances of considerable hardship, and all that he had to show for it was an MA. Sure, he was ABD for his Columbia doctorate and had completed all of the coursework and cleared the final exam for his MSc as well, with only the thesis remaining to be submitted, but being ABD and all-but-thesis were a far cry from holding the actual MSc degree and the coveted title of 'Doctor'. And sure, he was still a member in good standing of the Honourable Society of Gray's Inn, but that was a far cry from being a licensed barrister. Ambedkar thus informed the elders who sought to felicitate him that he had not done anyone any favours by winning a scholarship, going abroad and getting an education. It was something that every untouchable should be in a position to do. Any money that the organizers had gathered for the event, he insisted, ought, instead, to be given to untouchable youth to fund their education.[4]

As if all of these unfulfilled ambitions were not already bad enough, Ambedkar was also expected in Baroda to fulfil his part of the agreement of service to the state for a period of ten years. He would be attached to the accountant general's office as a probationer (earning Rs 150 per month), until the time he passed the Revenue Departmental Examinations and was absorbed into the regular grade. He had been to Baroda before, as a BA, and it was a miserable experience. Would it be any better this time around?

At least Ambedkar was now able to finance his voyage to Baroda. Thomas Cook had paid out the insurance claim for his sunken cargo, a welcome Rs 600.[5] On top of that, 'His Highness the Maharajah Saheb has been graciously pleased to give him Rs 300/- as a gift to cover the loss he has sustained through his luggage being sunk', read an order dated 21 September 1917 from the maharajah to the dewan of Baroda. Ambedkar gave half of the sum to his wife, Ramabai, and kept half for his travel and accommodation expenses. At the end of September 1917, Ambedkar, accompanied by his brother Balaram, boarded the train from Bombay bound for Baroda.

What happened upon arrival in Baroda sparked one of the most famous episodes from Ambedkar's life, frequently referenced and recounted. This is partly because it was inherently egregious, but also partly because Ambedkar himself brought particular attention to it by writing about it in his autobiographical fragments, *Waiting for a Visa*. This is how Ambedkar described the episode from the moment of arriving at the Baroda railway station from Bombay:

> I called [a carriage driver], and asked him if he knew if there was a hotel in the camp. He said that there was a Parsi inn,

and that they took paying guests. Hearing that it was an inn maintained by the Parsis, my heart was gladdened. The Parsis are followers of the Zoroastrian religion. There was no fear of my being treated by them as an untouchable, because their religion does not recognise untouchability. With a heart glad with hope and a mind free from fear, I put my luggage in a hackney carriage and asked the driver to drive me to the Parsi inn in the camp.

The inn was a two-storied building, on the ground floor of which lived an old Parsi with his family. He was a caretaker, and supplied food to tourists who came there to stay ... I went up [to undress] ... The caretaker came with a book in his hand. Seeing as he could well see from my half-undressed state that I had no *sadra* and *kasti*, the two things which prove that one is a Parsi, in a sharp tone he asked me who I was. Not knowing that this inn was maintained by the Parsi community for the use of Parsis only, I told him that I was a Hindu. He was shocked, and told me that I could not stay in the inn. I was thoroughly shocked by his answer and was cold all over. The question returned again, where to go? Composing myself, I told him that though a Hindu, I had no objection to staying there if he had no objection. He replied, 'How can you? I have to maintain a register of all those who stay here in the inn.' I saw his difficulty. I said I could assume a Parsi name for the purpose of entering it in the register ... He agreed, on condition that I pay him a rupee and a half per day for board and lodging ...

In the absence of the company of human beings I sought the company of books, and read and read. Absorbed in reading, I forgot my lonely condition. But the chirping and flying about of the bats, which had made the hall [to which my guestroom was attached] their home, often distracted my mind and sent cold shivers through me—reminding me of what I was endeavouring to forget, that I was in a strange place under strange conditions.

Sleepless in Baroda (1917–20)

Many a time I must have been angry. But I subdued my grief and my anger through the feeling that though it was a dungeon, it was a shelter, and that some shelter was better than no shelter. So heart-rending was my condition that when my sister's son came from Bombay, bringing my remaining luggage which I had left behind, and when he saw my state, he began to cry so loudly that I had to send him back immediately. In this state I lived in the Parsi inn, impersonating a Parsi.

It was the eleventh day of my stay in the inn. I had taken my morning meal, and had dressed up, and was about to step out of my room to go to office. As I was picking up some books which I had borrowed overnight, for returning them to the library, I heard the footsteps of a considerable number of people coming up the staircase. I thought they were tourists who had come to stay, and was therefore looking out to see who these friends were. Instantly I saw a dozen angry-looking, tall, sturdy Parsis, each armed with a stick, coming towards my room. I realised that they were not fellow tourists, and they gave proof of it immediately.

They lined up in front of my room and fired a volley of questions. 'Who are you? Why did you come here? How dare you take a Parsi name? You scoundrel! You have polluted the Parsi inn!' I stood silent. I could give no answer. I could not persist in impersonation. It was in fact a fraud, and the fraud was discovered, and I am sure if I had persisted in the game I was playing, I would have been assaulted by the mob of angry and fanatic Parsis and probably doomed to death. My meekness and my silence averted this doom. One of them asked when I thought of vacating.

At that time my shelter I prized more than my life. The threat implied in this question was a grave one. I therefore broke my silence and implored them to let me stay for a week at least, thinking that my application to the Minister for a bungalow would be decided upon favourably in the meantime. But the Parsis were in no mood to listen. They issued an ultimatum. They must not find me in the inn in the evening. I must pack off. They held out dire consequences, and left. I was bewildered. My heart sank within me. I cursed all, and wept bitterly. After all, I was deprived of my precious possession—namely, my shelter. It was no better than a prisoner's cell. But to me it was very precious.

After the Parsis were gone, I sat for some time engaged in thinking to find a way out. I had hopes that I would soon get a State bungalow, and my troubles would be over. My problem was therefore a temporary problem, and I thought that going to friends would be a good solution. I had no friends among the untouchables of Baroda State. But I had friends among other classes. One was a Hindu, the other was an Indian Christian. I first went to my Hindu friend and told him what had befallen me. He was a noble soul and a great personal friend of mine. He was sad and also indignant. He, however, let fall one observation. He said, 'If you come to my home, my servants will go.' I took the hint, and did not press him to accommodate me …

I decided to go to [my Christian friend] and ask him if he would accommodate me. When I put the question, his reply was that his wife was coming to Baroda the next day, and that he would have to consult her. I learnt subsequently that it was a very diplomatic answer. He and his wife came originally from a family which was Brahman by caste, and although on conversion to Christianity the husband had become liberal in thought, the wife had remained orthodox in her ways, and would not have consented to harbour an untouchable in her house. The last ray of hope thus flickered away. It was 4 pm when I left the house of my Indian Christian friend. Where to go was the one supreme question before me. I must quit the inn, and had no friend to go to! The only alternative left was to return to Bombay ...

This scene of a dozen Parsis armed with sticks lined before me in a menacing mood, and myself standing before them with a terrified look imploring for mercy, is a scene which so long a period as eighteen years has not succeeded in fading away. I can even now vividly recall it—and never recall it without tears in my eyes. It was then for the first time that I learnt that a person who is an untouchable to a Hindu is also an untouchable to a Parsi.[6]

Although Ambedkar wrote in these autobiographical fragments that he thus left Baroda for Bombay within a span of only eleven days, other accounts of the Baroda tragedy—including one by Ambedkar himself in his *Janata* newspaper[7]—differed in terms of chronology and a few other details. What we know is that Ambedkar's second sojourn in Baroda was as humiliating as his first one had been, if not even more so. He was treated contemptuously by his colleagues in the state bureaucracy and could find no comfort either at his tenuous accommodation or at his hostile office. His only refuge was a public library.

His mentor, Dada Keluskar, sought in vain to apprise the Maharajah of Ambedkar's unsustainable living and working conditions in Baroda. In fact, Keluskar himself narrated a shocking episode that Ambedkar had not mentioned in his own account of the Baroda days. According to Keluskar, as soon as he had learnt about the fiasco at the Parsee inn and that Ambedkar had boarded a train to return to Bombay, Keluskar had contacted a liberal-minded Brahman professor in Baroda, requesting him to offer boarding to Ambedkar. Upon learning of the Baroda professor's assent, Keluskar seated Ambedkar once again back on a train from Bombay to Baroda. When Ambedkar reached Baroda yet again, a servant of the professor's was waiting for him at the railway station with a letter. The letter implored Ambedkar not to come to his house, because although he himself was willing to accommodate him, his wife was averse to permitting an untouchable to stay in their house. Ambedkar thus returned again to Bombay then and there, this time without even having left the Baroda railway station.[8]

By 17 November 1917, Ambedkar was back in Bombay, with no intention of returning to Baroda to subject himself to further misery and humiliation there.[9] Ambedkar's previous return from Baroda to Bombay had been occasioned by the illness and subsequent death of his father. This time around, upon his return from Baroda, Ambedkar learnt of the death of Jijabai, his stepmother. The disaster that was Ambedkar's second sojourn in Baroda then opened up into a full year of further adversity and hardship in Bombay.

Chapter Six

Struggle, Sydenham, Southborough and Shahu Maharaj

Ambedkar was not close to his stepmother, but endeavoured to fulfil his filial obligations. What was much more devastating for Ambedkar was his elder brother Anandrao's death in the same month. Ramu—as Ambedkar called Ramabai—had already been taking care of Anandrao's wife, Laxmibai, and their son, Mukund. From this point onward, Ambedkar looked after the upbringing and education of his nephew, Mukund, with the same care and attention as his own son, Yashwant. Death hung over the Ambedkars throughout this long year of struggle, from November 1917 to November 1918.

His studies in London left incomplete, his dissertation for Columbia lost to the seas, his obligation to the state of Baroda unfulfilled and tragedy after tragedy besetting his personal life, Ambedkar had no career prospects and was desperate to earn some income. Notwithstanding the rough treatment and humiliation that Ambedkar had suffered at the hands of the Parsee mob in Baroda, he enjoyed a secure, reliable friendship in Bombay with his former Columbia University dormitory roommate, Naval Bhathena, who opened as many doors in the local Parsee community for Ambedkar as he could. Ambedkar worked for a short period as a personal secretary to an affluent Parsee businessman. He also picked up work tutoring young Parsee boys. He even seems to have tried his hand as a financial adviser, but his outcaste status stigmatized his efforts to find some footing in that trade.

While persisting in his hapless attempts to scrape together an income, Ambedkar did not forsake his regular studies. Even in India, he was still keeping the requisite terms for Gray's Inn, London.[1] Additionally, he was exercising his academic skills by writing a lengthy formal review of Bertrand Russell's then-recent book, *Principles of Social Reconstruction*, a review he would publish in the first issue of the *Journal of the Indian Economic Society*. The journal was a quarterly, edited by Chandulal Nagindas Vakil, a young man who had earned his MSc from LSE in 1921 along with Ambedkar, and who would later emerge as a well-known planning economist and professor of economics at the University of Bombay. It was published by the Indian Economic Society in Bombay (now known as the Indian Economic Association, boasting such distinguished figures as Amartya Sen and Manmohan Singh as past presidents). Ambedkar's review was largely an exercise in social philosophy, and he used the occasion to contrast Russell's critique of violence with John Dewey's distinction between force as violence versus force as energy—which Ambedkar had learnt by sitting in his Columbia University classroom. Evoking Dewey against Russell, Ambedkar wrote, 'It must be remembered by those who are opposed to force that without the use of it all ideals will remain empty just as without some ideal or purpose (conscious or otherwise) all activity will be no more than mere fruitless fooling.'[2]

In the very next issue of the journal, appearing in the autumn of 1918, Ambedkar published another article, this time more germane to the Economic Society than an exploration of social philosophy. It was titled 'Small Holdings in India and Their Remedies', a data-driven paper linking India's pathetically low agricultural productivity to its small and scattered land holdings. Aligning precisely with the interests and orientation of Vakil, the editor of the journal, Ambedkar's article must have made a favourable impression on its readership. One of those readers was a certain Professor Percy Anstey, a founder of the Indian Economic Society in 1917, and, since 1914, principal of the prestigious Sydenham College in Bombay. Thanks to the impact of these publications, as well as his contacts in London and formidable academic background, after a full year of struggle and hardship, in November 1918 Ambedkar finally caught a lucky break.

Sydenham College, which was modelled on LSE (and named, as we have already mentioned, after the former governor Lord Sydenham, who seems to have favoured Ambedkar), was holding interviews for a temporary (two-year) professorship in political economy. Ambedkar applied in December 1917. By the following April, the two shortlisted candidates were Ambedkar and a certain R.M. Joshi, who had also studied at LSE and was then working as a lecturer at Sydenham College. The principal, Professor Percy Anstey, another LSE alumnus and himself a former student of Edward Cannan, just as both Ambedkar and Joshi were, wrote their mutual professor in London for information about the two candidates' characters and capabilities. Anstey also wrote to the director of LSE, Sidney Webb, but Webb communicated that he did not know Ambedkar. Webb did, however, convey an opinion about Ambedkar that he had heard from Cannan: 'Professor Cannan, who saw him several times, judged him to be capable and well instructed with no lack of self-appreciation.'

Professor Cannan himself characteristically replied to Anstey's letter of query with his usual jocularity and a healthy dose of racist overtones:

> Both men are unusually good. I don't know anything about Ambedkar except that he came to do a thesis and attacked it and me in a way which showed he had quite extraordinary practical ability. 'And me' I say because if he wanted to prefer a request to the University, he would save me all trouble by recounting

all the relevant facts. He chose the subjects for the thesis, and got to work on it without giving any trouble. And so far as I could see, he was doing it very well indeed, and would in due time have got the M.Sc. quite easily ... I rather wonder if he is a pure Indian; his character is rather Scotch-American, though in appearance he is a fat Indian.

Joshi, on the other hand, is as lean as a tolerably healthy and well-fed person can be, and there is nothing European about him ... I should think he is much the best liked of all the Indians we have had. Not, I think, at all self-seeking. Ambedkar would do the job well in his own interest, while Joshi would do it for its own sake. I find it difficult to decide which of them would be the better teacher. Ambedkar would get up all that was required with ease and put the trusting students safely through his examinations, but I should think Joshi would be much more 'inspiring'.[3]

Anstey finally selected Ambedkar for the position, who taught at the college from 11 November 1918 to 11 March 1920. Bringing home a handsome salary of Rs 450 per month, Ambedkar's fortunes had finally taken a brighter turn. Limiting spending on himself to some 20 paise daily and handing over a purse of Rs 50–60 per month to Ramabai for household expenses, Ambedkar was able to save a sizeable sum of Rs 7,000 over the period of his teaching at Sydenham.

But Ambedkar and his family were not left alone to enjoy their improving fortunes in peace. Although Ambedkar had undertaken to repay Baroda state for failing to fulfil his part of the bond of service, he requested doing so only after landing permanent employment in the future. Maharajah Gaekwad instructed his administration that there should be no effort to recover the funds, as they had been spent towards education. Despite the fact that the Sydenham position was only a temporary appointment, and ignoring the Maharajah in their zeal, Baroda bureaucrats relentlessly hounded Ambedkar. They addressed letters to Sydenham College in January, March and May of 1920 with the subject line, 'Repayment of debts', reminding him over and over that he needed 'to expedite the matter' and 'take early action'. Other letters were sent to the Bombay Educational Department in 1920, proposing that his salary be docked and the funds diverted to the state of Baroda, and yet another in 1925 to trade union leader Narayan Malhar Joshi, who, later in the 1930s, cooperated helpfully with Ambedkar, although it is not clear how close of a personal relationship they had in the mid-1920s.[4] This harassment of Ambedkar and his employers and associates by Baroda bureaucrats to extract Rs 21,000, the total amount that Baroda state had spent on his studies, continued in various ways for a full fifteen years! It was not until 1932, when Ambedkar would meet Maharajah Gaekwad at the Round Table Conference in London and personally request that he intervene in putting an end to the harassment, that his Baroda file was finally closed.

The prior year of hustle in Bombay had taken Ambedkar throughout the streets of the city. Unlike when he had first arrived back in India from London and was a no-show at the event meant to felicitate him for his educational achievements, Ambedkar was now not shying away from public appearances. Perhaps his first major public appearance was a felicitation for Palwankar Baloo—untouchable cricketer and slow left-arm bowler, who was quickly becoming a sports legend in his own time. Indisputably one of the greatest Indian cricketers of his era, Baloo, from the Chambhar caste, had just dominated the field during a cricket tour in England, and Ambedkar was tasked by community members with writing the welcome address felicitating him upon his return to Bombay. An avid fan of Baloo's, Ambedkar was happy to oblige. Despite striking up a friendship at the time, their relationship would prove rocky in the coming years, as Baloo himself emerged as a political leader within the Chambhar community and Ambedkar faced constant headwinds in his efforts to unite the Mahars and the Chambhars into a collective movement. The felicitation ceremony brought Ambedkar in contact with another young Chambhar activist, S.N. Shivtarkar, who would become one of his closest friends and confidants for the next dozen years.

Now well established at Sydenham College, and known far and wide throughout Bombay as the sole Mahar with a post-graduate degree, on 27 January 1919, Ambedkar was invited to give testimony before the Franchise Committee headed by Lord Southborough precisely for this reason. Commonly known as the Southborough Committee after its chairperson, this committee had been set up by the British government earlier in 1918 to look into forthcoming constitutional reforms for all of the provinces of British India, especially with respect to franchise—the vote, voting rights, the representation of various minorities and communities, and so on. Not identified with any particular organization, unlike others who testified as leaders of specific communities or associations, Ambedkar did not limit himself to pleading on behalf of only the untouchables, but allowed himself to advise the British about comprehensive franchise reforms across the board:

> In ten pages of closely printed material, ranging far beyond demands for Depressed Class rights, [Ambedkar] urged joint electorates with reserved seats for Muslims ... and a low-pitched franchise for the Marathas ... allowing them a voice 'free from Brahman domination'. But he argued that Untouchables, whom he characterized as 'slaves', 'dehumanized', and so 'socialized as never to complain', must have communal representation 'in such numbers as will enable them to claim redress'. The franchise [bar] for depressed classes should be [set] 'so low as to educate into political life as many Untouchables as possible'.[5]

While demanding communal representation, Ambedkar referenced ideas he had first laid out in his 'Castes in India' paper three years earlier—specifically that untouchables were a different community from touchables, not because of any racial difference or because they were conquered pre-Aryan inhabitants, but solely on account of endogamic isolation. Buttressing his argument for separate electorates, Ambedkar evoked his professor John Dewey's words again (as he had the year prior in his review of Bertrand Russell's book): There was no 'like-mindedness' or 'social endosmosis' between untouchables and caste Hindus in India.[6]

In the end, however, Southborough's Franchise Committee declined to grant elected representation to the depressed classes in any of the reformed provincial legislatures; Bombay received only one nominated seat for untouchables. Finding this arrangement arbitrary and unfair, the British government themselves took steps to reverse it in the coming years. But for now, Ambedkar had certainly made his mark. He was described as highly intelligent even by those opposing his demands to the committee, and the learned and confident manner with which he spoke, not exclusively focusing on the interests of one section but placing its concerns more broadly within those of the very nature of democratic government, exhibited for anyone with ears to hear that the increasingly visible Mahar movement was about to inherit a leader of uncommon ability.

Indeed, one distinguished person, though not himself an untouchable, yet active and prominent in the movement, went as far as to call Ambedkar their 'emancipator'. This was Shahu Bhosale, popularly known as Chhatrapati Shahu Maharaj or the Shahu of Kolhapur. Ambedkar was introduced to the progressive-minded Shahu by Dattoba Dalvi, court painter for the Maharajah, and now renowned artist whose works are showcased at Jehangir Art Gallery in Mumbai, who was among Ambedkar's growing Bombay acquaintances and well-wishers. The Maharajah immediately took to Ambedkar for his intellect, knowledge, vision and oratorial skills. The admiration was mutual. The Maharajah was a pioneer in uplifting the depressed classes through various means, including reservation in employment, promoting schooling and offering free hostels for untouchable students, and even through his atypical social habits, such as insisting that his hunting companions take tea prepared by untouchables. He made a mark on

Ambedkar. Some twenty-five years in the future, Ambedkar penned a powerful book on the genealogy of the Shudra varna, and therein employed events that befell the Maratha predecessors of Shahu's lineage, descending back to the great Shivaji, as one of the main pieces of evidence for his argument. This was a thesis that harmonized well with motifs from the non-Brahman movement, to which Shahu Maharaj had lent all his regal weight.[7]

The Maharajah had made that dramatic remark about Ambedkar being the 'emancipator' at a conference for untouchables, for which he was the chief guest, in a small town called Mangaon in Kolhapur. The village *patil* (or headman) was a Jain called Appasaheb Patil, who helped the untouchables of Mangaon organize the conference, despite resistance from the Jains and Marathas (including a social boycott he was subjected to afterwards), the other two dominant communities of the area. The Maharajah had recommended that Ambedkar preside over the conference, and Ambedkar had accepted, spending two nights—20 and 21 March 1920—in two rooms of the simple village school that were prepared for him as accommodation. At the inauguration of the conference, Shahu spoke gushingly about Ambedkar—noting in typical aristocratic style that he had taken the trouble of cutting short his hunting trip only to be there to hear Ambedkar speak!

The Mangaon conference was soon followed up by a much larger one held in Nagpur, about which details are scanty. Many of Ambedkar's biographers have long claimed that the Maharajah presided over it and Ambedkar was called in to give the main speech.[8] However, an exchange of letters recently discovered in the Kolhapur archives shines a very different light on the events in Nagpur.[9]

From the letters we can confirm that the Nagpur conference was convened under the banner of the Akhil Bharatiya Bahishkrut Samaj Parishad (All-India Conference of the Excluded), organized by Ambedkar himself. It was to be held on 30 May 1920, and Shahu had accepted Ambedkar's invitation to be the chief guest. However, news reached Ambedkar that the Maharajah's daughter, Akkatai, was unwell and that the Maharajah would not be able to attend the Nagpur conference.

In an impassioned letter dated 11 May 1920, Ambedkar wrote that Shahu's absence would 'ruin everything' and that his support and presence were critical for the untouchable movement:

> It would seem rude to persuade you to attend the conference when there is illness at your home. But what can we do? Are we not your children like Akkasaheba? Do we have any other mentor? I beseech you to please accept the chairmanship of the conference for uplifting your beloved untouchable child.[10]

Ambedkar's strong appeal worked. In a reply to Ambedkar dated 13 May 1920, the Maharajah responded, 'Although my daughter is ill, I am going to take up your work. I shall set aside the obstacles and I will be there.'[11]

The 1920 conferences at Mangaon and Nagpur marked Ambedkar's initial entry into the theatre of grassroots politics that would evolve towards mass mobilization. Ambedkar began establishing himself as a leader with a unique vision and an unwavering principle of self-determination for the depressed classes. Forcefully challenging other untouchable leaders of the day, and especially touchable well-wishers of the untouchables, Ambedkar emphasized self-representation and self-led empowerment and uplift.

This new vision complemented his booming voice, and both began to be captured in local print, starting in 1920. With a financial injection of Rs 2,500 from Shahu Maharaj, Ambedkar launched a Marathi newspaper dedicated to informing the public about the untouchable movement. It was called *Mooknayak* (Leader of the Voiceless), and its inaugural issue appeared on 31 January 1920. The title of the paper was inspired by a quatrain of Tukaram, the seventeenth-century Marathi Bhakti poet celebrated for his egalitarian verses, which was printed in the masthead of *Mooknayak*:

Why should I feel shy?
I have laid aside hesitation and opened my mouth.
Here, on earth, no notice is taken of a voiceless creature;
No real good can be secured by over-modesty.[12]

While Ambedkar's first newspaper would not last long, it was succeeded by several others: the fortnightly *Bahishkrut Bharat* (1927–29), the fortnightly *Samata* (1928–29), which was later renamed *Janata* (1930–56), and the weekly *Prabuddha Bharat* (1956). The impact that Ambedkar's three and a half decades of journalistic endeavours must have had in raising Dalit consciousness can probably not be overestimated. The writing, always in accessible Marathi and absolutely no holds barred, punched through the ambiguities of social realities with remarkable clarity and insight. We can get a good sense of this through the imagery, power and forthrightness of Ambedkar's very first editorial.

Chapter Seven

A Loud Voice for the Voiceless (1920)

Ratnakar Ganveer, a Marathi writer who has explored Ambedkar's journalistic work, has pointed out that Ambedkar received all of his education in the English medium and was originally daunted by the task of articulating complex ideas in written Marathi. At first, Ambedkar penned his newspaper editorials confidently in English and then translated them into Marathi. Over time, with practice and after absorbing a great deal of Marathi literature, references to which are abundant in his editorials and commentaries, Ambedkar found as powerful a voice in Marathi as he enjoyed in the English language.[1] The pride that Ambedkar later showed in that achievement comes out clearly in a 1948 letter that he wrote to his fiancée, Sharada Kabir, who had written to him in an enviable Marathi that he found full of 'charm, simplicity, and grace':

> At one time, I had a mastery over the Marathi language. No one even now [could] claim to have read so much classical Marathi

literature as I have done. I was the editor of a weekly paper in Marathi for well nigh twenty years—and my writings, if they were collected together, would fill in at least three fat volumes.[2]

Mooknayak, a fortnightly, was published every second Saturday. Ambedkar was not the official editor, however, although he seems to have himself edited the first twelve issues within a span of six months. On paper, the first editor was Pandhurang Bhatkar, soon replaced by Dnyandeo D. Gholap. Gholap later became the first untouchable to be nominated to that one seat that was granted through the Southborough Committee reforms, becoming a member of the Bombay Legislative Council in 1921. Back in 1919, Gholap had assisted Ambedkar while writing his testimony before the committee, and the two were very close. A few years later (while on his second, much longer stint studying in London), Ambedkar received letters of complaint regarding Gholap's mismanagement of the paper. As a result, ties between Gholap and Ambedkar soured, and Ambedkar distanced himself from both Gholap and *Mooknayak* from 1923.

Ambedkar's first editorial was a tour de force. It is far preferable to read it for oneself than to have it described or summarized. It gives us a perfect snapshot of young Ambedkar's thinking just prior to his twenty-ninth birthday, at the dawn of 1920, a significant and eventful year. The English edition of Gandhi's *Hind Swaraj* had just been published in India (it had earlier been published in Gujarati and in English abroad, but not in India), Bal Gangadhar Tilak would soon die, and later in the year, the Non-Cooperation Movement would be launched upon outrage following the Jallianwala Bagh massacre in Amritsar. What visibility did the voiceless have amid all of these national(ist) events? Ambedkar sought, through his editorials in *Mooknayak*, to bring social issues to forums where only nationalist issues were being heard. The first editorial illustrates this beautifully:

> If anyone were to take stock of the sum-total of all the elements, of human as well as non-human origin, which constitute the

fabric of our nation, it would doubtless be revealed that India is most distinguished by the many disparities which characterise its composition. Among these disparities the most shameful is that which manifests itself in acute inequalities in material standards of living ...

Although Indians stand divided by many kinds of differences, the differences in religious affiliation are potentially more dangerous than those stemming from physical or intellectual factors. Often the differences on the basis of religion find expression in such extremities of conduct that they are the cause of bloodshed. The distinctions between the Hindus, the Parsees, the Jews, the Muslims and the Christians, and various other denominations, take diverse forms, but close scrutiny bears out that the stark hiatus between Hindus of different orders is both as incredible as it is reprehensible.

If a European were asked who he is, the answer provided by him, indicating his nationality—English or German or French or Italian—would be enough to resolve the matter. But the same cannot be said about Hindus. The statement, 'I am a Hindu', satisfies nobody. It is necessary for a Hindu to declare his caste in order to spell out his specific identity ...

The castes which constitute the so-called Hindu community are arranged in hierarchical order. Hindu society is like a tower, each floor of which is allotted to one caste. The point worth remembering is that this tower has no staircase and therefore there is no way of climbing up or down from one floor to another. The floor on which one is born is also the floor on which one dies. No matter how meritorious a person from a lower floor might be, there is no avenue for him to climb up to the upper floor. Likewise, there is no means by which a person entirely devoid of merit can be relegated to a floor beneath the one to which he has been assigned.

The inter-relationship between castes is not founded upon the logic of worth. However unworthy an upper-caste person might be, his status will ever remain high. Similarly, a worthy lower-caste person will never be allowed to transcend his lowliness. Because of the strict taboos against inter-dining and inter-marriage between members of lower and upper castes, the respective caste bodies are destined to remain always already segregated from each other. Even if bonds of intimacy are kept outside of consideration within the realm of caste relations, there is close surveillance of possibilities of contact which might transgress caste laws. While some castes are permitted limited mobility within the caste structure, some other castes, branded impure, are denied such movement altogether. The latter are the untouchable castes whose impure nature poses a threat of contamination to all caste Hindus.

At the pinnacle of the caste hierarchy are the Brahmans who regard themselves as the Gods of the earth. All other men and women have been born to serve them, or so they seem to believe. Hence they feel absolutely entitled to claiming the devotion of these subordinates. The Brahmans are convinced that they have earned their dues by their authorship of the sacred scriptures of the Hindus, notwithstanding the illiberal lessons which are preached through these texts. The writers of these scriptures seem to have been under the influence of intoxication while writing, otherwise they would not have tied such high thinking and sinister practices together. On the one hand, their scriptures preach that both living and non-living are forms of the same God, but on the other hand, they envision an extraordinary practice of inequality. This is not indicative of authors who are in their senses.

Right or wrong these Shastras have made an enormous impact on the minds of the innocent masses. That the masses are worshipping their enemies as Gods on earth—who would believe this? But we can actually understand why the masses have clung to such harmful, slavish religious practices, worshipping their enemies as their benefactors. The Brahmans, realising that if the masses are kept ignorant they can be led in any direction, have kept knowledge confined to themselves alone, making it their sole monopoly. The masses, thinking that this actually is their religion, follow it. There are enough examples of Brahmans, during their period of rule, punishing non-Brahmans who tried to acquire knowledge either openly or secretly.

Non-Brahmans have remained backward due to lack of resources and education. But their backwardness does not necessarily entail the misery caused by total deprivation. For, they have never lacked the means of subsistence obtainable through agricultural and industrial occupations, through trade and commerce, or other employment opportunities. It is the outcastes who have been the worst victims of social discrimination, who find themselves impoverished, weak and lacking in self-esteem. This is why it is their sorry plight that needs to be consciously highlighted. Their only redemption lies in self-emancipation from their chains of bondage, a process which has now happily begun.

They have long thought that the wretched condition in which they are placed is their lot ordained by God. This thinking can be removed from their mind only by imparting education to them. But education is a costly commodity and the untouchables, because of their poverty, are unable to purchase it. Even if a few of them can afford to purchase it, they are not allowed to enter schools because the stigma of untouchability is permanently attached to them.

The stigma of untouchability has also restricted their freedom of profession, and this in turn prevents their efforts to overcome their poverty. We cannot find untouchables in profitable professions like trade and commerce. With no other avenues open to them, they are constrained to remain manual labourers ...

There are people even among the untouchable communities who say that the untouchables are hemmed in from all corners and there is no way to escape from their insect-like existence. The untouchables have no education because they are poor and they are powerless because they have no education. The logic is correct, but it should not be forgotten that there are people who are fighting against the practice of untouchability. The real humanity lies in breaking barriers. It is a good sign that a sense of humanity or self-respect is now growing among the untouchables.

It is because of Hinduism's evil practices that crores of high caste people, unreasonable and obstinate, treat our people as untouchables. As long as other people treat us as untouchables, our people are bound to remain miserable. It is a happy occasion that our people have finally understood this whole social dilemma.

The untouchables have also now realized that upper caste Hindus are taking advantage of their easy access to the British Government in India to misrepresent the case of the untouchables to the Government. The untouchable communities have demanded that since casteism and caste hatred prevail in this country, for the realisation of genuine *Swaraj* the untouchables must have a share in the country's political power, through their own independently chosen representatives. Therefore, the untouchables have complained to the government over the stand taken by upper caste Hindus who oppose the demand made by the untouchable communities. The untouchables have now understood the tactics of caste Hindus who by gaining political power would surely use that power to perpetuate social inequality. This agitation of the untouchables against the designs of caste Hindus is a sign of growing awakening among us.

There is no better source than a newspaper to show the remedy against the injustices that are presently being done and will be done in the future to our people, and to discuss the ways and means for our progress. If we throw even a cursory glance over the newspapers that are published in Bombay, it will be found that most take care in protecting the interests only of some single upper caste. Not only do these newspapers show no concern for other castes, but sometimes they even go against the interests of other castes. Our warning to such newspapers is that if any one caste remains degraded it will have a negative effect on other castes too. Society is like a boat. Suppose a sailor with a destructive mentality, seeking to frighten or harm another sailor, strikes a hole in the other's compartment, the result will be that he too will sink sooner or later along with the one he tried to harm. Similarly, a caste which makes other castes suffer will also undoubtedly suffer directly or indirectly. Newspapers, therefore, interested in their own selfish interests should be advised not to follow the example of the clever fool who deceives others only to protect his own interests.

Unfortunately, there is yet hardly any institutional forum of communication, any media resource, which is prepared to foreground, frankly and fearlessly, the numerous problems which beset the outcastes. There are, no doubt, a few newspapers and journals which raise issues connected with the due need for resolution of the problems facing the so-called lower castes, but none of these really give exclusive attention to the question of the rights of the untouchables. It is for the purpose of filling this void that *Mooknayak* has been put into circulation ...

I end with the assurance that if subscribers are willing to extend their cooperation, then *Mooknayak* will courageously work for the great cause of our people, leading them on the right path. Their experience will ultimately show them that our assurance was not wrong.[3]

This was a powerful first editorial, followed by nearly a dozen more, equally strongly worded. The annual subscription price for *Mooknayak* was Rs 2.5. At first, the circulation was 700 subscribers. By 1922, it had risen to 1,000 subscribers. Nevertheless, the paper was chronically beset with financial and managerial problems. This was all, of course, exacerbated by Ambedkar's long absence in London. Although he exchanged numerous letters with his team in Bombay about the management of the paper, it ultimately fell apart. It was not solely on account of financial distress. Ambedkar's good friend Naval Bhathena had frequently stepped in to aid with that. In addition to donating money to support the publication, Bhathena even reached out to Bombay-based industrialists such as Godrej, asking them—successfully—to run ads in the paper! But it was impossible for Ambedkar to micromanage the activities of *Mooknayak* from afar. As mentioned, he finally broke his association with Gholap, and thus *Mooknayak*, in 1923. One important lesson he learnt in the process, however, was not to lightly delegate the management of his newspapers, but instead to keep them under tight control. This lesson served him well on his subsequent journalistic endeavours. Ambedkar himself would serve as editor for his next paper, *Bahishkrut Bharat*. And although in a later paper—first called *Samata* and then changed to *Janata*—he did appoint an editor, these future papers, unlike *Mooknayak*, mandatorily carried Ambedkar's name near the nameplate or flag.

Mooknayak faced financial hardship, but Ambedkar himself, thanks to scraped-up savings from his professorship at Sydenham, had solved the debilitating financial problem that he had faced back in 1917, when he was forced to leave in the middle of his higher education in London. He had been given a reprieve of four-years-plus-one term to find the means to return to LSE, and three of these years had already passed. Having saved the handsome sum of Rs 7,000 from work and borrowing a further Rs 5,000 from Naval, Ambedkar set his sights once again on England.

The family was by no stretch of the imagination financially comfortable, however. Moreover, yet another personal tragedy struck, when Ramu and Ambedkar's only daughter, Indu, died just after childbirth. Family stability remained tenuous as long as Ambedkar's budget was tight.

While Shahu Maharaj did not provide Ambedkar with financial assistance for his trip to London[4]—at least not yet, he would provide a loan the following year—he did support him in other ways, such as by bringing attention to him among important persons in England.

One such was his good friend Sir Alfred Pease, who had been a member of Parliament. Pease had visited the Maharajah's new schools in Kolhapur back in 1902 and spoken favourably about Shahu's many charitable and mobility projects during a function for the Maratha Education Society. The following year, when the Maharajah went to England for the coronation of King Edward VII, he was hosted by Pease. Later, Pease took the Maharajah on a tour of Scotland. In short, they were very close, and Shahu had often opened up to him about the tyranny of the Brahmans.[5] Hoping that Pease would open doors for Ambedkar during his stay in London, Shahu wrote:

> He is coming to England for study at the London School of Economics and at the Inns of Court. He will explain to you the difference between the Backward Classes and the Brahman bureaucracy. Also he will tell you what suffering one who tries to sympathize has to undergo at the hands of the bureaucratic Brahman, who claim to have democratic ideas, to wish to raise the backward classes, but who really crave nothing better than an oligarchy for themselves. He intends to lay before the enlightened public of England the viewpoint of non-Brahman Hindus, who are unanimous in the opinion that in asking for Home Rule, the real object of the Brahmans has been to regain and establish their long-lost power ... The non-Brahmans have failed to get a hearing from the several administrations in India but they hope to find sympathy at the hands of the British public.[6]

The Maharajah was as fond of Ambedkar as Ambedkar was of him, as was always apparent from his letters.[7] One such was sent on 13 June 1920, when Ambedkar wrote a letter (in Marathi) to Shahu to wish him on his forty-sixth birthday, which was on 26 June, and to inform him of a special issue of *Mooknayak* that was being published just for this occasion.[8]

With enough funds to relaunch the pursuit of his studies, and with the good wishes of his friends and mentor, Ambedkar bid farewell once again to his wife, Ramu (who, although they did not know it yet, was pregnant with a boy they would name Gangadhar), his only surviving child, Yashwant, his nephew Mukund, and the other family members under his care and support. In July 1920, he set sail yet again for London.

Chapter Eight
Lunchless in London (1920–22)

My dear Prof. Seligman,

You will probably be surprised to see me back in London. I am on my way to New York but I am halting in London for about two years to finish a piece or two of research work which I have undertaken. Of course, I long to be with you again, for it was when I was thrown into academic life by reason of my being a professor at the Sydenham College of Commerce & Economics in Bombay, that I realised the huge debt of gratitude I owe to the Political Science faculty of the Columbia University in general and to you in particular.

While I am in London I wish to utilise certain research facilities and I should be extremely obliged if you can send me a letter of introduction to Prof. Sidney Webb, Professors Marshall, Nicholson, and Foxwell. I am sure you know them and will not withhold this much kindness from your loving student,

B.R. Ambedkar[1]

Ambedkar arrived once again in London to finish what he had started precisely four years earlier, when he had first arrived in London from New York with the support of his supervisor, Professor E. Seligman. This time around, however, Ambedkar had changed—he was a different man. The prior three years in Bombay, marked by intense struggle and hardship—personally and professionally, leading then, thanks to his talents, tenacity and a few lucky breaks, to some signs of success and recognition for his efforts—had not only offered him formative life experiences but had also fortified his determination and resolve. The first editorial in *Mooknayak* already laid out what it was that Ambedkar now aimed to achieve in his lifetime: to 'remedy the injustices that are presently being done and will be done in the future to our people' and 'to courageously work for the great cause of our people'[2]—basically, nothing short of the emancipation of the untouchables. He saw the completion of his education in London as a necessary, albeit insufficient, prerequisite towards any hope for success along that arduous and ambitious path.

Some of these changes were visible in as mundane a document as his application of readmission to LSE. Unlike in his original application for admission in 1916, Ambedkar wrote his name this time as 'Bhivram', as his wife Ramu, his family, many of whom he had lost, and his close family friends in Bombay had been affectionally addressing him over the past three years. Now knowing what he wanted from life, and having grown more confident about who he was, he felt comfortable using his pet name 'Bhiva' even while in London—unlike the last time he had been there. If that hints at a bit of increased personal self-awareness, there is a strong mark of professional self-awareness on the application too. Under his home address, Ambedkar this time wrote '14 Hararwalla Building No 4, Parel, Bombay, India'. At a distance of just about two kilometres from his home at the BIT Chawl in Parel, the Hararwalla Building, now filled with banks that line the bustling NM Joshi Marg, contained a small office that Ambedkar and his *Mooknayak* team used, and that Ambedkar would continue to use in the future for his trade union activities.³ Giving his Bombay business address rather than his home address of the last full decade indicated that Ambedkar indeed meant business in London.

A third difference on the application form was that Ambedkar was enrolling not for the MSc coursework, which he had already completed, but exclusively for the submission of his MSc thesis. He thus selected 'evening' from the 'day or evening' option, which meant that he had no obligation to be present on campus, freeing him up for more intensive catch-up study for his bar examination at Gray's Inn, as well as to research and write the thesis itself. The reapplication form also showed that he had already decided upon the title of his thesis: 'The Evolution of Provincial Finance in British India.' That is more or less the same title as his doctoral dissertation at Columbia. And speaking of the latter, a fourth difference on this application was that, unlike on his 1916 application, where he had mentioned only his Elphinstone BA and his MA from Columbia, this time he added the Columbia PhD as well—Ambedkar had thus come to realize the significance of being 'doctorandus', the official title for a doctoral candidate who was ABD, quite unlike when he had first returned to Bombay in 1918, discounting his uncompleted academic achievements.

A fifth difference that Ambedkar's reapplication recorded was that, whereas in the original application he had left 'Occupation' blank, this time he wrote 'Ex-Professor of Economics'. As Ambedkar mentioned in the letter he had only just written to Professor Seligman, being 'thrown into academic life' in Bombay opened his eyes regarding the excellence of the education that he was privileged to have received at Columbia. And, finally, we also find Ambedkar's London address on his reapplication form: 95 Brook Green, Hammersmith, London, W6.

The 95 Brook Green accommodation was an absolutely charming Georgian three-storey brick rowhouse in an affluent neighbourhood of Hammersmith, overlooking the large Brook Green residential area park. As fine a place as it was, the landlady was miserable and miserly, and Ambedkar soon found himself searching for more hospitable digs.

The Marathi writer Prabhakar Padhye, in a chapter devoted to Ambedkar in his book portraying luminous personalities, wrote in 1939 that Ambedkar recounted to him, 'That landlady was a horrible woman. I am always praying for her soul; but, I am sure she will go to perdition!'[4]

With regard to these years in London, Ambedkar's two main early biographers, Keer and Khairmoday, both relied on Padhye, and all subsequent biographers have relied on Keer and Khairmoday, so details are both scant and dubious. But it is reported that Ambedkar shared quarters at Brook Green with another Marathi-speaking Indian law student named Asnodkar, who was from a rich family and not too studious. Asnodkar could thus himself afford to supplement the paltry meals that their mean landlady served, but Ambedkar, limited to an unyielding budget of £8 per month, was unhappily forced to subsist upon them. At breakfast, this was a piece of cold fish, a cup of tea and some toast with too little jam to cover it. As Ambedkar hilariously recounted to Padhye, the way one places a dob of red tika on the forehead of Ganpati, that's how much jam was placed on the corner of the toast. Lunch was not served, and he had no money to purchase any for himself, so this meal was skipped. Ambedkar learnt the hard way: There was no free lunch in London.

For dinner, the landlady served an unappetizing cup of warm Bovril (the trademarked name of a salty, viscous meat paste that is made into a drink by diluting it with hot water) with some biscuits and too little butter to cover them. Fortunately for Ambedkar, in those early days in London he had been in possession of a supply of papad given to him by a Gujarati friend. Each night at 10 p.m. he would ration out four to eat, along with a cup of milk, to stave off hunger through the night.

The oft-repeated story about this period that Ambedkar was the first to enter the British Museum at its 8 a.m. opening time and the last to leave at its 5 p.m. closing was told to Padhye by Ambedkar himself, but it is inaccurate. For the walking distance from Brook Green to the British Museum was a full two hours in one direction, and it was also over an hour even with public transport, which Ambedkar could not afford to regularly use. It is likelier that his routine study periods at the British Museum began after he had shifted into his new accommodation at Chalk Farm, only a forty-five-minute walk from the museum and a bit more to nearby LSE. From Brook Green, however, the spectacular collection of Goldsmiths' library (about which more in a moment) in its original South Kensington location would have been a mere forty-minute walk, and it is believed that Ambedkar often studied there.

Although Ambedkar had duly submitted his LSE application by late September or early October, there was some confusion regarding the enrollment process even as late as the end of November. But since he was not attending courses, the problem did not interfere with his progress. The LSE school secretary, Mrs Jessy Mair (whom history unkindly remembers as the cause of much gossip for being domineering with faculty, and especially for her influence over, and illicit love affair with, the director of LSE, whom twenty years later, in 1942, she would finally marry),[5] had asked LSE economist and world-famous book collector Professor Herbert Somerton Foxwell about Ambedkar. Ambedkar had already met Foxwell and handed over a letter of introduction written for him by his Columbia supervisor Professor Seligman, dated 23 September 1920. The gushing letter mentions that Ambedkar had 'passed his examination for the Doctor's degree with considerable distinction', signifying, of course, that he was ABD. However, the loose wording of Seligman's letter, along with Ambedkar's own LSE application form mentioning 'PhD' under the heading 'Degrees Taken', naturally led Professor Foxwell to infer that Ambedkar was already 'Dr Ambedkar'—which, of course, he wasn't. Thus, in a scribbled note to Jessy Mair from the LSE lecturers' common room, Foxwell determined that Ambedkar could not be identified with LSE, since 'there are no more worlds here for him to conquer'. He added a P.S.: 'We have no milk here.'

On 22 November 1920, Jessy Mair typed out a reply to Foxwell, thanking him for his note about Ambedkar. She did not mention the absence of milk from the common room, but what she did do was register Ambedkar anyway. Professor Cannan was assigned as his MSc thesis supervisor.

Professor H.S. Foxwell was one of the four professors whom Ambedkar had requested Professor Seligman in New York to write him letters of introduction to. The others were Professors Sidney Webb, the famous Fabian and co-founder of LSE; Alfred Marshall, founder of the Cambridge school of economics and teacher of John Maynard Keynes; and Joseph Shield Nicholson, an economist at the University of Edinburgh, whom Ambedkar sought to visit (he would later resourcefully use this letter from Seligman to Nicholson, which listed all of his academic qualifications, in lieu of an academic transcript for his application to study in Germany).

Although Foxwell was a well-known economist, especially influential with respect to the history of banking, his real claim to fame was his mammoth personal library, parts of which were acquired to make up the economics, finance and commerce collection of the University of London's famous Goldsmiths' library, which Ambedkar frequented, as well as the nucleus of the Kress Library of Business and Economics at Harvard University. As Foxwell had written to Seligman years before, 'The Goldsmiths' Company have bought my library. If it finds a home near me, I shall probably sell my duplicates, shall probably sell some "triplicates" in any case. I have an arrangement with Wm. Muller … I will tell Muller to send you his catalogues.'[6]

Ambedkar was himself an obsessive book collector, despite a chronic lack of funds. And even at this period in London he could be found shopping for books. He reportedly picked up at this time a massive set of annual reports of the East India Company covering the period from 1700 to 1858, which would have been essential for his thesis, a financial history of the period.[7] But he was also still coveting books not for his academic work but for his personal collection. He couldn't stop thinking about one book that he had passed up at a Bombay bookstall—every true book collector knows this feeling! He wrote to his friend and confidant S.N. Shivtarkar in Bombay, asking him to buy a second-hand copy of *The Works of David Ricardo* by J.R. McCulloch, which Ambedkar had seen for sale at a certain stall some months earlier. Although the book was widely available at the time in London libraries (having been published in London in 1888), Ambedkar was hankering for the one that had got away. Additionally, still keen on improving his Marathi prose, which he had been working on for *Mooknayak* editorials, Ambedkar also asked Shivtarkar to send him literary works by Ram Ganesh Gadkari, the Marathi poet, playwright and humorist.

Besides spending time working on his thesis in London libraries and passing his time in London bookshops, several receipts archived at LSE show that Ambedkar was busy at Gray's Inn, routinely paying his term fees, library charges and other dues there, some as high as £33. He had also paid £5.5 for the privilege of attending all the lectures and classes arranged by the Inn's Council of Legal Education. Thus, he was making steady progress on both his MSc thesis as well as his law degree. His dissertation for the Columbia PhD, however, was kept in abeyance.

With this much going on already in London (and New York), as well as back home in Bombay, it is nothing short of astounding to learn that in early 1921, only six months after his arrival back in the UK, Ambedkar decided to take on yet another course of study—and that, too, in another country and in another language!

In a handwritten letter in German, dated 25 February 1921, Ambedkar wrote to the Prussian Ministry of Science, Fine Arts and Public Education, requesting to enrol on a course of study for economics at the University of Bonn. He included a handwritten CV, also in German, detailing his past academic history (and over-optimistically claiming that he would be free from studies at London University by March), as well as his employment history (mentioning his stint at the finance and accounts department in Baroda as well as his professorship in economics at Sydenham). The letter also stated, 'I would like to mention that the University of Bonn, through the kind help of Prof. Dr. H. Jacobi, offered that I could submit a Ph.D. thesis in case I show adequate performance and am enrolled for three semesters there.'[8]

Professor Hermann Jacobi was not an economist but the leading German Indologist of the era. Ambedkar had no need for a third PhD in economics. His true intention was to get enrolled at Bonn University to study Sanskrit with Jacobi. However, he had no academic background in Indology or Sanskrit, whereas he was well qualified—both academically and professionally—for officially enrolling on an economics course. The ministry in Berlin had granted him the permission to do so, and on 29 April 1921, Ambedkar signed the registration docket in Bonn, Germany. Penniless for the travel expenses or fees, however, Ambedkar had earlier written to his trusted friend Bhathena, asking him for another loan of Rs 2,000, which he would use to purchase rapidly deflating German marks.[9]

The reason behind Ambedkar's haste in early 1921, as well as the reason that the entire enterprise of studying in Germany ultimately fell through, was due to Jacobi's impending retirement in 1922. Ideally, Ambedkar could have wrapped up at least one or two of his open courses of study in London and then headed to Bonn afterwards, but this conflicted with Professor Jacobi's plans. Although he had enrolled at Bonn, Ambedkar was never able to stay present in Germany long enough to attend lectures due to his many obligations in London. Finally, on 12 January 1922, Ambedkar was taken off the university register. There was no point pursuing the programme in Bonn after that, as Professor Jacobi had retired. Yet another opportunity to study Sanskrit fell through. However, Ambedkar would again come back to it, but not until nearly thirty years in the future.

Although the LSE Registrar's Office has been (mis)informing people since the 1970s that Ambedkar lived at the Brook Green, Hammersmith, address until 6 April 1921 and shifted to Chalk Farm on 7 April 1921, his 25 February 1921 letter to the Berlin ministry is addressed '10 King Henry's Road, Chalk Farm, London, NW 3' (as is an earlier 10 February letter to Bombay about the financial troubles of *Mooknayak*). He had managed to escape the mean and miserly landlady in Hammersmith and shifted into a far less beautiful but more welcoming three-storey brick rowhouse in Camden, where he would reside for the rest of his time in England—now the site of the Ambedkar Museum in London.

Here, Ambedkar was a lodger in the house of a widowed woman whose name biographers universally report as Frances 'Fanny' Fitzgerald, although her legal name had actually been Frances Proust (widow of Gaston Proust), and her maiden name had been Frances, or 'Fanny', Brooks.[10] Very little is known about her, despite her rather deep personal significance to Ambedkar. Ambedkar and Frances seem to have first met in Geneva, Switzerland, through a mutual acquaintance. But it is more commonly reported in all of the biographies that they had met at the India Office in London. Frances worked as a typist in the House of Commons of the British Parliament, at least part-time. Khairmoday writes that she worked at the India Office. However, there is no record of Frances ever having been employed at the India Office, and I think Khairmoday has got almost all of the information about Fanny quite wrong.

Census records show that Frances had four very young children living with her—and thus also with Ambedkar at the time—at 10 King Henry's Road. They were Gaston Albert Proust (born 23 March 1918); Dolores E. Proust (born 11 October 1915); Roy Eric Proust (born 12 June 1913); and the eldest, Frances Edwina Proust (born 28 September 1911). With these children ranging in age from two to ten years old, it must have been incredibly difficult for Frances to manage work. By 1939 she was no longer employed, as the census that year records her occupation as 'unpaid domestic duties'.[11]

Ambedkar and Frances struck up a close, and indeed romantic, relationship, which carried on through an exchange of letters over the next twenty or so years, until her death in 1946 (Khairmoday says she died in 1945)—around the time that Ambedkar published a long, full-page dedication to her in his new book on Gandhi and the Congress party. Ambedkar's dedication ended: 'To F., In Thy Presence is the Fullness of Joy.' The letter F is generally the way that Frances signed off on all of her letters to Ambedkar—either as 'F', or as 'Fx', or as 'Little Pal'. And the 'Fullness of Joy' passage is from the Book of Psalms in the

Bible: 'Thou wilt shew me the path of life: In thy presence is fulness of joy; At thy right hand there are pleasures for evermore.'[12]

Her many letters—usually starting 'My darling Bhim'—clearly reveal that Frances was hopeful of marrying Ambedkar, and in 1937, a Bombay newspaper even claimed that they had married during a trip that Ambedkar was taking to England at that time. One such love letter contained a candidly passionate passage:

> I want you to kiss me. I want to feel your strong arms holding me tight. I want you so much, your photograph is on the table beside me but it does not answer me, it does not kiss me back when I kiss it, the other one hangs over my bed, the little bed you had, I sleep in it now.[13]

Ambedkar did seriously consider marrying Frances, but after a great deal of anguished deliberation, ultimately decided against it. He would sacrifice love for the pursuit of his life's aim and mission. But all of this comes later. We will delve more deeply into the long-lasting relationship between Frances and Ambedkar in the next volume.

Let's return to 1921, when, by the first week of April, Ambedkar, the LSE Secretariat, the University of London Registrar's Office and Ambedkar's thesis supervisor Professor Cannan were all four exchanging a volley of letters trying to get Ambedkar registered for his thesis examination. Earlier in the year, Ambedkar had filled the wrong application form and had also submitted his supporting paperwork late. The LSE team prevailed over the University of London administration, and an exception was granted so that Ambedkar's thesis could be accepted for examination. In June 1921, Ambedkar was bestowed an MSc (Econ) for his thesis titled 'Provincial Decentralization of Imperial Finance in British India'. The thesis comprised 151 typewritten pages, with a three-page preface.

As happy an occasion as this was, it was still far from what Ambedkar had set out to London to achieve. And yet, by the end of the summer, he had begun to run out of the funds he had saved. After consulting with his friend Dattoba Dalvi, Shahu Maharaj's court painter, on 4 September 1921, Ambedkar penned a two-page letter to his 'dear Maharajahsaheb', laying out his financial predicament and requesting help to the quite modest sum of £200. Ambedkar explained how he had found himself in these financial straits despite his efforts at budgeting and financial planning, and stated that he needed £100 for a further payment towards his law degree and would need £100 for his eventual travel back to India. He said that he would return the money to the Maharajah with interest upon his return and that a bond for the same could be written up.[14]

Things back at home in Bombay were not great either. Letters to his wife Ramabai and to his friend Shivtarkar reveal both family and professional problems. Ramu was worried about their newborn son, Gangadhar, who had fallen ill. Ambedkar tried consoling her, telling her not to worry. Ambedkar's optimism was quite misplaced, however, as the Ambedkars lost yet another child when Gangadhar subsequently died of the illness. As for his surviving son, Yashwant, and his nephew, Mukund, Ambedkar was growing anxious about their education. He asked Shivtarkar to hire a tutor for the boys to ensure that their studies were on track. In a later letter from October 1922, Ambedkar also informed Shivtarkar that he had himself fallen quite ill, but instructed him not to let Ramu know, lest she worry.

Ambedkar's future second wife, Savita Ambedkar, a practising physician whom he married in 1948, looks back at this 1922 letter to Shivtarkar and suggests that Ambedkar's frequent illnesses seem to have launched precisely from this period:

> If researchers were to examine Dr Ambedkar's letters from 1922 onwards, they would find repeated mention of his health in most of them. Dr Ambedkar's associates and friends were well aware of the delicate state of his health, and they would regularly make solicitous inquiries about it.[15]

Another thing that the letters from this period show is that Gholap was going rogue and Ambedkar was losing control of *Mooknayak*. This situation only worsened, until Ambedkar disassociated himself completely from the paper in the coming year.

Despite Ambedkar's occasional illnesses and relentless poverty in London, along with his many aggravating problems back at home, the period from the autumn of 1921 to the spring of 1923 was remarkably productive. Although early in the year 1922 it is apparent that Ambedkar had still not fully figured out how he was going to manage the doctoral dissertations for both LSE and Columbia University, he had clearly decided upon a plan by that summer, and in the coming year executed it to perfection—or, at least, to near perfection. There were a couple of unexpected hiccups along the way.

Chapter Nine

Mr Ambedkar, to Ambedkar Bar-at-Law, to Dr Ambedkar (1922–23)

In late 1920, just after Ambedkar's arrival in England, he and his Columbia University supervisor were exchanging letters regarding his new period of stay in London. On 23 September 1920, Professor Seligman pointedly asked Ambedkar, 'Are you ever going to finish your Doctor's dissertation? I shall be interested in knowing.'[1]

As late as 16 February 1922, Ambedkar had still not worked out an adequate response:

> *My dear Prof. Seligman,*
> *Having lost my manuscript of the original thesis when the steamer was torpedoed on my way back to India in 1917, I have written out a new thesis entitled 'The Stabilization of the Indian Exchange', which I hope with your permission to submit for the Ph.D. at Columbia.*

I hope to be at Columbia for the exam sometime in December next....

Trusting you will be pleased to do the needful, I am

Yours sincerely,
B. R. Ambedkar[2]

The new thesis on the stabilization problem was a work in monetary policy, a field in economics quite different from his earlier-proposed thesis on fiscal policy (or, as Seligman would refer to it, a 'financial history of India'). Monetary policy was very much Professor Cannan's expertise (though he modestly claimed to know little about monetary policy in India). The idea to submit it to Columbia, then, was not a very good one. It took a few more months, but Ambedkar finally devised a plan. This solution was completely different from what he had anticipated in his February 1922 letter to Professor Seligman, however. And, unlike what he wrote in that letter, by 'December next', he was not in New York defending his Columbia University dissertation, but rather in Bombay looking after something else entirely.

Ambedkar decided, more sensibly, to submit the dissertation on the stabilization of the Indian exchange—what ultimately become known as 'The Problem of the Rupee'—to LSE under Professor Cannan's supervision, and to rework and supplement his MSc thesis, 'Provincial Decentralization of Imperial Finance in British India', as his doctoral dissertation at Columbia under Professor Seligman's supervision. This made the most sense because fiscal policy was originally the field that he and Seligman had settled upon way back in 1916, when the PhD thesis was known under the title 'National Dividend'. Ambedkar worked feverishly throughout 1922 to make this plan work. This would certainly have been the period when he was the first to enter the library in the mornings and the last to be chased out in the evenings. And despite various distractions coming from Bombay, Ambedkar managed to pull it off. By the spring of 1923, he was sitting on not one, but two completed, full-length doctoral dissertations of quality and originality.

Among the many distractions, however, was the untimely death of Shahu Maharaj a month shy of his forty-eighth birthday. On 6 May 1922, Ambedkar wrote a heartfelt letter of condolence to his son:

My dear Yuvaraj Maharaj,
The news of the death of His Highness ... came to me as a shock. I am doubly grieved by [this] calamitous event. In his death I have lost a personal friend, and the Depressed Classes have lost a great benefactor and the greatest champion of their cause ...
I hasten to convey ... my deep and sincere sympathy for this sad bereavement.

Yours in grief,
B.R. Ambedkar[3]

A month further along, fortunately, brought Ambedkar the happiest possible news in compensation. On 28 June 1922, he was finally called to the bar at Gray's Inn, having completed his twelve terms and passing all the requisite conditions and examinations. In the *Order Books* of Gray's Inn, historical records that are still extant and intact, we find this entry for 28 June 1922: 'It is ordered that ... Bhimrao Ramji Ambedkar [and others] ... be called to the Bar and they are hereby published Barristers accordingly.'[4]

He was now not merely Mr Ambedkar, but Mr Ambedkar, Bar-at-Law.

He was still not Dr Ambedkar, though.

To remedy this, in October 1922, Ambedkar finally submitted the doctoral dissertation 'The Problem of the Rupee: Its Origin and its Solution' to the LSE faculty for examination. But there was one hiccup: For reasons that remain unclear today, Ambedkar's submission was at first rejected.

Why?

The earliest explanation that we have was provided by Keer in his biography of Ambedkar:

> On submitting his thesis to London University, [Ambedkar] went to study at Bonn University. Hardly was he there for a quarter of the year when in March 1923 he was called back to London by his professor Edwin Cannan as the terse exposition in his thesis had given offence to the British imperialist examiners, who asked him to rewrite his thesis without changing his conclusions. This was not, however, the first time that Ambedkar's writing had caused a furor ... [H]e had read a paper on 'Responsibilities of a Responsible Government in India' before the Students' Union ... and Ambedkar was suspected to be an Indian revolutionary; even Prof Harold J. Laski ... opining that the thoughts expressed in the paper were frankly of a revolutionary nature.[5]

Keer's explanation is that Ambedkar was asked to revise and resubmit on account of some of his highly critical claims against the British that offended his imperialist dissertation examiners. Every subsequent biographer of Ambedkar[6] has run with this explanation, despite the fact that there is absolutely no corroborating evidence for it. Khairmoday, more punctilious than Keer, attempted to corroborate it with LSE in the 1950s, but could not. In the late 1970s, the High Commission of India in London entered the fray in an effort to determine whether LSE had censored Ambedkar. An administrative officer of the university replied to the High Commission:

> At this distance of time, I fear it would be quite impossible to say what, if any, revisions were made in the thesis, nor what the examiners' detailed views of it were. Matters of that kind were until very recently strictly confidential to the University

of London and its central administration; we have no relevant information.[7]

In other words, LSE would neither confirm nor deny Keer's account. Granted, Keer's account was not only possible but also plausible—the academic system in the UK was deeply tied in with the government's imperial projects, and critical statements that could have been tolerated at an American institution such as Columbia University would have been quite unacceptable at the University of London. On the other hand, there are several red flags in Keer's account that ought to make us cautious. First, Keer opens his discussion of the thesis rejection by claiming that Ambedkar was called back to London from Bonn for this reason. But Ambedkar was not even in Bonn during the later period in question: Professor Jacobi had already retired by then and Ambedkar had abandoned the plan of studying in Germany. That Keer gets the surrounding details quite wrong casts a shadow on the main claim.[8]

Second, LSE was a Fabian stronghold, packed with socialists of an anti-imperialist bent. Thus, to assume that his dissertation examiners were imperialists is in itself prejudicial and problematic. On the other hand, the left-leaning LSE belonged to the more conservative University of London system, from where other dissertation examiners would likely have been pulled. Third, the evidentiary, supporting story about Ambedkar reading out a paper at the Students' Union that was deemed revolutionary by no less than Harold Laski, the staunch socialist who was later a leader of the Labour Party, has itself not been corroborated and is quite difficult to swallow. Consider that in 1950, Jawaharlal Nehru, who had studied under Laski in England, eulogized him thus: 'It is difficult to realise that Professor Harold Laski is no more. Lovers of freedom all over the world pay tribute to the magnificent work that he did. We in India are particularly grateful for his staunch advocacy of India's freedom, and the great part he played in bringing it about.'[9] Although it is possible that Ambedkar did present one of his writings—most likely one of a dozen editorials that he had earlier written for *Mooknayak*—at the Students' Union, there is no evidence that Ambedkar was widely regarded as a revolutionary during his stay in London, or that his dissertation examiners wanted anti-British statements expunged from his writing.

The far likelier reason for the initial rejection of Ambedkar's dissertation may have been that Ambedkar had taken on and disagreed with every single economist who had written on this topic prior to him, which included his own supervisor, who was thus at odds with so many of his substantive claims. We can get a sense of this from Ambedkar's preface to his later revised and accepted dissertation:

> The conclusions [John Maynard Keynes] has arrived at are in sharp conflict with those of mine. Our differences extended to almost every proposition he has advanced in favour of the exchange standard. ... I cannot conclude this preface without acknowledging my deep sense of gratitude to my teacher, Prof. Edwin Cannan. ... I can say that his severe examination of my theoretic discussions has saved me from many an error.[10]

We also see this problem raised in the foreword that Cannan wrote to the published version of Ambedkar's work:

> As [Ambedkar] is aware, I disagree with a good deal of his criticism. In 1893, I was one of the few economists who believed that the rupee could be kept at a fixed ratio with gold ... I do not share Mr. Ambedkar's hostility to the system, nor accept most of his arguments against it and its advocates. But ... even when I have thought him quite wrong, I have found a stimulating freshness in his views and reasons. An old teacher like myself learns to tolerate the vagaries of originality, even when they resist 'severe examination' such as that of which Mr. Ambedkar speaks.[11]

Rarely has a thesis supervisor remarked on disagreeing with 'most' of his student's arguments and that thesis has passed. Not to forget that Ambedkar himself admitted to disagreeing with almost everything that John Maynard Keynes had written on the topic! But whatever was the true reason that Ambedkar's dissertation was originally returned for revision and resubmission, Ambedkar did resubmit in August 1923, and in November 1923 his long-awaited doctoral degree was granted. He was finally a Doctor of Science (in Economics). He was, at long last, Dr Ambedkar. It took from 1916 to 1923, but he had finally done it!

But there was another hiccup in the interim that we have passed over.

The rejection of the dissertation by the examination committee disrupted Ambedkar's academic plans. He had wanted to return to India not only as a qualified lawyer but also as a full-fledged doctor. This would have equipped him both academically and vocationally with all the formal training required for his enormously ambitious social and political projects. But he was desperately short of funds abroad, and once he received news that he would need to rework the dissertation and resubmit it, he realized that it would be impossible to stay on in London during that period. He thus decided to return to Bombay, which he did in April 1923. It was in Bombay that Ambedkar revised his doctoral dissertation and from Bombay that he resubmitted it to LSE in August. Hence, again from a long study period abroad, Ambedkar returned to India this second time with a second master's degree as well as a law degree, but still not as 'Dr Ambedkar'!

As mentioned, thankfully and at long last, all of that changed in November of 1923, when, through LSE, Ambedkar was awarded the DSc from the University of London. The next month, December 1923, the now Dr Ambedkar published his doctoral thesis as a book titled *The Problem of the Rupee: Its Origin and its Solution*, with a foreword by Professor Edwin Cannan. The publisher was P.S. King & Son, located in Westminster, London, a very reputable publisher for all subjects related to the empire. As it was one of the few approved outlets for official publications and reports by the government of British India, Ambedkar had probably shopped there frequently during his time in London.

This book, Ambedkar's first, contained a touching dedication in the front matter:

> Dedicated to the memory of
> My
> Father and mother
> As a token of my abiding gratitude for the
> Sacrifices they made and the enlightenment
> They showed in the matter of my education

Ambedkar reminisced often about how much his parents—especially his father, since his mother had died when he was so young—had sacrificed for his education, as well as how his father had created an atmosphere that encouraged learning and study. He once wrote:

> It was my father who taught me how to find a good English word for an equivalent Marathi word, and how to use it in the right place. I feel that I have earned some fame for writing and speaking good English. But how to use the right word in the right place so that it would carry the greatest weight, that was taught to me by my father in a manner which no other teacher had ever taught me. He always used to ask me words at random from Tarkhadkar [English grammar] and thus test my knowledge of the English language. Similarly, my father also taught me about idioms and how to use the right style of language.[12]

Beyond these teachings on the formal side, with respect to the social angle, Ambedkar's father had also been an associate and great admirer of the social activist and reformer Mahatma Phule, who would prove deeply influential on Ambedkar's own path. This was already apparent from Ambedkar's relaunched sociopolitical activities in Bombay in 1923, for it was not only his doctoral dissertation that Ambedkar was working on that year. Indeed, one of Ambedkar's most significant engagements after he returned to Bombay, besides his academic and sociopolitical endeavours, was his official entry into the legal profession.

On 25 June 1923, Ambedkar applied to be admitted as an advocate to the High Court of Bombay. As he had only just returned from England and was yet to submit his revised doctoral dissertation, upon which he was meant to be focusing his attention in Bombay, it is quite clear that he had been eager to launch a legal practice. It was a respectable profession, wherein there was a chance to earn—although earnings for him would be slight, since it depended largely upon touchable Hindus. But it did provide independence—for example, from meddling bureaucrats in a government administrative job—as well as free time to pursue intellectual challenges (such as writing books) and for social work and grassroots activism. In fact, Ambedkar turned his legal practice itself into a form of social work—charging little to nothing for cases involving untouchables or poor labourers—and activism, operating as 'one of the earliest precursors of India's civil rights lawyers'.[13]

In his application (which was referred to as a *sanad*, or an official government certification in British India), Ambedkar annexed evidence that he had been called to the bar from Gray's Inn, a certificate of good character and skill, as well as a letter from the barrister T.B.W. Ramsay, certifying that Ambedkar had interned in his chamber for a full year while in London.[14] Ramsay was an interesting character. He had a bustling chamber at King's Bench Walk, just a stone's throw from the Royal Courts of Justice, near the Middle Temple and the Inner Temple Inns of Court, and just minutes from Lincoln's Inn as well as LSE. But sports history remembers Ramsay more than legal history does. As an avid lover of cricket, the famous Indian Gymkhana Cricket Club in Osterley, London—generously funded by the Maharaja of Patiala, with contributions by the Maharajahs of Kapurthala, Jaipur, Jodhpur, Cooch Behar and Indore, as well as the Nizam of Hyderabad—owed its existence almost entirely to Ramsay.

In his memoirs, another zealous cricketer, Manicasothy Saravanamuttu (from the prominent and distinguished Ceylonese Saravanamuttu family), a journalist and diplomat in Malaya credited with saving Penang during its invasion by the Japanese in 1941, had this to say about Ramsay:

> A word about T.B.W. Ramsay, who passed away in January 1957 when my son, Lakshman, was working in his Chambers at 10 King's Bench Walk. Ramsay had a big Privy Council practice, getting many cases from India and the African colonies. But he was always a true friend to Indian and Ceylonese students and I know many a case in which he signed as surety for students entering the Inns of Court, thus saving them from having to pay the deposit of £200. ... In 1952 when H.S. Malik was Indian Ambassador in Paris, and Duleepsinhji was Indian High Commissioner in Australia and I was Ceylon Commissioner in Malaya, [Ramsay] wrote and recalled that we all three had played in the Indian Gymkhana team against the M.C.C. in 1921.[15]

In the 1950s, Ramsay could be proud not only of his former cricket team players' later professional achievements, but also that he trained in his chambers the future chief architect of the Indian Constitution.

A Privy Council practice meant that Ramsay would appear before the Judicial Committee of the Privy Council, or JCPC, in London. The JCPC was the highest court of appeal for the British Empire. Hence appeals from British India's high courts in Calcutta, Bombay and Madras, or later from the Federal Court of India in Delhi, whether civil or criminal, could eventually make it to this court of last resort. The JCPC was India's highest appellate court even after Independence in 1947, but was, of course, discontinued with the establishment of the Supreme Court of India through the 1950 Constitution—in fact, it was Ambedkar himself, two decades later, who would move the 'Abolition of Privy Council Jurisdiction Bill' in the Constituent Assembly in September of 1949.

Training in Ramsay's Privy Council practice would have exposed Ambedkar to all of the finer questions of law that take salience over questions of fact in appellate cases. Biographers of Ambedkar follow Keer in his claim that Ambedkar joined the Appellate Side of the Bombay Bar instead of the Original Side because a successful practice on the Original Side would have required the kind of social capital that only upper-caste or British solicitors enjoyed. However, Ambedkar hardly made much of an income even on the Appellate Side, so this explanation alone is weak. Much more likely, Ambedkar's prior experience and training at an appellate level made him more confident on that side, and the questions of law that were the basis of appeals would also have been more intellectually stimulating.

That Ambedkar was always interested in the jurisprudential and intellectual aspects of the legal profession was evidenced, among many other things, by him joining the editorial committee of the *Bombay Law Journal* a few years later (from June 1927 to August 1928). The prestigious journal had been launched in 1923 by B.G. Kher, a local Congress party leader who occasionally worked with Ambedkar in the 1920s on social causes, and who later became the chief minister (the office at the time was called prime minister) of Bombay, and who would be instrumental in getting Ambedkar re-elected to the Constituent Assembly after Partition in 1947, despite their many disagreements in the interim.

Whatever be the reason for his decision to work on appellate cases, by the end of 1923, Ambedkar's legal career had begun. He was Dr Ambedkar, Bar-at-Law. But could these impressive credentials compensate for the stigma of his caste?

Chapter Ten

A Barrister in Bombay (1924–26)

Bhimrao R. Ambedkar, BA, MA, MSc, DSc, Bar-at-Law. At thirty-three years of age, this was an impressively learned young man for any caste or nationality. And to be sure, his erudition in law was always beyond dispute. It was even formally acknowledged by way of various offers of judicial appointment. As early as 1924, Ambedkar was offered the post of district judge, with an enticing promise of appointment as a high court judge within a period of three years. Writer Prabhakar Padhye recollects that Ambedkar was quite seriously tempted by the thought of becoming a judge in the high court. Yet he turned down the offer, preferring the freedom of retaining options for social service and activism to the allurements of authority and ease of high income. But an immediate offer of a high court judgeship in 1924—well, that it seems he actually would have jumped at, as British government documents retained in the India Office attest to.[1]

Following his resignation many years later as the law minister in 1951, Ambedkar gave a speech recalling another offer for a Bombay High Court judgeship that he had received back in 1942, which he had also turned down in favour of pursuing his 'life's aim', which was 'to work for the well-being and uplift of my fellow brethren'.[2] There is also an unverified claim that the Nizam of Hyderabad had offered Ambedkar the post of chief justice of his princely state.[3]

His education, training, erudition and skill, however, all failed to translate into prosperity in the profession. Rohit De captured the situation with a striking comparison:

> His cases were low in volume and value in the 1920s and he became a law professor in order to sustain a steady income. The contrast comes out starkly in a newspaper article that reported Jinnah representing an insolvency matter of Rs 2,57,000 on the same day Ambedkar represented a retired Muslim schoolteacher in a breach of trust case valued at Rs 24.[4]

Ambedkar's inability to earn adequately in the practice of law was explained some years later in an April 1948 letter that he would write to his fiancée, Sharada Kabir:

> Started practising!! There was that opposition from the Hindu people, particularly Brahmans. Opposition from the Hindu people because I was opposed to the Congress, opposition from the Brahmans because a Mahar was infiltrating into their profession. Not to let me get any court work was the resolve of both parties!! I somehow managed to survive under these circumstances.[5]

Between 1926 and 1928, there were a couple of cases that Ambedkar pleaded that attracted wide interest. There was one regarding Dinkarrao Javalkar's Marathi book titled *Deshache Dushman* (Enemies of the Country) and another, where Ambedkar was a junior assisting in a larger, high-profile case regarding charges of sedition against the communist agitator Philip Spratt. Ambedkar's side won both these appeals.

The *Deshache Dushman* case was especially interesting because it was a battle between prominent members of the non-Brahman movement (the author of the book Dinkarrao Javalkar and its publisher Keshavrao Jedhe,[6] both followers of Jyotirao Phule and supporters of Shahu Maharaj) and the powerful Brahman orthodoxy that followed Bal Gangadhar Tilak and Vishnushastri Chiplunkar, who had founded the papers *Kesari* and *Mahratta* along with Tilak. Ambedkar's victory was seen as a symbolic win for the non-Brahman movement and a kind of tribute to the reform efforts of the Maharajah who had died a few years earlier. Ambedkar must have felt a sense of fulfillment in this tribute to his deceased friend and mentor Shahu Maharaj, who, incidentally, disliked and distrusted Bal Tilak, regarding him as venomously casteist and possibly corrupt. The earliest exchanges between Ambedkar and the Maharajah were about precisely this.

In a letter from June 1920, Shahu Chhatrapati wrote to Ambedkar to request his help in dealing with the law firm Little and Company to see if they could file civil and/or criminal cases against Tilak on various grounds:

> Please consult Messr Little and Co on two points: Firstly—the point that the Mahars were called a criminal tribe by Tilak. Can they proceed against him civilly? And secondly, that the public funds are alleged to be misappropriated by him or his party. Long accounts appeared in the *Sandesh* [weekly newspaper] about them. From those accounts are the persons concerned liable to be proceeded with criminally or civilly or both?[7]

Nothing came of those concerns at the time. But four years later, the *Deshache Dushman* case arose.

In 1924, the Pune municipality had erected statues of Tilak and Chiplunkar in the city. Meanwhile, members of the non-Brahman movement proposed erecting a statue of Jyotirao Phule, but this was vehemently opposed by the Brahman orthodoxy. The latter began vocally critiquing Phule, claiming that he was a sectarian who performed no wider public service. In this context, Javalkar published his book aggressively critiquing Tilak and Chiplunkar, calling them foul names and arguing that they were not national heroes but rather enemies of the country—as were all of the advocates of the hierarchical ideology of Brahmanism. Chiplunkar's nephew then filed a defamation suit against Javalkar, Jedhe and others, and in September 1926, the city magistrate sentenced Javalkar to a year in prison and Jedhe to six months. They appealed from Yerwada jail, and in October, Ambedkar appeared on their behalf, getting them acquitted. The following year, both Javalkar and Jedhe played prominent roles supporting Ambedkar throughout the historic Mahad Satyagraha.[8]

On the topic of Ambedkar's legal practice during that period, there was also a case that Ambedkar lost that was quite peculiar. Ambedkar was arguing the appeal of a woman who ran a brothel, who had been convicted under Section 373 of the Indian Penal Code. Section 373 stated that any person managing a brothel who obtained possession of a minor female was presumed to have done so with the intent of using her for prostitution. In this case, Ambedkar argued that the owner of the brothel, Vithabai Sukha, had not obtained possession of the girl within the sense of the IPC, but rather that the girl was an independent agent who was permitted to visit the brothel for a few hours each night free of charge and who happened to prostitute herself! As the judge himself indicated, Ambedkar lost the case primarily because he wanted to dispute facts that were found by the jury in the original trial, instead of being able to point out challenges to questions of law, the appropriate domain for appeals.

Rohit De had mentioned in the passage cited above that Ambedkar 'became a law professor' so that he could earn a steady income. This is to put a favourable spin on the rather humble reality of it. True, he would eventually join the distinguished faculty of the Government Law College, Bombay, in June 1928, but from June 1925 until his appointment at the law college, Ambedkar—yes, Dr Ambedkar,

Bar-at-Law—had to settle for part-time lecturer at Batliboi's Accountancy Training Institute (BATI)! Just imagine, prior to the end of his three-year stint as a casual lecturer at Batliboi's, Ambedkar was already the most highly educated academic, from any caste, in all of India, having earned a BA, MA, MSc, DSc, and by 1927 a PhD too, along with his law qualification. Not that teaching at a training institute was necessarily humiliating, but it was a far cry from being a 'professor of law', both in terms of income and social recognition.

BATI, at the Navsari Building in Fort (just two minutes' walk from the future campus of Siddharth College, which Ambedkar would found in 1946), was instituted and run by the dynamic and entrepreneurial chartered accountant Jamshed R. Batliboi. J.R. Batliboi, whom Ambedkar had met through his close Parsee friend Naval Bhathena, was the author of numerous pioneering books and study guides on advanced accounting, on the principles of auditing, on double-entry bookkeeping and on every other subject that might help a student pass the examinations of the Institute of Chartered Accountants, or Bombay University's Bachelor of Commerce degree, or that of the London Chamber of Commerce. What was strikingly unique about BATI was how it reached out to aspiring 'graduates, matriculates, or even non-matriculates' through a range of specialized courses that were 'oral or postal', which is to say, could be followed from off-campus through the mail! As one advert for BATI from 1929 boasted: 'The Hours of Attendance for all Courses are from 8 to 10 a.m. The hours do not interfere with your present vocation or employment, and the whole day is thus left at your entire disposal.'[9] When founding Siddharth College two decades later, Ambedkar took this ingenious formula from Batliboi. As Savita Ambedkar put it, Siddharth College 'became the first college in the history of Mumbai University to begin morning classes. This made it possible for the untouchables as well as for the touchables to go for higher education while retaining a day job.'[10]

BATI was thus a sort of cross between a coaching centre and a community college, with distance learning to boot. And it was successful for quite a while. As Batliboi boasted in the preface to one of his accountancy books, BATI enrolled more than 200 students per year.[11]

Jamshed Batliboi, as principal and professor of accounting at BATI, said that he was 'assisted by a staff of most highly qualified and experienced experts who have specialised in educational work'. Among them were a vice-principal cum professor of accounting, two professors of law, a professor of banking and economics, a professor of statistics and an assistant professor of accounting. The two professors of law had BA degrees to supplement their LLBs. However, not a single faculty member had an MA, let alone two PhDs, as Dr Ambedkar did by 1927.

Biographers of Ambedkar state that he taught mercantile law at BATI, but that was a generic description and not one of the subjects offered by name. There were two law-specific courses taught—commercial and industrial law; and company law and practice. There was also a course in banking, currency and exchange, for which Dr Ambedkar, having recently published a definitive book on the subject, would have been an ideal instructor.[12] That book, to tie up some loose ends from the previous chapter, was *The Problem of the Rupee*, published in December 1923. It was his DSc dissertation, which he had returned to Bombay in April 1923 to revise and resubmit, and did so in August 1923, less than two months after his sanad at the Bombay High Court. As earlier mentioned, the resubmission was accepted and his DSc granted in November 1923, making him 'Dr Ambedkar'. Dr Ambedkar then published his *Rupee* book in the last month of that year.

Again, he had by then already begun his legal practice, but with that were cases rather few, far between and providing inadequate income. His book collecting had not abated, and indeed joining the legal profession only served to justify more costly book acquisitions. A letter from the Law Reports Office in Madras (now Chennai) to Ambedkar reveals that he was in the process of purchasing all twenty volumes of the Indian Law Reports, 1901–20, for all four high courts! Hence, it makes perfect sense that in 1925 Ambedkar turned to moonlighting—if one can call lectures from 8 a.m. to 10 a.m. moonlighting—at Batliboi's, earning Rs 200 per month.

In this period, then, Ambedkar remained as much in the academic world as in the legal one. This included serving as an examiner at Bombay University, which provided him a small supplementary income. And indeed, Ambedkar took a keen interest in the condition of Bombay University, as is evident from his reply to a questionnaire that the University Reforms Committee had sent to him in 1924, along with 320 other specially selected experts. Some fifty questions were asked across a broad range of potential reforms—structural, legal, academic, curricular and more. In a painstakingly detailed series of replies, extending to some 8,000 words, Ambedkar laid out very specific ideas for reform, exhibiting both a depth and breadth of understanding about university education in general and the issues facing Bombay University in particular.

Ambedkar placed a great deal of emphasis on academic freedom, effective pedagogy and the promotion of high-quality research. The prescience of many of his replies is astonishing—Mumbai University today continues to face several structural and pedagogical inefficiencies that Ambedkar had offered creative solutions to 100 years ago. But one thing to note in particular is just how much Ambedkar drew from the operations and protocols of Columbia University in his prescriptions for the reform of Bombay University. For example, consider Ambedkar's reply to the twentieth question that he was posed: 'When Bombay University further develops its teaching functions, what should be the duration of studies for post-graduate degrees? How would you award such degrees, whether by examination, thesis, original research or a combination of one or more of these?'

> The duration of studies for post-graduate degrees should be four years (I am speaking only for social sciences). There should be two stages of two years each. At the end of the first stage the candidate should be entitled to the M.A. degree. He should

specialize in one subject only which should be the subject of his major interest. The test should consist of a written examination accompanied by an essay of some 75 typewritten pages showing his familiarity with the art of using original sources and commenting upon them. At the end of the second stage the candidate should be entitled to the Ph.D. degree. There the test would include an oral examination and a thesis of a respectable size fit for publication. The thesis will embody the investigations of the candidate in a particular field lying within the scope of the subject he had taken at the M.A. as being of major interest to him. Besides this the candidate will present himself for an oral examination in two subjects to be known as subjects of minor interest which will be allied to the subjects of his major interest. This arrangement will allow specialization with a broad base.[13]

The structure and process that Ambedkar proposed here was in every step identical to that of post-graduate studies in the social sciences at Columbia University at the time. Ambedkar himself went through the initial stage of two years, specializing in one subject (economics), sitting for a written exam at the end and submitting a seventy-five-page research paper ('Ancient Indian Commerce'), thus entitling him to the MA degree. He then went through a second stage, where two minors (sociology and history)[14] were added to the major, concluding with an oral examination and the submission of 'a thesis of a respectable size fit for publication' ('The Evolution of Provincial Finance in British India'), entitling him to the PhD. Ambedkar had thus enjoyed the benefits of this well-designed programme, allowing him 'specialization with a broad base', and sought that the same be made available to students at Bombay University.

Ambedkar's passion about one area in particular, i.e., the accessibility of books via high-quality libraries, led him to speak beyond the scope of the questions asked in the otherwise-exhaustive questionnaire.

He raised this point, about which the questionnaire was silent, with an annoyance that he was unable to suppress:

> Before closing my replies to the questionnaire, I beg to express my surprise at the absolute disregard the University Reforms Committee has shown in the matter of organizing a good library. I cannot see how any University can function without a first-rate library attached to it.[15]

It is clear, then, that Ambedkar was deeply engaged with the academic world as well as the legal one. But he was also in the process of becoming evermore deeply immersed in the world of social work and social activism. At times, the simultaneous wearing of three hats—lawyer, academician and social worker—was mutually reinforcing, such as how Ambedkar's legal work turned out to be a kind of activism and social work in many cases. At other times, however, there was a sort of ambivalence caused. For example, during this time the post of principal at Sydenham College opened up, and Dr Ambedkar applied for the position. Padhye recollects that Ambedkar was quite keen on getting the position, although it was not to be.

The local government's member for education, Dr R.P. Paranjpye, was an associate of Ambedkar's in an important social organization that Ambedkar had just pioneered (more in the next chapter about this); nevertheless, he was unable to get enough backing to offer Ambedkar, despite being duly qualified, the principal's post. Ambedkar's well-wisher and mentor Dada Keluskar, who had himself been principal of Wilson College at an earlier period, met Dr Paranjpye at the hill station of Mahabaleshwar to lobby for Ambedkar's appointment. Paranjpye, according to letters exchanged between Keluskar and Ambedkar, said that he could only offer Ambedkar a professorship at Elphinstone College instead. This offer Ambedkar promptly brushed aside, communicating through Keluskar that pursuing social work was more important to him and that he would not want that hindered by a full-time professorship.

Still committed to academia, however, Ambedkar published his second book in 1925. It was titled *The Evolution of Provincial Finance in British India: A Study in the Provincial Decentralization of Imperial Finance*, and published by the Westminster publisher PS King & Son. The title sounds quite similar to his 1921 London School of Economics MSc thesis 'Provincial Decentralization of Imperial Finance in British India', but this 1925 book was actually—at long last—Ambedkar's submission for his PhD at Columbia University in New York.

A comparison of the table of contents of the LSE MSc thesis versus the 1925 book (which led to the award, in 1927, of the Columbia PhD) is indicative of how well Ambedkar finally managed to sort out the problem of owing both of his alma maters publishable books. The MSc had three main parts, with a page extent of 151:

Part One: Provincial Budget – its origin. Part One included three chapters.

Part Two: Provincial Budget – its development. Part Two also included three chapters.

Part Three: Provincial Budget – its mechanism. Part Three only included two chapters.

The 1925 book, however, had four main parts, totalling nearly 300 pages. The first three parts were almost identical to those of the MSc:

Part One: Provincial Finance – its origin. Part One of the book included basically the same three chapters as the MSc.

Part Two: Provincial Finance – its development. Part Two also included basically the same three chapters.

Part Three: Provincial Finance – its mechanism. Part Three of the book added a third chapter, whereas the MSc thesis had only two.

Then the book also added a fourth and final part:

Part Four: Provincial Finance under the Government of India Act of 1919. Part Four had three new chapters, symmetrical with each of the earlier three parts.

Thus, the 1925 book was like a continuation of the 1921 MSc thesis, updating the whole and adding four new chapters that doubled the length of the book—and it was for this, the completion of the dissertation on India's financial history that Ambedkar had begun in New York back in 1916, when he passed the doctoral examination and was declared ABD, that Columbia University finally granted him the PhD degree in June of 1927. The book is still available in microfilm format in the Columbia University library. On their copy, there is a thesis label mounted on the book's title page that reads: 'Submitted in partial fulfilment of the requirements of the degree of Doctor of Philosophy in the Faculty of Political Science, Columbia University, in the City of New York.'

There are two more personally meaningful ways in which Ambedkar's 1925 book differed from his 1921 thesis. First, just as *The Problem of the Rupee* contained a foreword from his LSE supervisor Professor Edwin Cannan, *Evolution of Provincial Finance in British India* contained a foreword from his Columbia supervisor Edwin Seligman.[16] And in his own author's preface, Ambedkar wholeheartedly thanked Seligman in *Finance*, just as he had thanked Cannan in *Rupee*. In this case, however, since the first half of *Finance* had an earlier iteration as his LSE MSc thesis under Professor Cannan, he had to thank Cannan in this book too: 'I am also thankful to Prof. Cannan, of the University of London, who has read the rough draft of a small part of the manuscript. My debt to Prof. Seligman, my teacher at Columbia University, is of course immense: for from him I learned my first lessons in the theory of Public Finance.'[17] Recall that it was with Seligman that Ambedkar had taken his first course in economics at Columbia, called 'The Science of Finance', Economics 101.

And finally, just as *The Problem of the Rupee* contained a touching dedication to his parents about their enlightenment regarding his education, *The Evolution of Provincial Finance in British India* contained this kind dedication to the progressive-minded man who granted him the Columbia scholarship:

A Barrister in Bombay (1924–26)

Dedicated to
His Highness Shri Sayajirao Gaikawad
Maharajah of Baroda
As a token of my gratitude for his help in the
Matter of my education

Despite that the PhD thesis was double the length of the MSc thesis upon which it was based, and despite that there were various qualitative differences on top of the quantitative ones, throughout Dr Ambedkar's life, he would never make mention of his MSc degree or list it among his achievements. It is never mentioned anywhere that his PhD was also listed. His stationery mentioned only his first MA from Columbia, as well as his PhD, and then his DSc from LSE, along with his Bar-at-Law degree. In an exceptional exercise of academic integrity and self-restraint, Ambedkar unilaterally chose not to take public credit for both of the degrees, as the two theses shared material in common.[18]

Ambedkar's education was, of course, protracted and immense, and its formal elements had now finally come to a conclusion. The early academic books that emerged from his formal studies continued to make an impact in later years, although Ambedkar's writing gave way to a less formal and more polemical style. Still, his writing until the end was scholarly and indicative of deep and wide study. Early on, in December 1925, Ambedkar's *Rupee* made waves in the British government, which was in the process of attempting to rationalize monetary policy in India and to stabilize the rupee. To that effect, in August 1925, the Royal Commission on Indian Currency and Finance was appointed and began hearing expert testimony. Dr Ambedkar submitted a 3,500-word 'Statement of Evidence' to the commission, offering numerous recommendations, and on 25 December 1925, he gave oral testimony before them.

The transcript of the testimony is intense! The chairman, Edward Hilton Young, along with eight of the other nine members of the commission (only the Bengali industrialist Sir Rajendra Nath Mookerjee remained silent), grilled Ambedkar for over one hour, with questions covering a wide range of theoretical, historical and statistical debates in agonizing detail. Ambedkar's written 'Statement of Evidence' was essentially abstracted from his book *The Problem of the Rupee*, and several of the members were sporting copies, continuously referring to page and line numbers during the interrogation. For Ambedkar, the testimony before the commission must have been like a replay of his doctoral dissertation defence at LSE. Except in this case, the results were not merely academic. The commission published its report in August 1926, putting forth many recommendations regarding a gold standard for the stabilization of the currency exchange, but most emphatically, regarding the creation of a central bank: 'The commission is of the opinion that India ... should perfect her currency and credit organization by setting up a central bank ...'[19] And thus was the Reserve Bank of India created.[20]

What was truly fascinating about Ambedkar's testimony was that he was seeking to advise on monetary policy from the explicit vantage point of labour and the working masses. In an exchange with the commission member Sir Purshottamdas Thakurdas, a Gujarati industrialist and one of the founders of the Federation of Indian Chambers of Commerce & Industry (FICCI) along with G.D. Birla, Ambedkar was straightforward about how his underlying ideology might conflict with that of the elite members:

Ambedkar: May I just explain it in my own way?

Thakurdas: If you please.

Ambedkar: The way in which I look upon the problem is this. Today we have one shilling, sixpence (1s. 6d.). That to my mind means a certain price level. If you want us to go back to 1s. 4d., it seems to me we have to raise our prices. ... Therefore the complete question to my mind is, shall we raise our prices from what they are today, so that we can go back to 1s. 4d.? Now I, being a member of the labouring community, feel that falling prices are better. That is my view of the matter.

Thakurdas: You say, as you put it, that, being a member of the labouring community, that means from the point of view of the labouring class it is undesirable?

Ambedkar: Yes, and I may go further and say that from the national point of view too falling prices are better than rising prices.[21]

What followed next in the exchange between the gentle plutocrat, Sir Thakurdas, and the learned egalitarian, Dr Ambedkar, was a remarkable dispute between the capitalist and socialist outlooks:

Thakurdas: Now I suppose you heard the arguments that are being advanced that a high exchange … is undesirable in the interests of the producer. What would you say to that?

Ambedkar: All that it means is a depression of profits. I do want to make a distinction—I do not know how far people will appreciate it—between depression of industry and depression of profits …

Thakurdas: In the ordinary course, for the adjustment to be complete, you would expect that the wages he pays to his labourers also go down?

Ambedkar: Yes. I mean if he wants to get the same amount of profit, I would say yes.

Thakurdas: And in cases where the [producer is a] farmer who is just able to make both ends meet, he loses?

Ambedkar: No. He does not get profits, but he does not lose. Profit is something else; it is surplus.

Thakurdas: He will make less profit?

Ambedkar: Yes; there would be a depression of profit.

Thakurdas: To that extent of course the producer will be a loser?

Ambedkar: If you think that he had a legitimate right to that profit, then of course you would be right in saying that he loses.[22]

This same labour-conscious and people-centric ideology that underlay Ambedkar's monetary policy equally underlay his jurisprudence, as well as his everyday practice of law. He could not make a fortune as a barrister-at-law, but he could make a difference. This desire to leverage his economic and legal qualifications for the uplift of the common and labouring people also pushed him to create institutions dedicated to that aim.

Chapter Eleven
'Educate, Agitate, Organize'

The first major institution that Ambedkar formed was the Bahishkrut Hitakarini Sabha (BHS), literally translated as the 'association for the benefit of the excluded', but referred to in English as the Depressed Classes Institute. The term 'Bahishkrut' (also commonly spelt 'Bahishkrit', with an 'i')—excluded, outcaste, excommunicated, ostracized—is interesting because it constituted a sort of first effort at self-naming by the identity community that would eventually settle around the term 'Dalit'. There had been a small organization in the Akola district (in Berar, now in north-central Maharashtra), which had been formed sometime prior to 1920, that used this term. They even fitfully published a newspaper titled *Bahishkrut Bharat*, which Ambedkar mentioned in his first editorial for *Mooknayak* back in January 1920. In 1927, as we shall see, Ambedkar would purloin this name for his own newspaper launched to help propagate the activities and ideology of the BHS.

The BHS endured for around ten years, active mostly in Bombay, although it seems to have been conceived farther out in the province—in Barshi, a town near Solapur. Judging from one of the weekly letters exchanged between Ambedkar and Frances Fitzgerald during this period, something very important was brewing for Ambedkar on 10 and 11 May 1924, which kept him too busy to write to her that week. It was likely the Provincial Depressed Classes Conference held in Barshi, where a resolution was passed that an institution needed to be formed for the 'amelioration and uplift' of the depressed classes: the BHS. Fortunately, we know a great deal about the formation and activities of the BHS because the *Rules of Constitution*, written by Ambedkar, as well as the Annual Report for 1925 and 1931 are still extant.[1]

The BHS was officially founded on 20 July 1924 in the Damodar Hall of N.M. Joshi's Social Service League (SSL), literally just a few steps from Ambedkar's home in the BIT Chawl in Parel. It was not unique insofar as there were already several service organizations targeting social reform in general and the amelioration of the poor and marginalized in particular. However, the vast majority of these were charitable services of 'high-caste' bodies, political parties and the like, meaning that untouchables were the objects of charity as opposed to being the agents of change. Ambedkar referred to this distinction as one between help and self-help. The BHS was fundamentally an organization for self-help. This important idea of self-help, being the agent of change oneself rather than an object of charity, did not mean that help, financial or otherwise, would not be taken from the 'upper classes': 'The Founders of the Sabha have been conscious that without their cooperation and sympathy it would not be possible for the Depressed Classes to work out their salvation.'[2] However, it did mean that all financial decisions and executive functions would be in the hands of untouchables themselves. To establish this, the constitution of the BHS required that 'the Board of Trustees will at all times include a member or members of the Mahar, Chambhar, Mang and Dhed communities'.[3]

Ambedkar was the chairman of the council of management of the BHS, his close friend S.N. Shivtarkar (from the Chambhar community) was the general secretary and N.T. Jadhav was the treasurer. The board consisted of many important people from among Bombay's social and political elite, including Parsees, Marathas and Brahmans. The president of the board was Sir Chimanlal Harilal Setalvad, a jurist from a prominent Brahmakshatriya family who was sometime vice-chancellor of Bombay University and a member of the governor of Bombay's executive council. Other board members included Dr R.P. Paranjpye, the minister for education, and B.G. Kher, future chief minister of Bombay State. Since the stated objectives of the BHS were reformative and amelioratory, there was no problem garnering the support and cooperation of these eminent upper-class well-wishers. These objectives were: to promote the spread of education among the depressed classes by opening student hostels and educational institutions; to promote 'the spread of culture' among the depressed classes by opening social centres, libraries and study circles; to advance the economic condition of the depressed classes by launching industrial and agricultural training; and to 'represent the grievances' of the depressed classes.[4]

With such a high-powered board profile, the BHS occasionally experimented with punching well above its weight in its efforts towards self-representation of the depressed classes. For example, in anticipation of the arrival in 1926 of the new viceroy of India Lord Irwin (who was replacing Lord Reading, who had served from 1921 to 1926), Ambedkar shot off a letter to the private secretary of the governor of Bombay to inform him that 'the Council of Management of Bahishkrut Hitakarini Sabha has resolved to present an address of welcome to the incoming Viceroy on his arrival in Bombay on the 2nd of April 1926 on behalf of the Depressed Classes'. Dr Ambedkar was not *asking* the governor whether the BHS could do this—he was informing him that they were doing it. After a volley of confidential letters were exchanged between the Bombay governor's private secretary, the home department's special branch and the Bombay police commissioner, who had the BHS surveilled and assessed, the answer came back in March 1926: 'Not good enough to present the address to the Viceroy.'[5]

The motto that the BHS used was 'Educate, Agitate, Organize', and as apparent from the stated objectives, there was at first much more emphasis on *educate* and *organize* than there was on *agitate*. Later, however, as the activities of the BHS evolved from educational, cultural and social betterment to much more radical agendas, including satyagrahas and other political agitation aimed at the annihilation of caste, the elite 'upper-caste' members of the board slunk away one by one.

There were non-negligible achievements in terms of education and culture in 1924 and 1925. Students' hostels were opened in Solapur, Jalgaon and Panvel, where students were not only accommodated, but also had their clothes, books and boarding covered. In the heart of a mill workers' area called Mahar Colony in Byculla, a reading room and a library were opened. Recreational centres to divert the youth were also opened or maintained in slum areas, including a Mahar hockey club.

Ambedkar biographer and eminent sociologist Christophe Jaffrelot cites all of these developments—hockey, for example, being regarded as an elite sport—as evidence for his (rather specious) claim that 'the values of Sanskritization remained deep-rooted in Ambedkar's psyche at that time'.[6] Jaffrelot suggests that all through the 1920s, for Ambedkar 'the road to equality first passed via an attempt to persuade untouchables to conform to Brahmanical virtues …'; and he inferred this not merely in the demands of the BHS, but even from Ambedkar's speeches at Mahad (about which more will be written in the next chapter).[7] But Jaffrelot's interpretation is both reductionistic and insensitive to the social realities of destitute communities lacking avenues of social mobility. The call of a leader for her community to take steps to overcome their abject poverty does not necessarily mean that she unconsciously desires them to become robber barons!

Jaffrelot compounds his errors by failing to realize that the BHS slogan of 'Educate, Agitate, Organize' was not indicating the desire to emulate the 'upper castes' through achieving education, but was a reference to the Fabian socialist, playwright and LSE co-founder George Bernard Shaw, who had summed up the mission of the Fabian Society with those three words.[8] Perhaps, however, Jaffrelot might argue that Shaw's *Pygmalion* was effectively a play about Sanskritization.

The concept of 'self-help' is another that seems to confuse Jaffrelot, who interprets it as being high-caste emulation and Gandhian, when, in fact, the move towards agency that it actually implied was later used by Ambedkar in the 1930s in specific contrast to Gandhi's harijanization (i.e., what Ambedkar saw as the undermining of the untouchables' agency by treating them as objects of charity). But the main reason, I believe, for Jaffrelot's seeming inability in his biography to really understand who Ambedkar was most likely lies in Jaffrelot's palpably Eurocentric worldview. For example, Jaffrelot ends his discussion of Ambedkar's struggle to overcome Sanskritization by concluding: 'By the end of the 1920s, he had rejected the logic of Sanskritisation … [and] he gradually came to reject Hinduism in favour of Western values—especially egalitarian individualism—and looked for a new strategy of emancipation.'[9] This is not the place to lay out why egalitarian and individualist values are not inherently Western, but it is worth noting that Ambedkar himself spent several years towards the end of his life composing a massive book showing that Buddhism arose in ancient India as an egalitarian movement.[10] Contrary to Jaffrelot's Eurocentric framework, Ambedkar was not stuck between only two alternatives—Sanskritization or Westernization.

Placing this theoretical discussion to one side, Ambedkar's task, his calling, remained the uplifting of the downtrodden. He pursued this intellectually, leveraging his prodigious ability and education, and he pursued this institutionally by way of the BHS. He also pursued it through his legal practice. In addition, he pursued it with community organization and activism. The latter two areas saw Ambedkar travel frequently in the provinces and beyond. In the mid-1920s, he spoke at gatherings and conferences in Nipani (now in Karnataka), Malwan (south-west Maharashtra), Jejuri (near Pune) and Goa, among other occasions. His wife, children, nephew and accompanying family were also out of Bombay for much of this period, in the countryside, where it was thought that Ramu's frequent ill health might improve (she appears to have contracted tuberculosis). There they kept a small pet deer, and in a March 1925 letter from Frances Fitzgerald, we learn that Ambedkar was quite distraught over its death. Ambedkar was always fond of pets, and greatly attached to his dogs—and he had many.

Ambedkar's speeches during this era displayed a wide range of concerns, rather than just a specific thrust of focus. On some occasions he spoke of national politics, on others about the need for the depressed classes to agitate collectively for their rights, and occasionally he also chastised the untouchables for behaviour indicative of a lack of self-respect or ambition. Entertaining a vast field of social and political possibilities, he weighed the options of mass agitation for entry into temples or, on the other hand, conversion away from Hinduism altogether. During his speech in Jejuri, he even pondered the suggestion that untouchables should colonize land for themselves where they could live free of persecution by caste Hindus! He often spoke of the events unfolding at Vaikom in 1924, showing some cautious admiration for Gandhi's position. In Vaikom, in Travancore State (now Kerala), untouchables had launched a satyagraha for access at least to the road in front of the local temple, if not to the temple itself. Gandhi had visited the city and sided with the untouchables. At the conference in Nipani, Ambedkar commented at length on these events:

> For us, the most important event in the country today is the Satyagraha at Vaikom. Most of you know what sort of debate is going on. The Untouchables of Vaikom insist that they should be allowed to use a road which is used by all the people and animals as well ... The fact to remember is this: that even after a whole year of protest, there is no result. Before Mahatma Gandhi, no politician in this country maintained that it is necessary to remove social injustice here in order to do away with tension and conflict, and that every Indian should consider it his sacred duty to do so. According to Mahatma Gandhi, social and political causes are not separate but are one and the same ... However, he does not insist on the removal of untouchability as much as he insists on the propagation of Khaddar or Hindu-Muslim unity.

> If he had he would have made the removal of untouchability a precondition for membership of the Congress as he made yarn spinning a precondition of voting in the party. Well, be that as it may, when one is spurned by everyone, even the sympathy shown by Mahatma Gandhi is of no little importance.[11]

Later in the same speech, prophetic of events to come in the following years, Ambedkar launched an attack on the sacred texts that the Brahmans were appealing to in order to prohibit the untouchables from gaining access to the road in front of the temple:

> This clearly indicates that we should burn all these scriptures to ashes, or verify and examine the validity of their rules regarding untouchability … and if we are unable to prove their falseness or invalidity, we are to suffer untouchability till the end of time! Truly these scriptures are an insult to the people. The government should have confiscated them long ago.[12]

Two years later, Ambedkar exercised the first option, burning the *Manusmriti*.[13] And twenty-two years later, he undertook the second option, researching and publishing books on the inaccuracies of scriptural dogma with respect to the origins, practices and justifications of untouchability.

Another topic of importance to Ambedkar, about which he spoke regularly at these various conferences, was the Bole resolution. This was a pioneering resolution put forward in the Bombay Legislative Council in 1923 by Sitaram Keshav Bole, a social reformer who worked to improve the condition of mill workers and was especially known for his contributions towards the Bhandari community (erstwhile toddy tappers). Bole was fond of Ambedkar, and indeed had been there at the felicitation of young Bhiva back in 1908, when he had matriculated from Elphinstone High School. Ambedkar admired him too, and even thought of Bole as the most likely candidate to succeed him—though he was his predecessor by many years—in leading the Dalit movement in the political realm, in the event that Ambedkar had to step back from politics (for example, by being appointed as a high court judge).[14] There is a charming photo of Bole and Ambedkar from many decades later at a function in Bombay in 1951. As the photo illustrates, in candid photos of Dr Ambedkar, he would most often be found smiling or even laughing, although he always put on a more serious countenance for staged photos. This candid photo captured Bole sitting on Ambedkar's lap, as only two chairs had been set out, for Dr Ambedkar and his wife.[15]

The Bole resolution, however, was a most serious matter, and ignited the consciousness of the depressed classes everywhere. It had been implemented by the government on 11 September 1923, and read:

> The Council recommends that the Untouchable Classes be allowed to use all public watering places, wells, and dharmshalas which are built and maintained out of public funds or administered by bodies appointed by Government or created by Statute, as well as public schools, courts, offices and dispensaries.[16]

Though officially implemented, the resolution was scarcely enforced. Consequently, in August 1926, Bole moved another resolution in the Bombay Legislative Council (BLC), recommending that the government not give grants to any municipality or local board that refused to give effect to the 1923 Bole resolution. Ambedkar not only supported the resolutions, but he would soon even launch legal proceedings as well as direct action in an effort to force municipalities to comply with their requirements.

Towards the end of 1926, Ambedkar was himself nominated to the Bombay Legislative Council as a depressed classes representative. This opened a new chapter for him, as well as a new avenue into the political domain, to complement his already-existing engagements in the academic, legal and social fields. As to be expected with a person juggling so many diverse obligations, Ambedkar was occasionally absent from the council for extended periods. However, there were also periods—especially in the first couple of years—where he was fully engaged and active there, delivering some of his most powerful speeches and moving significant and even historic pieces of legislation. But there is no question that the heavy responsibilities that came along with the nomination initially overwhelmed him. As he wrote to a close friend:

> My own responsibilities as you know are great enough, and this entry into the Council has added quite a lot more. I don't know how I will cope with them all. People expect so much from me that I fear it will be humanly impossible to satisfy them. All I can say is that I shall try my best to discharge the duties that have befallen me. In this, of course, I count upon the support of my friends. For, one cannot fight a battle single-handed.[1/]

This letter, incidentally, was written upon a new letterhead, listing not only Ambedkar's recently awarded PhD from Columbia University, but also his recent nomination to the council. As his address, he used Damodar Hall, Parel, Bombay-12. As discussed in Chapter Ten, Ambedkar would decline to list the MSc that he had earned from LSE, and after adding his PhD, he never mentioned his MSc again. He does, however, continue always to list the MA that he had earned even earlier from Columbia. This enumeration of his degrees and qualifications, as well as the address, would be the format for the stationery that he would use all the way up until 1935:

Bhimrao R. Ambedkar,
MA, PhD, DSc, Bar-at-Law,
Member, Legislative Council,
Bombay

Despite the added workload, serving as a member of the BLC afforded Ambedkar the opportunity to become familiar with the arcane procedures and protocols of a formal parliamentary body. This learning experience would serve him well in the future.

By the end of 1926, some three years after returning to India from London, Ambedkar had made great professional strides towards establishing a foundation for his lifelong effort to liberate his people. But on the personal front, things were far from happy. In July 1926, tragedy struck. Ambedkar and Ramu lost yet another child to illness. This one hit Ambedkar particularly hard, perhaps because, unlike on previous occasions when he was living abroad for long periods, he had been there with the boy, Rajratna, from the day of his birth to the day of his death.[18] A month after the tragedy, Ambedkar wrote a poignant letter to his longtime friend Dattoba Pawar from Kolhapur, which revealed his state of mind as 1926 came to a close:

> There is no use pretending that I and my wife have recovered from the shock of my son's death and I don't think we ever shall. We have in all buried four precious children, three sons and a daughter, all sprightly, auspicious and handsome children. The thought of this is sufficiently crushing, let alone the future that would have been theirs if they had lived. We are living no doubt in the sense that the days are passing over us as does a cloud. With the loss of our kids the salt of our life is gone and as the Bible says: 'Ye are the salt of the earth; if it leaveth the earth, wherewith shall it be salted?' I feel the truth of this every moment in my almost vacant and empty life. My last boy was a wonderful boy the like of whom I had seldom seen. With his passing away life to me is a garden full of weeds. But enough of this. I am too overcome to write any more.
>
> With best regards of a broken man,
> Yours in grief,
> B.R. Ambedkar[19]

Chapter Twelve

From Bhima Koregaon to the Mahad Conference (1927)

On the banks of the river Bhima, watch how the valiant soldiers fight.
The Mahars defeated the Peshwas that day.
This battle has nullified your pothis and puranas.
Where was your spirituality when you were torturing us?
But don't blame us for the fall of your Peshwas—it was the vengeance of destiny itself.

— Shahir Rajendra Kamble
Sung (in Marathi) at Bhima Koregaon, 01 Jan 2017[1]

While 1926 concluded in grief, 1927 was more promising. Indeed, it was life-altering for Dr Ambedkar, and thus historic for all of us who have been in some way or another impacted by his life and work.

This year, replete with history, was busy and significant from day one. On 1 January 1927, Ambedkar and his colleagues visited the Bhima

Koregaon *vijay stambha*, an imposing obelisk erected by the British to serve as a victory memorial for the Battle of Koregaon, fought on 1 January 1818 between the British East India Company and the Peshwas. The site, not far from Pune, commemorates the company forces' fallen soldiers, many of whom were Mahars, who had fought valiantly despite being massively outnumbered. In chronicles of the era, their heroism became the stuff of legends: The vastly outnumbered victorious forces exhibited 'the most noble devotion and most romantic bravery under the pressure of thirst and hunger almost beyond human endurance'.[2] As the plaque on the obelisk reads, the forces 'accomplished one of the proudest triumphs of the British army in the East'.[3]

From a simplistic nationalist point of view, it seems gauche to celebrate a battle that led to the further triumph of the British in India. But the realities of the time were more complex—indeed, the Peshwa forces, here belligerents against the British, had fought alongside the British on previous occasions. The British forces comprised numerous 'natives', and the 'Indian' forces themselves were often majority foreign mercenaries, such as Arabs, as was the case in the Koregaon battle. A pan-Indian consciousness to anchor a nationalist sensibility was only inchoate at the time. What was more immediate and concrete, however, was awareness of community and self-identification with caste.

From the point of view of caste, especially from the vantage point of a marginalized, degraded, outcaste community, the battle bore testament to the fighting spirit of the Mahars, to a martial valour that belied the demeaning social status to which they were relegated by 'higher' castes, especially by the likes of the Peshwas. Earlier Peshwa rule had been notorious for its brutal and inhumane treatment of Mahars.[4] For Ambedkar and all of his allies gathered at the memorial, some veterans and some still active military, the 1 January commemoration represented a rallying point of triumph in the Mahars' enduring battle for dignity and self-respect, equality and recognition. The monument served as a proud and sombre gathering point for Mahars throughout the late

1920s, 1930s and onwards, with the symbolics of the old battle inspiring courage and fortitude for the new battles to come.

The following month, on 18 February, the Bombay Legislative Council kicked off with its first session for 1927, and Ambedkar's tenure in the council began. As mentioned earlier, he had been appointed to the council by the governor of Bombay late in the previous year and was completely new to a formal body of this kind.

The council assembled at the magnificent neoclassical Town Hall of Bombay, overlooking Horniman Circle. With a massive flight of thirty steps leading up to the Grecian portico entrance, the facade of which boasts eight imposing Doric columns with wings of wrought-iron terraces and an interior adorned by spiral staircases, the impressive architecture of this building conveyed a sense of gravitas that must have struck Ambedkar. And, of course, there was its imperial pomp—all of the stones for the enormous structure had been brought by ship from England.

The business of the council on that first day was the swearing in of the new members—Ambedkar was sworn in on that day itself—and the election of the new president of the council. The following day, assembling at noon, there was again only formal business. New members continued to be sworn in; a deputy president was elected; various committees were set up, their chairs nominated; and ballots were handed out for the election of members to the committees. On the third day, Ambedkar found himself elected to the finance committee, and moments after that to the public accounts committee as well. It was also on this day that the substantive work began. The governor of Bombay addressed the newly formed council and its various officers now placed in their functions, and then at length the budget was presented, launching three full days of debate.

Up until then, Ambedkar had hardly spoken a word, other than for his swearing-in or for proposing or accepting nominations. By now five full days of sessions had passed, including two days of lengthy debates on the budget, and the majority of the council members probably assumed that a freshman such as Ambedkar would remain relatively silent throughout the length of his first year. But on the sixth day, 24 February, Ambedkar did speak, and at surprising length and depth with respect to the details of the budget, and with totally unexpected candour.

Ambedkar primarily addressed his remarks directly to the government's new finance minister—an Indian, Sir Chunilal Mehta, who had earlier been the revenue member[5]—and raised the many inequities of the process of collecting taxes: 'I think the revenue system of this presidency is inequitable and indefensible,' he argued, pointing out the regressive tax policies that overburdened the poor as well as the government monopoly on liquor, which was ostensibly for limiting the consumption of alcohol but was actually just to earn more revenue (he later reiterates this in another speech on 10 March, when the excise tax is being debated). Turning to spending rather than to the collection of revenue, Ambedkar strongly criticized the government's heavy and ever-increasing expenditure on administrative costs rather than on social advancement. Raising the level of the debate on the budget from merely demanding frugality and a balance of revenue and expense, Ambedkar closed his speech by admonishing his fellow members:

> I hope ... this Council is really earnest in its desire for compulsory education, for medical relief, for freedom of the people from the habit of drink, and for providing all the amenities of life ... The good things of this earth do not fall from heaven. Every progress has its bill of costs and only those who pay for it will have that progress.[6]

Ambedkar made a mark not just by speaking—many new members refrained from doing so, including P.G. Solanki, the other member representing the depressed classes, who had been appointed to the Bombay Legislative Council—but by speaking forcefully and articulately on matters well beyond the interests of the depressed classes. Often, members representing specific interest groups (for example, Anglo-Indians, Indian Christians, depressed classes, etc.) spoke up only with respect to matters directly affecting the group they represented. As became clear to everyone from the early days, Ambedkar would never permit himself to be limited in this way.

Not that Ambedkar in any way forsook his duty to represent the interests of the depressed classes. Quite the contrary, he took every opportunity to safeguard their interests, as is well attested in the council records. The 5 March session captured this well. On this day, just after the swearing-in of a new member, Ambedkar launched the question-and-answer period with a question to the government about a certain M.K. Jadhav from the depressed classes, who had applied for one of the three available positions as deputy collector in the revenue department but was rejected. Ambedkar wanted all of the details to ensure that Jadhav's application had been properly handled.[7] He followed this with a request to the government to outline the measures they had taken to implement the 1923 Bole resolution regarding the access untouchables had to all public places.

Perhaps Ambedkar's most impressive speech of this sitting was on education, about which he spoke at length on 12 March. It was certainly the most moving, as several members would later mention in their own follow-up remarks.[8] He began the speech by noting the dismally slow pace of bringing children into the educational system, at the same time that administrative expenditure on education was rapidly increasing. He then proposed, radically, that at least as much money should be spent on the education of people as was being taken from them in the form of excise duties. He also hinted at enforcing compulsory education at least until the fourth standard, and demanded that more money be invested in ensuring the lasting literacy of the entire population. He then critiqued the increasing commercialization of education and pointed out that if secondary and tertiary education were only possible by demanding high tuition fees, the lower classes would never be able to benefit from education.

Ambedkar was relentless. He moved on to address the glaring inequalities in education among different communities. He highlighted that the depressed classes and other backward classes (including tribals) had nearly zero students enrolled in higher education for every two lakhs of their population, whereas advanced Hindus had 1,000 students enrolled for every two lakhs of their population. He thus concluded: 'All these communities are unequal in their status and progress. If they are to be brought to the level of equality, then the only remedy is to adopt the principle of inequality and to give favoured treatment to those who are below the level.'[9] Ambedkar closed his speech by making several recommendations to the minister for education that would better ensure that students from the depressed classes had a real chance of receiving quality education.

The first session of the Bombay Legislative Council concluded on 17 March, and Ambedkar had attended every single day of the session, eager to learn the ropes, the processes and the protocol, as well as to contribute and make his mark. The next session of 1927 began on 18 July, but a great deal happened within this break of four months. When Ambedkar returned to the council for the second session in July, the unique and profound experience of participating in a dangerous direct action had changed him in some way—and this did not go unnoticed by the other members.

This direct-action event went by many names, such as the Chavdar Tale Satyagraha at Mahad, the Satyagraha Conference and the Mahad Satyagraha. All of this actually describes a protracted struggle with numerous facets and all sorts of repercussions—personal, social, professional, institutional, political and legal. There were two primary, or culminating, events—the first in March 1927 and the second in December 1927. For the sake of clarity, I will refer to the March 1927 event as the Mahad Conference and the December 1927 event as the Mahad Satyagraha.

The concrete origins for this momentous struggle in Mahad date back to 1923-24, with the proclamation and fitful adoption of the Bole resolution, whereas the legal closure of the Mahad case did not come until a decade later, in late 1937. In that year the Bombay High Court finally ruled in Ambedkar's favour. Since then, the historical and symbolic significance of Mahad, just as with Bhima Koregaon, has continued to grow right up to the present day.

Mahad is a town in the Konkan region of Maharashtra, about 160 km from Mumbai. It is the site of the naturally fortified Raigad Fort, the capital of Shivaji's Maratha kingdom. After the passing of the Bole resolution in 1923, the Mahad municipality—through its local, self-governing council—had complied, at least on paper, by declaring the Chavdar *tale*, or lake (often referred to as the Chavdar 'tank', since it was artificially constructed), open to access by untouchables. However, untouchables refrained from drawing water from Chavdar lake, both due to the distance of the water source from the Maharwada, the area where Mahars lived, as well as to the palpable hostility of the 'upper castes', primarily the Brahmans, whose houses occupied the area around the lake. By May 1924, a year after the Bole resolution, no untouchable had yet dared to draw water from Chavdar tale.

That month, an intelligent and energetic local young Mahar activist, Ramchandra Babaji More (later known more as R.B. More, or, rather, as Comrade R.B. More), held a meeting at the Maharwada, where he proposed to hold a conference at Mahad and invite Dr B.R. Ambedkar to preside over it. More had suffered from vicious casteism at the hands of Brahmans in Mahad for the entirety of his young life. This included the unjustified imprisonment of his father for two years due to a conspiracy that Brahmans had hatched only out of envy for the single-storey house that More's father and grandfather had constructed and lived in. He was also at first not admitted to the Mahad high school, despite being an exceptionally gifted student and winning a government scholarship. Under advisement from Ambedkar's brother Balaram, with whom More lived for six months as he 'interned' at *Mooknayak* (actually sleeping in the *Mooknayak* office), More wrote an open letter to the government to expose the discrimination, which embarrassed the school enough to grant him admission. But he was still not permitted to sit inside the classroom, lest he pollute the caste Hindus. More relished the thought of bringing such a highly educated and articulate Mahar as Dr Ambedkar to Mahad to shame the haughty caste Hindus, as well as to inspire untouchable students of the area to pursue higher studies and awaken them to their rights.

In 1924 itself, More travelled to Bombay to invite Ambedkar to lead the conference. Ambedkar accepted in principle but said that he would have to decide the dates later. In the meantime, More, with the help of Ambedkar's colleague Bhai Anant Vinayak Chitre (from the Chandraseniya Kayastha Prabhu [CKP] caste and one of the founders of the Social Service League, which strongly supported Ambedkar at the time), devised ways to raise money for the conference. This included putting on a play at the League's Damodar Hall in December 1924, called *Sant Tukaram*, written by G.B. Kadam of the Sahakari Manoranjan Mandal, the 100-year-old dramatic society that continues to operate to this day. Because of Ambedkar's insistence, it was More who stood up in front of the crowd after the play and nervously delivered a vote of thanks to the drama company and the SSL.

As More sweetly recalled later: 'This was the first public speech that I had given in my life and interestingly it was with the motivation from none other than the great icon-to-be of the Dalits. I always cherished it as one of the landmarks of my public life.'[10]

It took More three long years to convince Dr Ambedkar to set firm dates for the Mahad Conference. Some of this delay can be attributed to an increase in Ambedkar's bouts of debilitating ill health in this period, as a letter he wrote to Dattoba Pawar dated 7 February 1927 hints at:

> You must be wondering at my silence. But I have been so ill since I returned from Panhala that I could not work. I am just getting better and the first thing I am doing is to reply to

the heaps of letters that have reached me in the matter of my nomination to the Council.[11]

In the interim, in December 1926, More successfully led the Crawford Lake Satyagraha in nearby Dasgaon, asserting the untouchables' right to access that water source. Ambedkar's protracted deliberation over when to hold the Mahad Conference resulted not merely from his poor health, but also from the fact that More and others had direct action very much in mind. This was very unlike the kind of social work that Ambedkar's Depressed Classes Institute (BHS) had been consistently pursuing until then. It meant that the very nature of Ambedkar's means and methods would be undergoing a substantial, radical shift.[12]

At long last, Ambedkar set the dates: 19-20 March 1927 in Mahad. Ambedkar was formally announced as its president (at this time the conference was called the Kolaba District Bahishkrut Parishad). Bapusaheb (Gangadhar Nilkanth) Sahasrabuddhe, a socially conscious Brahman activist from the SSL, would be the main speaker. And Sambhaji Gaikwad, a resident of the Bombay Improvement Trust Chawl like Ambedkar, who had started a library there that would become an important centre for the BHS, would be the chairman of the reception committee. Everyone set off diligently to work, disseminating information not only throughout Bombay, but to untouchables all across the Konkan region.

Ambedkar began working on his presidential speech for the conference. He selected a young graduate named C.B. Khairmoday to take the dictation. Khairmoday, decades later, would be responsible for archiving all the material related to Dr Ambedkar's movement and pen his monumental twelve-volume biography in Marathi. Khairmoday has described the process of drafting the speech, which is worth recounting as it was quite characteristic of Ambedkar. He said that the main composition took about a week to complete, but that Ambedkar made markings, changes and corrections right up till the day he left for Mahad. Ambedkar would dictate to Khairmoday but be continually interrupted by others who would urgently need to speak to him, and then would suddenly turn back to the job of dictating. Multitasking was the only way Ambedkar could possibly complete his huge scope of work as a social leader, a practising lawyer, a teaching professor, a husband/father and the primary earner of an extended family—and, of course, as a member of the Bombay Legislative Council, which was in session daily (except on Sundays) during this entire period—right up to 17 March 1927.

Anand Teltumbde, grandson-in-law of Dr Ambedkar and influential scholar (who had been imprisoned on nebulous charges linked to Bhima Koregaon commemoration-related protests), has written in his admirable book about the Mahad struggle that Ambedkar left Bombay by boat on 16 March, took stops along the way and reached Mahad on 19 March at noon. This cannot be correct, however, as Ambedkar was at the Bombay Town Hall for the final day of the BLC session, which started at 1 p.m. on 17 March. Indeed, quite late that afternoon, Ambedkar posed harsh questions to the government about what he described as 'the tyranny' that Mahars were forced to endure in *gaonkaris*, or self-governing private villages.[13] Thus the earliest that he could have left for Mahad would have been on 18 March.

More recollects bringing Dr Ambedkar, along with his elder brother Balaram, the primary speaker Sahasrabuddhe, the other main speaker Bhai Chitre, Ambedkar's close friend Shivtarkar and others from Bombay on the early morning of 19 March, reaching Mahad's Dak Bungalow (where Ambedkar would be staying) by early afternoon. He said that some 5,000 untouchables from all over the Konkan region had amassed by then.[14] The conference began in the late afternoon, and More introduced the leaders and persons of prominence to the crowd. Then Ambedkar, handsomely dressed in a white dhoti and blue suit jacket, read out his presidential address.

This was a speech of some 3,500 words, which would have thus taken at least half an hour to deliver. It was packed with information and exhortations, and so much of it would have come as a revelation to the crowd. Ambedkar started with some personal, autobiographical remarks, which was something he usually did in any speech where untouchables were the main audience, but which, interestingly, was something he almost never did when delivering speeches to a general audience. He began by indicating his reluctance to accept the presidentship of the conference, which he attributed to his nature—presumably by which he meant more cerebral and scholarly than activist. After mentioning that he had spent his childhood in the area and regarded it as his motherland, he launched into an elaboration of all of the opportunities gained and lost by the untouchables through military employment. His concerns from Bhima Koregaon at the start of the year were obviously still very much on his mind.

Indeed, a great deal of the speech, despite appearing to be an objective rendition of facts, was in so many ways intimately connected to Ambedkar's own life—from his early upbringing in a military environment due to his father's career, to his own academic orientation and personal hobbies, and even up to current challenges in front of the Bombay Legislative Council. For example, early on, while speaking of the myriad opportunities that the army had provided Mahars, Ambedkar evoked an idea from his Columbia University seminar paper 'Castes in India'. 'Recruitment of Untouchables in the military', he said, 'had brought about a revolution in the structure of Hindu Society', since touchable castes were forced to comply to orders issued by their 'inferiors' in the social hierarchy—and, of course, to eat, sleep and socially interact with them.

The education of girls and women, also a perennial preoccupation for Ambedkar, was another focal point of his speech. Earlier in the British army, when Mahars were recruited in high numbers, education was effectively compulsory. This led to high levels of literacy and basic education for girls, a phenomenon that has reversed ever since the British ended the recruitment of Mahars in the army. And as Ambedkar had just argued in the BLC one week earlier, the British had still not instituted free and compulsory primary education in Bombay, meaning that the untouchables would remain largely illiterate and uneducated unless they managed to get their ban on recruitment to the army lifted. This was one of Ambedkar's primary exhortations—they must strive to convince the government to reopen the military profession to the untouchables.

While speaking of high levels of literacy among the untouchables in the previous century, Ambedkar brought up a subject that would seem to have been utterly random. He said, 'Due to this spread of education the collection of books amongst the Untouchables was disproportionately large.' He went on to speak for another minute or two about rare books in the possession of untouchable book collectors—a deeply idiosyncratic topic for a large-scale public speech!

Back on the main track, there were more exhortations to action made by Ambedkar. They centred on promoting education within the community, thus opening the doors to government service, not only in the army, but in white-collar jobs within the bureaucracy. He emphasized the need for untouchables to cherish and preserve their dignity, which would be helped by their economic independence from relying upon the touchable classes. He then closed his speech by conveying urgency about creating a sense of awakening among the untouchables—this was the task of emancipation.

The following morning, 20 March, Ambedkar met Sahasrabuddhe, Shivtarkar, Bhai Chitre and others at the house of Surbanana Tipnis, a local activist from the CKP caste who had been deeply influenced by Ambedkar over the previous years and who had, as chairman of the Mahad municipality, led the local self-governing council to officially embrace the Bole resolution. At Tipnis's house it was decided that after the conference proceedings of the day (which included a number of speeches and the passing of several conference resolutions—see Appendix 2), they would all march to the Chavdar tale and make the Bole resolution a living reality. And this they did. Around noon, the delegates lined up in file behind Dr Ambedkar and marched in a long procession to the lake. Once they had reached, Ambedkar drank water from it with cupped hands, amid loud cries of various slogans, including '*Shivaji maharaj ki jai* (Victory to Shivaji Maharaj)', '*Har har Mahadev* [an appeal to Lord Shiva]', and reportedly even '*Mahatma Gandhi ki jai* (Long live Mahatma Gandhi)'.

Ambedkar and his colleagues returned to the Dak Bungalow without incident, and the large crowd made its way back to the conference venue to eat lunch before heading off to their various villages throughout the region. Sometime around 2 p.m., however, violence began to erupt as rumours spread that the untouchables had polluted the Chavdar tale and were now planning on entering—and thereby defiling—Mahad's historic Vireshwar temple, dedicated to Shiva and believed to have been used by Shivaji Maharaj. Ambedkar reported to the police superintendent that his people had concluded their programme at Mahad and had no intention of entering the temple. But the crowd of angered savarna Hindus that had built up was bent on violence—some sixty-five untouchables were wounded in random attacks spread out around Mahad, twenty of them seriously injured. Well-known leaders, including P.N. Rajbhoj, the Chambhar activist from Pune, were beaten to the point of needing hospitalization. Ambedkar and other leaders, committed to non-violence, urged the untouchables not to retaliate; they were forced to suffer the blows and stone pelting as best they could, often seeking shelter in the houses of Muslims and other locals from the Kayastha caste.

After the crowds had dispersed, Ambedkar and his colleagues who had come from Bombay shifted out of the Dak Bungalow (which had been reserved for use on 20 March by other visitors) and into the local police station—presumably using the cells as bedrooms. Ambedkar stayed on for a further two days to ensure the police complaints over the attacks were properly filed and evidence collected. This strategy bore fruit. In June 1927, five of the nine arrested perpetrators of violence against the untouchables were sentenced to four months' imprisonment.

For their part, the orthodox inhabitants of Mahad gathered at the Vireshwar temple to assess the situation and do some damage control. Two steps were taken, one sacred and one profane, although it is difficult to discern which was which. Pitching the gathering as an ad hoc meeting of the Mahad municipality—Tipnis, of course, not in attendance—the group revoked the earlier resolution to adopt the Bole resolution. Henceforth, untouchables were not within any explicit rights to draw water from Chavdar tale. The other hateful step taken was to purify the Chavdar tale, so that touchable Hindus could drink from it again. Brahman priests were brought in at a considerable cost to conduct the purification. As appropriate mantras were chanted, 108 earthen pots of 'polluted' water were removed from the tale and then 108 pots of a 'purifying' mix of cow dung, cow urine, curd and milk were submerged into it.[15] The status quo ante had been restored.

Chapter Thirteen

From Doctorsaheb to Babasaheb

Upon Ambedkar's safe return to Bombay, his family, especially Ramu, vented her frustration and anxiety over the new path that his social service had taken—direct action that courted danger. Ambedkar downplayed the danger, but little did any of them know then that his next visit to Mahad towards the end of 1927 would entail even higher risks—likely imprisonment, possible disbarment and perhaps even death.

At that moment, with every newspaper in the Bombay Presidency covering and commenting upon the dramatic events that had ensued in Mahad, many supportive but many also critical, foremost upon Ambedkar's mind was having his proper say. To that end, on Sunday, 3 April, Ambedkar launched the fortnightly *Bahishkrut Bharat*, a newspaper of between eight and twelve pages that came out every other Friday until September, but then only sporadically until 19 November 1929, when its final issue appeared. The Social Service League's Damodar Hall functioned as the office for the paper, where Ambedkar would dictate the editorials and content to enthusiastic student volunteers, none of whom accepted any money. Thus, the main operating expenses were Rs 258 and 8 annas for annual rent, Rs 98 as salary for the peon, and printing and postal costs. Despite the low expenditure, the paper suffered financial losses to the tune of Rs 500 per year, forcing Ambedkar to shut it down.

Perhaps an editor specially dedicated to the paper would have helped its viability. But Ambedkar had learnt his lesson from *Mooknayak*, and this time around *Bahishkrut Bharat* explicitly carried his own name as editor. This, however, added yet another responsibility on his already-overburdened shoulders, on top of serving as member in the BLC, practising as a lawyer, lecturing at Batliboi's, leading the BHS in its mission of social work and, of course, heading a household. Nevertheless, Ambedkar wrote prolifically for the paper, writing twenty-four columns over the course of the paper's brief run.

The first editorial—titled 'We Are on the Scene Again'—was another tour de force (see Appendix 3 for the full text). Ambedkar used the occasion of this first issue of *Bahishkrut Bharat* to reflect and comment upon his first editorial from *Mooknayak* that had appeared 'on the scene' seven years earlier. Through that device, he was able to draw attention to salient differences in the political realities of the two time periods—and thus renew his call to action. He wrote:

> This writer had started a fortnightly newspaper called *Mooknayak* ('Leader of the Voiceless') on 31st January 1920. There he had stated in the first issue itself that there was no more effective means than a newspaper to voice the injustices done to the untouchables by Caste Hindus, and also to suggest the ways and means for their progress and total liberation from their slavery ... We ended by assuring that if our subscribers encouraged us by subscribing to the paper, then *Mooknayak* would not fail in showing our people the right path, and that their experience would show them that our assurance was not wrong ...
>
> But the writer who had given this assurance could not keep his promise. This was due to unavoidable circumstances in his

life mission. After some experience running *Mooknayak*, its founder realised that he must find a profession which would keep him free for social service and at the same time to earn his livelihood. For this he had to go to England to complete his Barrister course, which he had kept incomplete when he had returned to India in the first phase of his education in America and England. Returning to England, he had handed over the running of *Mooknayak* to a young man whom he had trained, hoping to see the paper prosper upon his return. But his hope proved futile. *Mooknayak* no longer continued by then …

The views that had been expressed in the editorials of *Mooknayak* had all appeared prior to the Reform Act of 1919 being implemented. Now the Reform Act is in full force. The power that was earlier in the hands of the British Government has, in some proportion, fallen into the hands of upper-caste Indians. Without bothering for the representation of the untouchable communities, the British Government handed power over to Caste Hindus like the owner of cattle hands them over to a butcher. The condition of the untouchables has since deteriorated from bad to worse. Hence, right-minded persons among the untouchable communities will certainly agree that to stop the injustices being done to the untouchables and to place their problems before the world, there is no better remedy than a newspaper entirely dedicated to their cause.

There will likely be another Reform Act in 1930, and whatever power the British Government has retained till now will also fall into the hands of Indians. If this happens, and if untouchables do not get adequate representation, their fate will be sealed once and for all. According to this writer, if the untouchables are to avoid this coming tragedy, they must launch their movements and start their agitations from this very moment. May God bless us for our success![1]

The paper, though far from a financial success, certainly aroused curiosity and interest. Editors of other papers would cite Ambedkar's words from *Bahishkrut Bharat* and take issue with them. In turn, Ambedkar would take up the challenge and offer his own harsh rebuttals to them in subsequent issues of his paper. In the earliest days of the paper, however, Ambedkar was laser focused on explaining and justifying his actions at Mahad, and the larger meaning he drew from that event.

After the 3 April inaugural issue, the next three editorials of *Bahishkrut Bharat* were entirely devoted to the Mahad Conference. The 22 April issue was titled 'The Religious Battle of Mahad and the Responsibility of Savarna Hindus'. The 6 May issue was titled 'The Religious Battle of Mahad and the Responsibility of the British Government'. And the 20 May issue was titled 'The Religious Battle of Mahad and the Responsibility of the Untouchables'. Thus, Ambedkar systematically laid out what he believed should be the position taken and actions undertaken by the touchables, the government and the untouchables, each in turn.

As a person, Ambedkar had always been regarded as outspoken, even blunt. But his overall affability generally served to counterbalance whatever offence his frankness might cause. His writings in *Bahishkrut Bharat*, however, were pure fire. He held back no punches in any of the three editorials—they raised alarm in each of the audiences that they were addressed to, caste Hindus, government and, yes, even the untouchables. The last major writing by Ambedkar that had been widely available to people or to the government was his 1925 book *The Evolution of Provincial Finance in British India: A Study in the Provincial Decentralization of Imperial Finance*. That was a sober work of academic erudition. Now, two years later, he was publishing writings of outright social revolt.

To be sure, this seemingly quantum change didn't come from nowhere. Between the publication of *Provincial Finance* in 1925 and *Bahishkrut Bharat* in 1927, Ambedkar had been touring widely and giving speeches that pondered the radical ideas that would ultimately crystallize in his editorials. He had already spoken at length on matters of national politics from the point of view of the depressed classes, on the need to agitate collectively for their rights; he had weighed the options of mass agitation for entry into temples, or on conversion away from Hinduism altogether. But in these many speeches over the past years, he had been rather more reflective than decisive. The violence in Mahad changed that for him. It catalysed Ambedkar's decision-making. He had now achieved a certain clarity and with it a bold resolve. The editorials laid out the path forward.

In 'The Religious Battle of Mahad and the Responsibility of Savarna Hindus', Ambedkar started out by correcting the widely held opinion that Mahad was simply about the use of a water facility. On the contrary, the heart of the Mahad agitation was far more significant: It was about establishing whether there was religious equality within Hinduism and the overall justness of that religion. Water was just the means used. Equality and justice were the real issues at hand.

> At the root of Mahad was the issue of whether the Untouchables, as members within the Hindu fold, had equal rights to other members. Now the world knows that the answer to this question has been given in the negative by the upper castes of Mahad attacking our crusaders … Any outsider would of course be quite surprised to see people resort to physical violence against members of their own religion just to prove that they were socially inferior.[2]

That Hindus practise such a violent inequality is ironic, since Hindu theology—even more so than that of Christianity and Islam, which are both nevertheless more egalitarian in practice—espouses the consummate basis for social equality, through its doctrine that Ambedkar would later (around 1950, in a celebrated but controversial book he called *Riddles in Hinduism*) dub as Brahma-ism, in striking contrast to the Brahmanism that Hindus actually practise:

The tenets of Hinduism are even more congenial to promoting equality than those of Christianity and Islam. Hinduism does not stop at saying that all human beings are 'children of God'; it fearlessly propounds that they are all *forms* of god. There cannot be any such thing as someone being superior or inferior to the other. Such is the lofty principle of Hinduism. It is difficult to conceive of a superior basis for establishing equality than Hinduism. Despite this, one cannot find even a trace of social equality within Hindu society like one finds in Christian or Muslim nations. On the contrary, people who call themselves Hindus violently obstruct those who try to establish equality.[3]

So what ought the savarna Hindus have done instead? What was and is their proper responsibility? Ambedkar laid it out plainly, even appealing to their higher self-interest:

High-caste Hindus should have made efforts to remove the hypocrisy of mouthing that all humans are forms of god while treating some of them, just because they are born in a particular caste, as impure. It was their duty to deflect the religious fanatics who habitually mistreat Untouchables, bringing a blot to their great religion. These people should have halted those sinister attempts at oppressing their own co-religionists. They should instead have served as role models, thus consolidating the ranks of the Hindus by treating the Untouchables with equality and justice. But those who regard themselves as high-caste elites did nothing of the sort. They did not even stop with the violent clash. If they had, we would not have felt as bad as we do now in learning that these Hindus have performed purifying rites for the tank. This is a heinous crime that they have committed, reifying the orthodox notion that Untouchables are impure and that contact with them is polluting. There is no doubt that the people who performed and supported this purification have insulted the Untouchables.⁴

Ambedkar rounded out the editorial by informing the savarna Hindus of an attitudinal shift that was under way within the untouchable communities. The upper castes should take heed of this, because the beatings mercilessly meted out to the untouchables at Mahad were to be the last that they would bear without reprisal. Ambedkar thus ended by issuing a stark warning to savarna Hindus—their violence would beget retaliatory bloodshed.

> Until Mahad, we agreed with Mahatma Gandhi that untouchability was the biggest blot on the Hindu religion. But now we have changed our view: untouchability is a blot on our own body. When we thought it a blot on Hinduism, we had relegated the task of eradicating it to you. Now that we see it as a blot on ourselves, we are determined to wash it off ourselves. We will not hesitate to sacrifice our lives in the process. You may take obscene actions like purifying the Chavdar tank in an effort to try to prove our impurity, but we will not sit quiet until we have forced you to admit that we are not impure. Mahad was only the first battle in the war for establishing equality. Sure, there will be some battles lost and some battles won, but we have no doubt that ultimately victory will be ours. In these noble battles for our emancipation we do not wish for blood to be shed. But if those infected with the disease of Brahmanism resort to bloodshed, do know that we will not retreat—the responsibility for what results will be theirs and not ours. Let them keep this warning in mind.⁵

Exactly two Fridays later, the next issue of *Bahishkrut Bharat* appeared. The editorial this time was addressed to the British government rather than to touchable Hindus. 'The Religious Battle of Mahad and the

Responsibility of the British Government' marshalled together a great deal of earlier case laws to establish the rights of the untouchables, including their specific right to draw water from Chavdar tale. Ambedkar used these same legal precedents within the court, after a legal battle was launched later in the year. Here, however, he was equally interested in panning out further to show the wider implications of the Mahad struggle—it was, again, not just about the isolated act of accessing water, but about the denial of civil rights to untouchables, and about the nature of human rights as such. He brilliantly argued:

> The custom of untouchability is not a lawful custom. This custom has neither granted any rights to the touchable community against the untouchable community, nor has it abolished any of the rights of the Untouchables. Human rights in public life cannot be established by someone issuing an ordinance. It is inherent in every human being. Just because a right was not used or there was a gap in its usage, that does not mean that it ceases to exist. It is as foolish to forbid a person from using a water source because he had not used it before as it would be to say that a person cannot walk on a particular road because he had not used that road before. Therefore, the Untouchable people have not committed any crime by going to the Chavdar tank. Nobody could have accused them of an unlawful act even if they had entered the Vireshwar temple. The only crime was committed by the touchables. They opposed the Untouchable people unlawfully while in the exercise of their rights.[6]

Ambedkar was making a case against the common practice of the British government to claim not to interfere in age-old customs and traditions. Ambedkar's point was that, when rights were at stake, the justness of those customs and traditions had to be taken into consideration. Furthermore, it had already been secularly established that public roads were equally accessible to all, irrespective of age-old customs barring untouchables from using certain roads lest they pollute touchables in the process. Ambedkar argued that the law that applied to roads should equally apply to other public things, such as water bodies.

If the untouchables had the right to draw water from public sources, the government had the responsibility to protect the untouchables who were exercising their right. It was a primary function of the government to protect those exercising their rights from unlawful opposition by others. Moreover, any government failing to act always encouraged lawlessness. Indeed, if the British government carried out its legitimate police powers effectively, the rioters who had attacked the untouchables at Mahad with impunity would have never dared to have done so in the first place. Alas, Ambedkar was not optimistic about the British government moving either quickly or effectively in this regard:

> We doubt whether the government will accept our suggestion and implement it without delay. Although our British government is not reactionary, it is extremely slow. It has developed an attitude of marking time instead of marching on. And when a social issue is involved, it gets invariably paralytic.[7]

That being so, Ambedkar felt he needed to give some warning of dire consequences, should the government neglect to act. Echoing the closing warning that he had given to savarna Hindus in the previous editorial, Ambedkar cautioned the government that, in the present circumstances, inaction on their part would prove far costlier than taking action would.

> The Untouchables had tolerated the outrage, highhandedness and the injustices of the touchables at Mahad only in the hope that the government would provide them due protection. If that hope were belied, it would not be possible for them on future occasions to maintain the peace that they had maintained

at Mahad. They would be compelled to pick up sticks in self defense.[8]

The next editorial to appear was of yet another tone altogether. In 'The Religious Battle of Mahad and the Responsibility of the Untouchables', Ambedkar embarked on a highly charged, impassioned, yet systematic appeal. He started off by suggesting that the hardened stance of the touchable community was based partly on their narrow self-interest, but also partly on an unthinking and blind adherence to religious traditions—traditions to which even the untouchables had not strongly enough objected in the past. Hence, the untouchables needed to operate keeping touchable-Hindu self-interest in mind and, of course, to emphatically voice their objections to the customary religious practices by which they were oppressed.

> The importance of the Mahad conference lay precisely in the fact that it communicated the objection of the Untouchables to their treatment. It has brought the touchables face to face with their evil customs. Until now, they followed them because it did not cost them anything. Now, however, they have begun to realise that it could cost them their life. Although the Untouchables did not raise their hands against the touchables at Mahad, the have amply communicated that in the future they would not take their beating lying low.[9]

With the touchables recalcitrant and the government inactive, it was now Ambedkar's decided opinion that the untouchables needed to act through a two-pronged strategy, appealing both to the moral conscience of touchables as well as to their narrow self-interest. On the one side, direct action like in Mahad was required everywhere. On the other side, untouchables had to leverage the current culture war between Hindus and Muslims to their own advantage. That is, they needed to begin threatening conversion.

> All Untouchables need to start taking similar actions everywhere as they did in Mahad. Nothing will change without such acts of resistance. Otherwise the thoughtless touchable people will not be forced to think about the custom of untouchability, and this thousand-year-old custom will continue for the next thousand years … The Untouchables also need to ponder over the ways in which they can make a dent in the interests of touchable people. It is only then that we would succeed in bringing about the desired change in their opinion … The touchable Hindus should consider what would happen to Hindu society if the Untouchables boycotted Hinduism and converted to Islam.[10]

Realizing that he was now not just making waves but possibly ushering in a tsunami, Ambedkar spent the majority of space in the editorial explaining and justifying his call to weaponize conversion in the battle for liberation within Hinduism:

> I am fully aware that some touchable people will call me crazy for suggesting such options to the Untouchables. But I would ask them a counter-question: what else should the Untouchables do? It is the tradition of the moderates that they expect the Untouchables to peacefully place their unanimous demand before the touchables. But what has this achieved, since the history of the movement over the last 25-30 years? Irrespective of how moderately the Untouchables presented their views, howsoever rational their position, well-founded their complaints, and just their demands, the touchable Hindus had always haughtily ignored them.[11]

Ambedkar pressed on, brushing aside these feckless cries for moderation:

> Untouchability is such a grave sin and such an enormous injustice that we demand its immediate eradication. This is our ideology.

We might consider an alternative suggestion to accomplish it from those who agree with us, but we are confident that there may not be a better option ... The people who have become insensate by enjoying unbridled power need such shocks to bring them to their senses.[12]

Concluding his lengthy justification for the controversial strategy of leveraging conversion, Ambedkar returned to the first course of action. He noted that resistance and direct action would take a great deal of courage and determination:

It is true that the option of resistance that we suggested is difficult. We also know that when you resist, there will be reprisals from the touchables. That is not something that should make you fear. Rather, Untouchables should be prepared for that moment, and to fight back if attacked. It will not work without that. The Untouchables must show their might ... You do not sacrifice ferocious animals like tigers; it is chickens and goats that get slaughtered.[13]

Having raised the point of courage and valour, Ambedkar closed this powerful exhortation by hearkening back to the prowess of Mahar soldiers over the ages. Many battles gone by had shown that the untouchables were lions and tigers, not meek sacrificial goats:

To which *rashi* other than *Sinha* would those ancestors have belonged when they fell in the battle that would bury the Peshwas, and for that brave act, whose names are engraved on the victory pillar of Koregaon? Is the option of resistance going to be so difficult for a people whose ancestors have achieved such great feats with their bravery and prowess, even under the severe constraint of untouchability? We do not think so at all. They do have bravery. What they do not have is consciousness.

Therefore, those among the Untouchables who have realized their self-identity should now come forward for the crusade that has just begun. They will wash off the blot on their clan and be the role model for their community.[14]

Such a call to action was not restricted to writing. Ambedkar continued touring and addressing conferences, and on many of these occasions he reiterated all of these same points that he had written in his newspaper. The paper itself is a wealth of information on so many of Ambedkar's activities and engagements, documented for the length of its print run. We learn from the 1 July 1927 issue, for example, about an unfortunate experience of untouchability that Ambedkar suffered when visiting the Thakurdwar temple in Bombay. This temple, built by the ascetic Atmaram Baba in 1838, was not far from Wilson College, at the junction of Thakurdwar Road and Girgaum Road, where it still stands today. Some local papers had boasted that it had been open to all Hindus ever since its inception. Ambedkar, along with his friend Shivtarkar, went to meet the head of the temple to learn details about its progressive policies. Upon entering, Ambedkar was mobbed and harassed by a crowd that had gathered. The head of the temple, fearful of the crowd, cancelled his planned meeting with Ambedkar there and then, and Ambedkar and Shivtarkar had to leave in haste under threat of violence. Later, the head went so far as to perform purification ceremonies, the temple having been regarded as defiled by the untouchable Ambedkar's feet.

Ambedkar was not keen on entering temples anyway. He was already drawn strongly to a Buddhist outlook and was spotted by an admirer on a local tram reading one of Dharmanand Kosambi's early books on Buddhism the same week that his colleagues were up in arms about the scandal of the temple purification.[15] But temple entry was a serious public issue, irrespective of Ambedkar's personal ambivalence. There was a movement stirring in the town of Amravati, between Bombay and Nagpur, for the right of untouchables to enter its historic and ornately constructed Ambadevi temple. Amravati had a reputation for progressive social reforms and was the site of the earliest Mahar-run schools and hostels. It had also replaced the notorious *baluta* system (a topic we shall cover in Chapter Fifteen, where we find Ambedkar representing in the Bombay Legislative Council against it) with cash payments. The agitators for temple entry held a conference in Amravati, over which Ambedkar was invited to preside. In his presidential speech, Ambedkar reportedly spoke against separate temples for untouchables, used his public roads analogy from *Bahishkrut Bharat* to claim the legal right to enter temples open to the Hindu public, and spoke of the untouchables' sizeable historical contribution to Hindu culture, or Hindutva.[16] Even in progressive Amravati, the temple-entry campaign met with no success, and eventually the movement faded away entirely.[17]

The Bombay Legislative Council returned to session on 18 July for one month. In this session, Ambedkar introduced a new resolution: 'This Council recommends to Government to appoint a committee with a majority of non-official members of the Council to enquire into the conditions of the depressed classes and aborigines in the Presidency and to recommend measures for the alleviation of their condition.'[18] The resolution passed. The BLC met again on 20 September for its final month of 1927. Ambedkar was exceptionally active during both the July and the September sessions, especially with respect to a bill before the Council to reorganize and overhaul Bombay University. He was also actively engaged in a bill designed to address small agricultural holdings, but we will speak more about that in Chapter Fifteen. And as always, he interpellated numerous questions to the government, always taking them to task for the treatment of the untouchables, and to try to ensure compliance with the Bole resolution.

The Bombay University Act Amendment Bill was put forward by the member for the University of Bombay, K.M. Munshi, whom Ambedkar clearly mistrusted if not disliked—their clashes throughout the 1920s and 1930s in the BLC would make it rather awkward for them at first to work so closely together on the drafting committee for the Constitution of India in the late 1940s. But that was a future obviously unknown. Here, in 1927, Ambedkar liberally railed against Munshi for all of the glaring defects of the bill: 'I do not personally understand how this Government can strut about with a report brought about by men who were absolutely inexpert in their job ...'[19]

Ambedkar spoke at length on the organization of the university itself, and his position here was more or less the same as it had been in 1924, when he had painstakingly completed a questionnaire on university reforms. But Ambedkar was also particularly animated over the need to have representation for the depressed classes within the new composition of the university senate:

> Mr Munshi said that if it had been a question of division of any material benefits he would probably consent to the introduction of communal representation on the Senate. But I wish to remind him that the backward classes have come to realise that after all education is the greatest material benefit for which they can fight.[20]

A particular change that had manifested in Ambedkar since the first session early in the year was the open and emphatic manner in which he called out the hypocrisy of all the members of the council itself, along with his usual righteous upbraiding of the government:

> No Member in this House can say that he is non-communal in his attitude. I challenge any honourable Member to deny it ... There can be no doubt in my mind that every member in this House as well as outside is bound to look at every question consciously or unconsciously from a communal point of view ... We are so minded that we cannot associate with other communities on terms of equality.[21]

Ambedkar had by this time witnessed too much and experienced too much to stand by in silence as hypocritical claims about caste and community were espoused by would-be reformers. The long year of 1927 had been a consequential one, historic, but also tragic in many ways—and it was not even close to over. In this year, too, Ambedkar's eldest brother, Balaram, died at the age of fifty-five. Away in Amravati, Ambedkar had not been able to attend the funeral in Bombay.[22] But the year brought joys as well. The PhD certificate that Columbia University had bestowed upon Ambedkar on 8 June finally reached him in Bombay. His protracted period of education was officially completed and recognized. But Ambedkar's wife Ramabai needed to be sure. She cautiously asked her husband, who had been so long absent in the past, 'You aren't thinking of getting any more degrees, are you?' She was visibly relieved when he confirmed that he was indeed done.[23]

Ambedkar's achievements up until 1927 did not only earn him the title of doctor, twice over. His tireless social work and manifold struggle for his people, personally, legally and politically, was winning universal accolades among the untouchable community. In recognition, his aid and archivist, and also his future biographer, C.B. Khairmoday, reverentially referred to Dr Ambedkar as 'Babasaheb'.[24]

This name stuck.

To the wider world he was Dr Ambedkar, but 1927 onwards, he would forever remain Babasaheb for the untouchables.

Chapter Fourteen

Mahad Reloaded: The Satyagraha

Liberty is never received simply as a gift—it has to be fought for.
—B.R. Ambedkar (1927)

Towards the end of June, *Bahishkrut Bharat* ran an announcement that stirred untouchables all over the Bombay Presidency. The announcement called forward anyone from the depressed classes who was eager to wash off the stigma of pollution thrust upon them by the Mahad Hindus' obscene ceremony of tank purification and who sought to denounce the atrocities committed by the Mahad Hindus on the untouchables who had taken water from the Chavdar lake. These volunteers should enlist themselves at the Bahishkrut Hitakarini Sabha in Bombay.

Yet another movement for agitation in Mahad began to organize. The police kept an eye on the developments. On 4 July, the Bombay police commissioner wrote a note on a large gathering the day before:

> Under the auspices of the Bahishkrut Hitkarini Sabha, a public meeting of the depressed classes was held at the Cowasji Jehangir Hall [in Colaba] on the evening of July 3rd to protest against the hardships inflicted upon the Untouchables of Mahad in Kolaba district. Dr Bhimrao Ramji Ambedkar, Bar-at-Law, presided over an audience of about 1000 people. Speeches were made by the president, and … Sitaram Namdeo Shivtarkar … They decided in order to carry on a peaceful agitation against this treatment to enlist volunteers and collect funds. They would first have a conference at Mahad after the Diwali holidays and then it would be decided to start satyagraha in order to enforce their rights as citizens. A resolution to this effect was passed.[1]

Young R.B. More impressed upon Ambedkar that the orthodoxy in Mahad was not going to sit back and watch while the untouchables asserted their rights. Untouchables all over the Konkan region were already being punished in their various villages through boycotts from the caste Hindus. At the next Mahad Conference, they would have to bring the entirety of their needs along with them—food and water, sleeping supplies, tents and materials for a makeshift stage and meeting venue, etc.—as no one in or around Mahad would sell them anything. To meet this problem, More formed an organization of Dalit youth, calling it 'Dr Ambedkar Seva Dal'. The idea pleased Ambedkar but not the name. He soon changed its name to Samata Sainik Dal (SSD) (or Social Equality Army). The SSD would later be a crucial component of Ambedkar's political party, the Independent Labour Party (ILP), in 1936.[2]

There was also the likelihood that they would be met with violence in Mahad, just as last time. For this reason, in addition to the youth volunteers who were enlisting in the SSD, Ambedkar sought to cultivate a team of disciplined volunteers, many from a military background, to manage security. A unit of fifteen members was fashioned from people in his own Bombay chawl.

The leaders of the non-Brahman movement, Keshavrao Jedhe and Dinkarrao Javalkar, for whom Ambedkar had acted as attorney and successfully had them released from prison, and who had participated in the initial Mahad Conference back in March, also pledged their full support. This meant they would bring masses from their non-Brahman organization, the Satyashodhak Samaj, along with them. But there was a hitch. Their support of this new Mahad agitation was conditional upon no Brahman being permitted to take part in it. This condition irked Ambedkar and was generally unacceptable to him. There were several progressive Brahmans committed to social equality and justice who worked closely with Ambedkar, both from the SSL and within the BHS itself, and whose involvement was important. For example, there was his own Sanskrit tutor, with whom Ambedkar would cull out and translate objectionable passages from the *Manusmriti* to raise awareness of its sinister teachings. Moreover, Ambedkar was already in the process of forming the Samaj Samata Sangh, an inter-caste organization designed to promote the idea of social equality among various castes and communities, including many Brahmans (we will look more closely at the activities of the Samaj Samata Sangh in the next chapter).

Ambedkar published his opposition to this condition in the 29 July issue of *Bahishkrut Bharat*. He explained that it was not Brahmans but Brahmanism that was the enemy of the untouchables. A non-Brahman imbued with the inegalitarian, hierarchical beliefs of Brahmanism would be as repugnant to Ambedkar as a Brahman free of Brahmanical thought and practices would be welcome to him:

> We do not believe that persons born into the Brahman caste cannot be liberal in thought. And we need all people who are sympathetic to our cause, whether they be Brahman or non-Brahman. To exclude Brahmans would not only be wrong in principle, but also wrong in strategy ... There should not be any objection to the participation of all such people along with

Untouchables who genuinely believe that the eradication of untouchability is extremely necessary from the viewpoint of reform, justice, human compassion, and national unity.³

In the end, Jedhe and Javalkar assented, and Ambedkar's agenda received support from the Satyashodhak Samaj.

Meetings in preparation for the Mahad Satyagraha proliferated, not only in Bombay but also in smaller towns all throughout the presidency. Ambedkar was occupied day and night with planning and fundraising, especially in early September, prior to the BLC third session, and late October onwards, upon the conclusion of the BLC work for 1927. Ambedkar estimated that a sum of no less than Rs 2,000 would need to be raised to fund the post-Diwali Mahad gathering. And that was another thing—no specific dates had yet been fixed. Ambedkar set about addressing this in the second week of September.

On 11 September, a public meeting was held at Damodar Hall, and the official satyagraha committee was formed and announced, with Ambedkar as the president and Shivtarkar as the secretary. Four days later, this committee met at Ambedkar's office and fixed the dates of 25-26 December for the satyagraha in Mahad. On 17 September, another public meeting was organized in one of the mill chawls in the Elphinstone Road locality, and full organizational details were disseminated through a communication written by Ambedkar:

> All untouchables are hereby notified that it has been decided to hold a conference on 25 December at Mahad. When we had already held a conference at Mahad on 19 March, why is this conference being held at the same place? The answer is that when the untouchables exercised their right of drinking water from the Chavdar tank, the touchables brutally attacked them, with the intention of preventing them from doing so ... This issue concerns humanity. We have to wash off the blot put on us by the touchable people ... We need funds for this. Those who

wish to make a contribution either in the form of money or grains should do so…

Yours sincerely,
Dr Bhimrao Ambedkar, M.A., Ph.D., D.Sc., Bar-at-Law, MLC, President-Satyagraha Committee.[4]

Ambedkar became creative in fundraising. After requests for donations from lawyers in the high court failed (Hindu lawyers generally refused, and only Rs 100 could be raised from Muslim and Jewish lawyers), Ambedkar approached actors and playwrights. Baburao Pendharkar, founder of the *natak mandali* Lalit Kaladarsha and soon-to-be silent film star, agreed to perform a charity play at the Elphinstone theatre on Grant Road, which raised Rs 200. Soon thereafter, other drama companies put on more shows, and another Rs 250 was raised. The remainder of the funds were contributed by the untouchables themselves.

Ambedkar continued using *Bahishkrut Bharat* as a mouthpiece for promoting and justifying the Mahad Satyagraha. In an intriguing editorial from 27 November, Ambedkar delved into the lessons that all satyagrahis could take from the Bhagawad Gita. He thought the Gita a suitable guide as it was at that time acceptable to both the savarna Hindus and the untouchables. In the process of explaining his own position on non-violence, contrasting it with that of Gandhi's, Ambedkar laid out the dictum that should guide all of the satyagrahis in Mahad: 'Non-violence wherever possible; violence whenever necessary!'[5]

But Ambedkar and his allies were not the only ones in the process of preparation. On the very same November day that Ambedkar published his article on the Gita, orthodox Hindus and their allies held a meeting at the Vireshwar temple in Mahad with the aim of developing a strategy to prevent Ambedkar and the untouchables from drinking water from Chavdar lake. Sympathizers of Ambedkar and a delegation of Brahmans from Pune who, to keep the untouchables in the Hindu fold and prevent them from converting, had come to Mahad to urge the Brahmans there not to stand in Ambedkar's way all disrupted the meeting before a strategy could be devised. Nevertheless, such a strategy was devised— and it proved to be successful.

On 12 November, a group of orthodox Hindus filed a suit in the local court in Mahad, and two days later an injunction was granted, prohibiting Ambedkar (the defendant) and other allied parties from taking water from Chavdar lake until the case was finally decided. The order granting the injunction stated:

> This is an application asking the Court to grant to the applicants a temporary injunction restraining the opponents from going to the Chaudar Tank or taking water therefrom. The applicants have, on 12th December 1927, filed in the Court, Regular Suit No. 405 of 1927, for obtaining a Declaration that the said Chaudar Tank is of the nature of private property of the touchable classes only and that the Untouchable classes have no right to go to that tank, or take water from there, and also for obtaining a perpetual injunction restraining the defendants from doing any of these acts … The application states, among other things, that for hundreds of years since the tank has been the exclusive enjoyment of the touchable classes only, that on 19th March 1927, a number of persons of the Untouchable classes led by the defendant, entered the tank all of a sudden, washed their hands and faces with the water and thus contaminated it, that in consequence of this contamination, the touchable classes could not take water from the tank for over 24 hours, i.e., until the water was purified at great cost by performing ceremonies laid down by the Hindu Shastras. A great hardship was thus caused to the touchable classes …[6]

Irrespective of the injunction, the formal programme of the Mahad Satyagraha conference scheduled in both a morning and an afternoon 'march to the Chavdar tank to fetch water' on Day 1 (25 December),

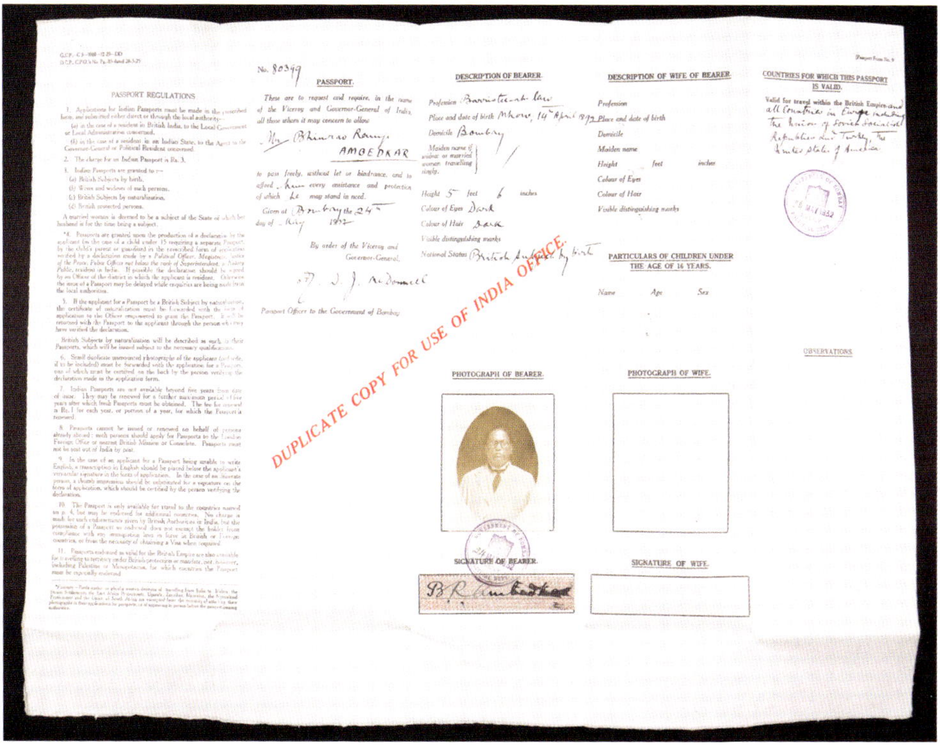

B.R. Ambedkar's passport, which shows his height, and his year of birth as 1892.

S.K. Bole sitting on Ambedkar's lap.

Damodar Hall
Bombay-12
18-2-33

Dear Dr [Moonje],

Many thanks for your letter inviting me to Ratnagiri to open the Temple on the fort to the untouchables. I am extremely sorry that owing to previous engagements I am unable to accept your invitation. I however wish to take this opportunity of conveying to you my appreciation of the work you are doing in the field of social reform. As I look at what is called the problem of the untouchables I feel it is intimately bound up with the question of the reorganization of Hindu Society. If the untouchables are to be a part and parcel of the Hindu Society then

The 1933 letter from Ambedkar to V.D. Savarkar.

it is not enough to remove untouchability; for that purpose you must destroy Chaturvarna. If they are not to be a part and parcel, if they are only to be an appendix to Hindu Society then untouchability so far as temples is concerned may remain. I am glad to see that you are one of the very few who have realized it that you still use the jargon of chaturvarna altho you qualify it by basing it on merits is rather unfortunate. However I hope that in course of time you will have courage enough to drop this needless and mischievous jargon. With best wishes and hoping to meet you some time. I am

Yours sincerely
B R Ambedkar

Number 1 Chawl of the Bombay Improvement Trust (BIT) in Parel, where Ambedkar lived in rooms 50 and 51 for more than twenty years.

Ambedkar (extreme right) with the faculty of Sydenham College, Bombay, in 1919.

The Ambedkar House Museum in London.

Ambedkar, Bar-at-Law, after being admitted to the Bombay High Court.

Ambedkar with the Samata Sainik Dal (1928).

Ambedkar (sitting on the extreme right) with the faculty of
the Government Law College, Bombay, in 1928.

Ambedkar with the Samaj Samata Sangh, 1929.

Ambedkar in his thirties.

Ambedkar, around the age of forty.

as well as a morning and an afternoon march to the tank for water on Day 2 (26 December). On Day 2 the schedule even details that '250 people will be asked to stay back and through them the program of fetching water from the tank would be continued until 2 January 1928'!⁷ This written programme, issued by Shivtarkar in his capacity as secretary of the satyagraha committee, concluded with a special note: 'The Satyagraha committee requests all the delegates to conduct themselves with extreme humility and peace during the course of the Satyagraha and hopes that on no occasion they will allow peace to be compromised.'⁸

At 9 a.m. on Saturday morning, 24 December, Ambedkar, along with some 200–250 others, boarded the capacious, ocean-faring *Padmavati* from Bhaucha Dhakka wharf on Bombay's eastern seafront, bound for Hareshwar Bandar, about 100 nautical miles to the south. Ambedkar was dressed in a khadi dhoti with a traditional Maharashtrian *uparne* flung over his shoulders, over a crisp, white sadra—the front pocket of which was stuffed with folded government papers sanctioning a peaceful assembly in Mahad, as well as the order enjoining Ambedkar from accessing Chavdar tale. Two groups of the Samata Sainik Dal (still called the Dr Ambedkar Seva Dal then), one batch from Ambedkar's own chawl and one from nearby St. George's Hospital Chawl in Fort, had reached the wharf an hour before Ambedkar, all smartly dressed in khaki uniforms, resembling army men.⁹ Upon Ambedkar's arrival, amid cheers from the hundreds of volunteers and supporters, the *sainik*s flanked Ambedkar and escorted him to the ferry. Bystanders were under the impression that Ambedkar had received a military send-off.

Shivtarkar had widely published a pamphlet instructing satyagrahis to bring their own plates, cups, blankets and food provisions to last them three days, since they would be boycotted by savarna Hindus and unable to purchase any such supplies in or around Mahad. In it, he also advertised that he would be leaving Bombay by ship on 24 December, inviting them to deposit Rs 5 for transport costs at the BHS office if they wished to accompany him. Thus, everyone knew the route that Ambedkar would be taking that day, and at every pier where the *Padmavati* halted along the way—Mandve, Alibag, Revdanda, etc.[10]— large crowds were waiting to cheer on the leaders of the satyagraha and catch a glimpse of Babasaheb Ambedkar.

They finally reached Hareshwar Bandar that evening. The navigable Savitri river, leading almost due east to Mahad, empties into the Arabian Sea at Hareshwar, guarded by the historic Bankot fort commanding its southern shore. Ambedkar and his party were received and hosted by supporters from a village called Kolmandale a few kilometres east of the coastline. The next morning, 25 December, at 8 a.m., they all boarded river boats from Bankot and plied up the river, passing very close to Ambedkar's ancestral village of Ambadawe along the way. They reached Dasgaon around noon, where more than 3,000 people were enthusiastically awaiting Ambedkar's arrival. Also patiently waiting was the Kolaba district superintendent of police, who served Ambedkar with a summons from the district collector and then drove Ambedkar in his police car, along with Sahasrabuddhe, to a meeting with the collector in Mahad. The thousands gathered there became agitated, believing that their leader had been arrested before the satyagraha conference had even been launched. But R.B. More, Bhai Chitre, Shivtarkar and other leaders managed to calm the crowd down, lined everyone up in a long column of five and marched in a procession onwards to Mahad, shouting slogans such as '*Mahad Satyagraha ki jai*' along the way.

The district collector attempted to persuade Ambedkar to abandon the satyagraha, but in vain. Ambedkar did agree, however, to allow the collector to address the conference with his concerns, and told him that he would send word of a suitable time on the following day. Ambedkar and Sahasrabuddhe were escorted back to the other leaders at the main conference pandal, and Shivtarkar officially inaugurated the conference. Soon thereafter, Ambedkar read out his presidential speech—it was a lengthy script of nearly 5,000 words, which must have taken some forty-five minutes to deliver. Given the action-orientated occasion and

Mahad Reloaded: The Satyagraha

the lack of even a basic level of education for the vast majority of the audience, Ambedkar's decision to focus so much of his speech on the French Revolution, supplementing it with remarks on the patricians and plebeians of an even-more-distant ancient Rome, seems rather eccentric. But what it shows is that Ambedkar had a strong sense that Mahad was historic in some way, and not at all ordinary. An event of historical consequence required ambitions commensurate with it. And on this occasion, Ambedkar announced an agenda as ambitious as could possibly be imagined at the time—not merely the abolition of untouchability, but the very annihilation of caste.

> Do not have any misunderstanding that you have been invited by the Satyagraha Committee for drinking water from Chavdar tank ... This conference has been called to make a start toward establishing equality. If you conceive of the conference in this manner, I am sure that you would not have any doubt that it is unprecedented. This day has no parallel in the history of India. For a comparable meeting in the past, you have to look at the history of France ...
>
> By abolishing untouchability we might become *Shudras* instead of our present status as *atishudras*. Does that root out untouchability? ... If you want to kill a snake, you do not strike at the tail but at the head. To destroy a harmful disease, you go after its root causes—you attack only after understanding where its roots lie. Here, you must understand that untouchability does not get eradicated merely by abolishing *loti bandi* [i.e., prohibition of using common dishes or cups for drinking water] and *bheti bandi* [prohibition of socializing with other castes]. With the abolition of these two prohibitions, untouchability in public might disappear, but in private it would still thrive in the home. To abolish untouchability inside and outside, we must undermine *beti bandi* [prohibition of inter-caste marriage] ...

Roti bandi [prohibition on inter-dining], *loti bandi, bheti bandi*—these have all emerged from out of *beti bandi* … I would not insist upon the abolition of the *varnashrama* order if it were possible to abolish untouchability some other way … In my opinion, the eradication of untouchability lies in the annihilation of the prohibition against inter-caste marriage. Only then can we establish true social equality.

This mission is for our own interest, but it is also in the national interest. Hindu society has no other option for survival than to abolish untouchability and the *chaturvarna* system … *Chaturvarna* is a disintegrative social order whereas a single varna would integrate all people. It is not surprising that a society that sings the praises of a disintegrative social system has faced repeated defeats throughout its history. If this plight is to be overcome, the framework of the *chaturvarna* system has to be smashed, so all of Hindu society can be seen as just one varna.

Therefore, if we want to make Hindu society strong, we will have to annihilate *chaturvarna* and inequality, and reconstruct it on the principles of equality and one varna. The path of the eradication of untouchability and the path of strengthening Hinduism are the same path. The mission we have undertaken is thus as much in the interests of the nation as it is in our own self-interest. This mission is a true social revolution.[11]

After Ambedkar's speech, the conference passed four resolutions: a declaration of human rights; a repudiation of the *Manusmriti*; a demand that all followers of Hinduism be identified simply as Hindus, whereas identification by varna (Brahman, Shudra, etc.) and caste (Mang, Mahar, etc.) should be prohibited; and a reform of religious institutions, including opening the priestly profession to any duly-qualified Hindu. Several other speeches were delivered with comment and explication on the resolutions, and then towards the end of the evening, an audacious and unforgettable ceremony was solemnly conducted—the burning of the *Manusmriti*.

There was already a dedicated area for the pyre, which, along with the presence of untouchable hermits and the ritualistic mannerisms adopted by Ambedkar and Sahasrabuddhe—as though this were a holy offering, *homa havan*—projected this unprecedented iconoclasm as a veritable sacred rite. Ambedkar handed specially selected sheets from the book one by one to Sahasrabuddhe, who read aloud their violent shlokas mandating horrific punishments to be meted out to uncompliant Shudras, before dropping each page into the fire.

Thus concluded the first day of the Mahad Satyagraha Conference.

On the morning of 26 December, the second day began with Ambedkar giving a short speech to propose the satyagraha, after which a dozen other speakers gave talks of various lengths and topics, but all expressing support for the satyagraha. The non-Brahman party leaders Jedhe and Javalkar also gave speeches in favour of the satyagraha. Other prominent delegates of the conference, on the other hand, gave speeches against it, but far fewer than those who were in favour. In the meantime, Ambedkar had informed the district collector to make his way to the conference, and when he reached, he was invited to convey his position—which, though an English bureaucrat, he did in fluent Marathi. The collector spoke in earnest sympathy of the plight of the untouchables and stated outright that between the two conflicting parties, the touchables and the untouchables, he and the government were on the side of the untouchables. But a court injunction had to be respected, and if they disrespected the court they would be turning the government from an ally into a foe—and thus it would be not only the touchables but also the government that would be blocking the path of the untouchables to the Chavdar tale. The collector's speech did not seem to make much of an impact on the crowd overall, who heard more speeches for the rest of the evening, both for and against the satyagraha—those who spoke against it were often booed, while those who spoke in favour of it were cheered. But his words did impact the majority of the satyagraha committee, who met in the evening to come to a final decision about whether or not they would march the following day to the tank.

Surprisingly, the consensus among the leaders that night was to not go through with the satyagraha. Instead, they decided, in a show of strength, to march in an enormous procession to and around Chavdar lake, but not to violate the injunction against drawing water from it. The committee rightly foresaw that the only way they could possibly convince the thousands of eager satyagrahis not to proceed with the satyagraha was if Ambedkar himself were the person to propose the resolution against it. The following morning, that is what he said:

> This conference was called to offer a satyagraha against those savarna people who were not allowing the untouchables to access Chavdar tank … [We are now in a situation] where the satyagraha offered by this conference against the savarnas will automatically change into one against the government. In view of this fact and the explanation offered by the District Collector that the government … has all sympathies with them in their struggle for equal rights, this conference decides to suspend the satyagraha until the court pronounces its verdict in the civil case.[12]

The delegates were dismayed, and there was a great deal of chatter and confusion. Ambedkar spoke up again:

> You will obviously think that I am a featherbrained person, since yesterday it was I who proposed the resolution for doing the satyagraha and today I am the one who proposed the opposite. Actually, I have done both of these things after proper consideration. Yesterday I needed to know your degree of determination. In the past it has been a serious defect in us that

we lacked strong determination. You people have now overcome that defect. No one could possibly doubt your determination anymore. I am taking due cognizance of that when I ask you now to suspend the satyagraha. You do not have to deploy your strength the moment you realize that you have it. We can strike with all of our new-found strength at the appropriate time and the appropriate target. A sympathetic government is not the appropriate target ... No one can say that you have suspended the Satyagraha because you are timid. At most they could tease you about your leaders going back on their resolve. But do not take offence from that ... Personally, I take it as a matter of great pleasure, nay, great pride, that my followers have gone four steps ahead of me. While I ask you to suspend the satyagraha today, I am as determined as you are that we should not give up this struggle without capturing the Chavdar tank. Keep it in mind that I will not sit quiet until we have accomplished this task.[13]

Ambedkar's explanation and the sincerity which with he delivered it was effective. Fifty sainiks from the SSD organized the thousands of would-be satyagrahis into a massive, snaking procession with four people to a row, headed first by the organizers, followed by a troop of fifty women participants and then the several thousand others. At 10.30 a.m. they started marching, and though the distance to the tank and back was not far, because the column of protesters itself stretched for nearly a kilometre, they did not return to the conference pandal until noon.

Once back, the conference restarted. There were votes of thanks and other orders of business, but for the most part, that was it. Some 2,000 participants left that afternoon. Ambedkar made an announcement that he would like those who were prepared for it to stay another night, so the rest of the participants did not leave Mahad until the following day. News of the procession had spread fast, and though few, if any, people from the local Chambhar community had participated in the conference, the Chambharwada decided to hold a meeting that evening and sent a request to Ambedkar to attend. Ambedkar complied, and went along with his friends Shivtarkar and P.N. Rajbhoj, both from the Chambhar caste. Despite this and numerous other attempts made by Ambedkar over the years to reach out to the Chambhar community and to ally with them, no lasting strategic unity between the Mahars and the Chambhars could ever be formed.

Ambedkar also held a special meeting with female delegates of the conference. Khairmoday kept an imprecise summary of what Ambedkar told the group, and different biographers give differing accounts. All witnesses agree, however, that Ambedkar's remarks on how they should feel free to dress and adorn themselves howsoever they wished, not how they were compelled to in order to indicate their caste, made an immediate impact. The following day, hundreds of untouchable women were seen around Mahad wearing their saris in the style normally exclusive to 'upper-caste' women, and they had discarded their tin and other cheap metal ornaments with the aim to replace them one day with silver and gold. Ambedkar's focus, naturally, was not on clothes and the like, but on encouraging, above all, the education of the girl child. The women had to commit to sending their girls to school, irrespective of whatever immediate compulsions made it more expedient for them to stay home and work. Characteristically he added, 'you also need to take a role in conferences such as this in the future.'[14]

After the Mahad Satyagraha Conference had finally closed and the delegates had all cleared out, Ambedkar and his core group took a day to see the nearby sights, including the Gandharpale Buddhist caves, by which Ambedkar was visibly moved. Later they trekked to Shivaji's Raigad fort, some 25 kilometres from Mahad, and camped the night there. Reportedly, some orthodox Brahmans from the region, appalled at Ambedkar's burning of the *Manusmriti*, had hired some local goons to murder Ambedkar as he slept unprotected at Raigad fort. Members of the Seva Dal, along with untouchable military pensioners from the surrounding area, caught wind of the plot and made their way in a sizeable number to Raigad. Armed and experienced, they stood guard throughout the night at the base of each of the several paths up to the fort.

What happened that night at Raigad turned a new page in Ambedkar's life story, for it was only the first assassination attempt of what would ultimately amount to ten documented attempts against him over the coming years.[15] He survived them all.

Chapter Fifteen
Between Mahad and the Round Table Conference (1928–29)

It was around this time that Dr Ambedkar's deification began. Mahar sadhus, or ascetics, of different sects (Kabirpanth, Nathpanth, etc.) had been brought together by one of Ambedkar's associates who sought to prevail upon them to actively engage in social work, rather than just wander around begging from the community. At first, they agreed that they would spread awareness about the Mahad Satyagraha. But then a bizarre debate erupted between them, consuming all of their focus and attention. Dr Ambedkar, most certainly, was an avatar of God—but which god? One sadhu asserted that Ambedkar was obviously Rudra, since they had the same demeanour. But another countered that Rudra could not manifest in full form into the body of an untouchable. After an animated debate, consensus slowly emerged that Ambedkar was an incarnation of half-Rudra, although a couple of sadhus remained unsatisfied even with this cunning solution. Later, when all of this was recounted to Ambedkar, at first he burst out laughing at the absurdity of it. But then his face changed and he grew serious, telling everyone around him that it was with baroque theological preoccupations such as this that Brahmans had poisoned the Indian mind.[1]

A crowded photo of Ambedkar with the volunteers of the Samata Sainik Dal (see inserts) taken in 1928 is perhaps evidence of at least one of the benefits of his metamorphosis into a mortal god in the eyes of many in his community. The picture shows some 400 sainiks, looking disciplined and remarkably well organized. He would have no trouble recruiting manpower for any of his future pursuits. Still, Ambedkar had little patience with being worshipped. He was not a humble man, but he was the furthest thing from egotistical or in need of flattery. Above all, he was rational, practical and earnest—qualities at complete odds with being regarded as divine.

The futility of it aggravated Ambedkar, who felt, and often bluntly told his worshippers, that it would be far better if they sloughed off their slavish mentality and even their belief in gods, and focused, instead, on social work for others and on their own self-respect.

Throughout Ambedkar's life, for the entire time that he was Hindu, his thoughts and actions on various aspects of religion and spirituality remained indecisive and even ambiguous. It was only after Ambedkar had become sure that he would convert to Buddhism, something that seems to have crystallized for him right around 1947-48, that his variegated views on religion, and spiritual thought and practice became much more clear, decisive and confident—although still not fully consistent until around the official conversion itself, another eight or nine years further along.[2] In 1948, Ambedkar published a unique and fascinating book polemically exploring the origins of untouchability in ancient India, intimately interlacing those origins with the religious and social struggle between Hinduism and Buddhism. He dedicated that book to the untouchable saint Chokhamela (as well as Nandanar and Ravidas), indicating that by that time, Ambedkar had become fully at ease with acknowledging the positive religious and even social contribution that saint-poets such as Chokhamela had made. But that was twenty years ahead in time from what we are discussing now.

In January 1928, a meeting of the depressed classes was held in Trimbak, a town near Nashik, where the Trimbakeshwar Shiva temple is located. The meeting was convened to contemplate the ways and means to construct a temple to Chokhamela for use by the untouchables. Ambedkar was asked to preside—a clear strategic mistake on the part of those who sought to build the temple. Ambedkar prevailed upon the group to forego building the temple, arguing that it would be a far more apt memorial to this great saint to use their resources of time, money and energy towards social causes instead. At this period in his life, Ambedkar could not actually see that untouchable saints such as Chokhamela had contributed anything substantial to the social sphere, despite their eloquent advocacy for the equality of all devotees. He was reading all of the available literature on the Bhakti Movement, on Chokhamela, on Tukaram, on Dnyaneshwar and about his father's own Kabirpanth tradition—his obsessive book-collecting had by no means ebbed in late 1920s' Bombay—and across all of these various devotion-based movements, he could discern only the advocacy of equality of believers, as opposed to the more radical and relevant demand of social equality as such. It was also not lost upon him how easily any such Hindu-based spiritual movement, howsoever egalitarian, could be assimilated into the overpowering paradigm of Brahmanical Hinduism, thus working against social emancipation instead of towards it.

This latter threat loomed large in Ambedkar's mind throughout this era, where temple-entry satyagrahas were taking centre stage, even dislodging the unambiguously civil-rights-based struggle for untouchables' equal access to public water sources, exemplified by Mahad. The status of temples as public-versus-private was always more opaque an issue than that of water sources, schools or roads. And the British government was generally averse to interfering in religious matters unless they could see a practical benefit to themselves. Constantly weighing heavy on Ambedkar's mind, too, was just how viciously violent temple-entry campaigns always were. Hindus never shied away from spilling blood when it came to upholding the 'purity' of their temples. The Parvati temple satyagraha in Pune in October 1929 was a good example of this.

The Parvati temple satyagraha was not one that Ambedkar was directly involved in, in part because there were so many savarna Hindus in leading roles on its satyagraha committee, including members of the Arya Samaj. Ambedkar did support the satyagraha, however, in both writings and speeches. There were three prominent Mahar leaders, as well as Chambhar leader and Ambedkar ally P.N. Rajbhoj. There were also the Brahman founder of the Social Service League S.M. Joshi and a future minister in Nehru's first Cabinet, N.V. Gadgil. Non-Brahman leader K.M. Jedhe also took a central role, despite the prominent participation of Brahmans. These satyagrahis, as well as four women, attempted to climb the long flight of stairs leading to the main temple gate, but were attacked with rocks and sticks by orthodox Hindus bent on keeping them out of the temple. Most of the satyagrahis were wounded, and Rajbhoj had to be hospitalized at the nearby Mission Hospital.[3]

The second of the ten documented attempts against Ambedkar's life was also during a temple-entry campaign in Bombay. His associate, Shankaranand Shastri, recalls that several 'upper-caste' Hindus attacked Ambedkar with lathis while he was leading a satyagraha at the Mumba Devi temple in the Bhuleshwar area of Bombay in 1928. I believe it may have actually been at the nearby Bhuleshwar temple itself where newspapers reported on a three-year-long struggle that Ambedkar and others waged to open both the temple and its water tank to the untouchables. A *Times of India* headline summed up the scene: 'Fight at Temple, Untouchables Beaten.'[4] Ambedkar, calling for direct action, said that one lakh Dalits would be ready to lay down their lives in the Bhuleshwar satyagraha. This was one of the unique cases where the agitation actually bore results. In 1932, the Bhuleshwar temple, along with four other Bombay temples, were at last opened to the untouchables.[5]

The Bhuleshwar campaign involved the courts, although Ambedkar was not a party to any of the actions. He was still in the middle of the

Mahad litigation, however, and with good results. On 13 June 1929, the Mahad court decided the civil case in favour of Ambedkar. *Bahishkrut Bharat* trumpeted the victory, but the celebrations were cut short by an appeal against the decision by persons purporting to represent Mahad Hindus. Ambedkar won this too, on 8 June 1931, but yet another appeal was filed. This, in turn, was dismissed on 30 January 1933, but there was still no scope for celebration: The caste Hindus filed yet another appeal, with the Bombay High Court finally deciding the case in Ambedkar's favour on 17 March 1937—the final judgment (see Appendix 4) coming a full decade after the satyagraha.

Although Ambedkar sought to continue practising law after the Mahad Satyagraha, he felt that he was being silently boycotted by the Hindu legal fraternity, as no cases were coming his way. On 31 March 1928, his contract of teaching at Batliboi's expired, meaning that he would be losing out on his income of Rs 200 per month, an amount that was not getting supplemented by any paying legal cases. Around that time, a temporary professorship opened up at the Government Law College, which Ambedkar fortunately secured, commencing in June 1928 and continuing until March the following year, thus rescuing him from penury. But he did not give up his effort to get cases, or at least on being prepared in the event that a case did come to him. We can see this from a letter that he wrote to a colleague of his named Dattoba, dated 2 October 1929, where he stated that he had fully paid his library fees and his state income taxes, and was only awaiting a support letter from Dattoba to attach to his application for the renewal of his sanad for the practice of law.

In the third week of February 1928, the new year of the Bombay Legislative Council set off, starting as usual with the Budget. As in the previous year, Ambedkar stood to speak critically of the Budget, and again did so with a great deal of sophistication and detail. But his critique of the Budget in 1928 was also peculiar, because it seems to have been targeting the defects of the unpopular finance minister (called 'finance member' in the Bombay Presidency) Sir Chunilal Mehta, just as much as it targeted the defects of the Budget itself. Ambedkar styled the Budget 'deplorable' and 'a grave scandal'. But the real scandal for Ambedkar seemed to have been in the person of the finance minister,[6] and Ambedkar did not shy away from calling him out: 'What good is an Indian Finance Member if he is not to respond to the wishes of his countrymen?'[7]

Ambedkar was enthusiastically active in the BLC of 1928—even more so than in 1927, when he had also attended each day of every session—but then, as we shall see, he had a total drop-off in 1929, not attending at all. How serious and significant an institution he regarded the BLC came out strikingly in an interview he gave to the Simon Commission later in 1928 (about which more will be said shortly): 'A Legislative Council is more than a museum; it is a place where, for instance, social battles have to be fought, privileges have to be destroyed, and rights have to be won.'[8]

One such social battle began in the BLC during that first session, when Ambedkar introduced a bill: 'Bill No. XII of 1928, a Bill further to amend the Bombay Hereditary Offices Act, 1874.' The bill's objectives were to properly define the duties of, and properly remunerate (in cash rather than in *baluta* [i.e., a share of a village's agricultural harvest]) the thousands of *watandars* (a '*watan*' was a hereditary rent-free grant of land to a villager—the watandar—in lieu of perpetual services that he performed for the village), most of whom were untouchables kept at subsistence levels. In an exhaustive speech introducing the bill to the council, Ambedkar spoke for over seventy minutes, alternating between closely reasoned argument and heartfelt passion, calling the watan system 'atrocious' and blaming it for keeping untouchables in a servitude that they could not transcend as long as the system remained in place. It was due to the failure of Ambedkar's bill to pass—or, more accurately, because the select committee to which Ambedkar had entrusted it mangled it beyond all recognition—that Ambedkar finally withdrew the bill in July 1929 and fully absented himself from the BLC for much of the remainder of his first term.[9] He had threatened precisely this while moving the bill:

> I can assure the House that the Mahar people are absolutely determined to have the bill, and I may tell my honourable friends that if the Government refuse to liberate these people on grounds of finance, on grounds of convenience, or on any other grounds, that it will be a war between the Revenue Department and the Mahars. If this bill does not pass, I for myself am not going to be in the Council; I am going to spend the rest of my time seeing that the Mahars organise a general strike, and bring the Honourable, the Revenue Member to feel that the principles of this bill are absolutely essential for the welfare of the Mahar people. I am speaking from the bottom of my heart.[10]

Ambedkar remained true to both his word and his heart. But it took a full decade to achieve the reforms he so passionately sought. It was not until 1937 that he found himself in the position to reintroduce a nearly identical bill for getting the watan system reformed.

The Ambedkar of 1928 certainly seemed to be a changed Ambedkar from the pre-Mahad days. He had, of course, always been a confident person, courageous, proud of his achievements and forthright, but now he was moving far more unapologetically and outspokenly against the grain. Everything he engaged with in the BLC seemed to run counter to the majority opinion. He did rise to speak in vigorous defence of a bill granting maternity benefits, but otherwise with all other legislation and committee work he found himself nearly always in dissent. There was, for example, the Small Holders' Relief Bill, which had been introduced the previous year. Recall that Ambedkar had already researched the problem of small holdings in India and published his proposed solutions in a journal article a decade earlier. The government in 1927 had proposed very different remedies from those of Ambedkar's,[11] but at the same time, the BLC nominated him to work on passage of the bill in the select committee. Ambedkar was in a tight spot. Ultimately, he did sign off on the report of the select committee in 1928, but only subject to a written dissent. The dissent was sharp, arguing that the effect of the bill would be to 'reduce landowning farmers into landless labourers'.[12]

Ambedkar was also going strongly against the grain—at least against both the Indian National Congress (INC) and the Muslim League—by agreeing to cooperate with the newly assembled Indian Statutory Commission, tasked with preparing for constitutional reform. It was popularly known as the Simon Commission, after its wealthy and charismatic chairman, John Simon. Simon was formerly a leader of the Liberal Party, and a future foreign secretary, home secretary, chancellor of the exchequer and lord chancellor—the only person in British history to have held all four of these high-level posts. But at that time, he had the misfortune of leading an all-British commission to India, no Indians included, which was thus wildly unpopular. When they arrived in Bombay in February 1928, the commission was met by protesters holding black flags and banners reading, 'Simon, Go Back.' It was during one such protest against the commission that Lala Lajpat Rai was severely beaten by the police and soon thereafter lost his life.

Although mainstream parties boycotted the commission, numerous depressed classes' parties and organizations from across India participated (including those with the support of Periyar E.V. Ramasamy, who personally encouraged Ambedkar to participate as well), legitimately fearful that otherwise the INC and the Muslim League would exclude them from adequate representation and power-sharing in any future constitution for India. This concern was soon borne out by the INC's Nehru Committee Report, an all-Indian alternative to the Simon Commission, aiming to produce an Indian-drafted constitution for India. Although this proposed constitution, envisioning India as a dominion within the British Commonwealth with internal self-government, included an unprecedented, progressive enumeration of basic rights,[13] it completely neglected any share of political power for the untouchables:

> In our suggestions for the constitution we have not made any special provision for the representation of the 'depressed classes'

in the legislatures ... We feel strongly however that the 'depressed classes' must be abolished, or rather that they should be raised socially and economically so that they may take their proper place in the community. The only way to do this is to give them educational and other facilities for this advance and to remove all obstacles ... Some of the articles in the Declaration of Rights ... will go a long way to remove the disabilities from which these classes suffer ... We are convinced that the 'depressed classes' will rapidly disappear ...[14]

Participating on behalf of the Bahishkrut Hitakarini Sabha, Ambedkar submitted two written statements that he thought would be of use to the commission. One was a 'Statement concerning the safeguards for the protection of the interests of the depressed classes as a minority in the Bombay Presidency and the changes in the composition of and the guarantees from the Bombay Legislative Council necessary to ensure the same under Provincial Autonomy'—quite a mouthful! The thirty-page document called for universal adult suffrage, and granting that, for no separate electorates for any caste or community (not even Muslims), but with reservations for various minorities (including the depressed classes) within the legislature and public administration. Separate electorates would be necessary, however, if the franchise were not universal.

The other written statement that Ambedkar submitted on behalf of the BHS was a 'Statement concerning the state of education of the depressed classes in the Bombay Presidency'—a twenty-page document outlining precisely what its title says, arguing, among other things, that a focus on university education for the untouchables would remain a futile gesture as long as sound, fully participatory primary and secondary education continued to be only apathetically pursued. Now, it is not entirely clear why Ambedkar submitted a report on education to a commission tasked with constitutional questions, but the timing of the submission may account for it. Only two weeks later, in mid-June 1928, Ambedkar launched the Depressed Classes Education Society (DCES), a body that would take over all education-related matters from the BHS.[15] The separation of the DCES from the BHS gave needed distance from the increasingly radical public perception of the BHS, and allowed Ambedkar to win a government grant of Rs 9,000 per year in sponsorship of five hostels for use by untouchable students. The government funds proved insufficient, however, and Ambedkar was forced to seek out charitable donations for the education society, which, by 1929, had already run into debt.

It was not only on behalf of the BHS that Ambedkar participated with the Simon Commission. He had two quite different roles. Each of the presidencies assembled provincial committees out of their legislative councils, tasked with working alongside the Simon Commission—or, rather, under it. Shortly after Ambedkar had submitted his two written statements to the commission, he landed up on the provincial committee created by the Bombay Legislative Council. In May 1929, the provincial committee submitted its report to the Simon Commission. This time, Ambedkar did not even sign on to the provincial committee's report with a dissenting note. Instead, he submitted an entirely separate report of his own, longer than that of the provincial committee's!

It was titled 'A Report on the Constitution of the Government of Bombay Presidency' and was ninety pages long. The document began:

> I regret that I have not been able to agree in the tenor of the report prepared by my colleagues on the committee or to accept the more important of the conclusions on the matters falling within the scope of our inquiry. I have therefore submitted this separate report containing my own views and recommendations.[16]

The views and recommendations in this rival report echoed those that Ambedkar had laid out in his written statement submitted the year before on behalf of the BHS. It launched off, in its first section, with a turn of phrase that has often been repeated over the years:

> For, I am of the opinion that the most vital need of the day is to create among the mass of the people the sense of a common

nationality, the feeling not that they are Indians first and Hindus, Mohamedans or Sindhis and Kanarese afterwards, but that they are *Indians first and Indians last*.[17]

In October 1928, Ambedkar was in Pune with the Simon Commission, which—along with the provincial committee upon which Ambedkar sat—was interviewing witnesses. At one point, Ambedkar switched his chair from that of committee member to that of witness, and himself gave testimony on behalf of the BHS. P.G. Solanki also sat with him, representing the depressed classes, but hardly spoke, except to support Ambedkar. The commission overall, but especially the chairman, was sympathetic to Dr Ambedkar and accorded him a great deal of respect. It was quite otherwise with the members of the provincial committee, who attacked Ambedkar's position at every given opportunity—the Muslim members, above all, were aggrieved and aggressive, as Ambedkar's proposals denied them separate electorates or other special concessions, treating discrimination based on caste with the same seriousness as that of community.

One member of the Simon Commission, future leader of the Labour Party and Prime Minister of Britain, Clement Attlee, sought to understand from Ambedkar some of the nuances between untouchables as a labouring bloc and the labour movement as such. This was timely because precisely in that moment, Ambedkar was deeply embroiled in a struggle over how to respond to the strike of Bombay mill workers, so many of whom were untouchables, being led by the communist organizers of the largest mill labourers' union (called the Girni Kamgar Union). Ambedkar's view was that the communists were far more motivated by politics than by the material improvement of the lives of the labourers—and this was certainly true in the case of untouchable labourers, whose interests were perennially forsaken by the largely Brahman-run communist outfits.

Ambedkar thus went directly against the communists, going so far as to help cultivate and lend full support to a rival union, the Bombay Textile

Labour Union, which met at Damodar Hall, with Ambedkar presiding. Ambedkar's union supplied strike breakers, primarily untouchable labourers who could not afford to strike and who would bring ruin to their families if they lost their tenuous employment, for a number of mills during the 1928 strike. When the Girni Kamgar Union called for a general strike again in 1929, Ambedkar's union once again rallied against it—the previous year's strike had already resulted in the debt of so many untouchable labourers to extortionate money lenders. As Ambedkar argued in *Bahishkrut Bharat*, it was the right of labour to resort to a strike with a view to bettering their conditions. But in these strikes called by the communists for their own political ends, the condition of labourers always worsened rather than improved. The communists were behaving like doctors trying to cure a disease by killing the patients.[18]

Attlee seems to have been intimated about Ambedkar's trade-union activities, and posed him a remarkably difficult question:

> Attlee: I wanted to get this point from you. You put forward a claim for representation of the depressed classes on the basis of numbers. Now, we have claims put forward on a different basis altogether; on, say, the labour basis. You get a cross-division in that way, because a man can be a depressed class man and he can also be a labourer?
>
> Ambedkar: He is usually, if not always, a labourer.
>
> Attlee: That is rather a play on words, isn't it? I am speaking of capital and labour, of labour in big industries, not of ordinary un-organised labour. I am speaking of organised labour. How are you going to get over the difficulty? If you are going to have representation by social status in one case and by industry in another, you are going to get a cross-division. How will you get over that?
>
> Ambedkar: There will be some provision for organised labour, and the majority of the depressed classes are labourers.[19]

The trenchant question posed by Attlee was not adequately responded to by Ambedkar within their brief exchange—and, indeed, this type of question posed a century ago continues to hang over the Dalit movement even today, with many Dalit groups and individuals aligning themselves with leftist labour ideology, but more still remaining opposed, often on account of the long-standing indifference of the left to the persistence of caste.[20]

The caste question remained foremost for Ambedkar throughout 1928–29. The new Social Equality League (Samaj Samata Sangh, or SSS) that he had formed towards the end of 1927 continued increasing its activities. Just as the DCES had taken over educational activities from the BHS, the Social Equality League (or SSS) had taken on all inter-caste activities that may have earlier been supported by the BHS. The latter, after all, had basically lost all of its 'upper-caste' members due to its evolution from educational, cultural and social work to radical direct action—and, of course, the burning of the *Manusmriti* as well as the irrepressibly burning words of *Bahishkrut Bharat*. The Social Equality League's narrow focus on eradicating untouchability and creating inter-caste alliances made it a good home for all of Ambedkar's caste-Hindu well-wishers and supporters.[21]

Two such Brahman supporters who were active in this period were Devrao Vishnu Naik and Shridhar Balwant Tilak (known as Shridharpant), the youngest son of Bal Gangadhar Tilak, already referred to as 'Lokmanya' at the time. D.V. Naik, just three years younger than Ambedkar, had been with Ambedkar since the Mahad Satyagraha and grew to become a faithful and reliable pillar for him. One of the most active members of the SSS, Naik leveraged his status as a Brahman to conduct numerous radical measures—at least according to orthodox Hindus—such as ceremonially bestowing the sacred thread upon untouchables (at one depressed classes conference in Ratnagari that Ambedkar presided over, Naik gave the thread to as many as 6,000 people!), conducting Vedic rituals for untouchables that were ordinarily reserved for savarna Hindus and officiating over inter-caste marriages.

One Vedic wedding ceremony was co-organized by Naik and the SSS in June 1929 and held at Damodar Hall. Naik did not serve as the priest, but it was significant in that Vedic rites prohibited to untouchables were used. It was the wedding of the son of pioneering Mahar activist Govind Ramji Adarekar, who had been one of the leaders of the Mahad Satyagraha and who had earlier formed the Mahar Samaj Seva Sangh in Bombay. Elder statesman Bole was in attendance, as was P.G. Solanki and, of course, Ambedkar himself—and so was his wife Ramabai and sister-in-law Laxmibai.

It was rare for Ramu to have been there, as her health—never very good—was rapidly deteriorating from unknown causes since the previous year. Although the actual cause was presumed to be tuberculosis, most people in the community, including Ambedkar himself on occasion, attributed it to the emotional trauma arising from the death of their son Rajratna. Ambedkar was preoccupied with worry. This worry was amplified by the fact that his elder sister Tulsa had passed away on the day before his thirty-eighth birthday, in 1929.[22]

If the irrepressibly radical *Bahishkrut Bharat* served as the mouthpiece of the now-well-established, albeit increasingly notorious, Bahishkrut Hitakarini Sabha, how was the Social Equality League meant to get its message out? A new fortnightly paper, *Samata*, was launched on 29 June 1928, with Devrao Naik serving as the editor. The date 29 June was a Friday, and thus *Samata* and *Bahishkrut Bharat* (still edited by Ambedkar) were published every alternating Friday, at least as long as *Samata* ran—which was until 15 March 1929, when it ceased with its nineteenth issue. Meanwhile, *Bahishkrut Bharat* continued running until 19 November 1929, when it folded for lack of funds. Recall that this fate had already been anticipated back in November 1928, when the first issue of the second year appeared with Ambedkar warning about the debts run up by the paper. By the start of 1930, then, Ambedkar had no papers for disseminating his message. Fortunately, at the end of November that year, he was able to launch a new paper, titled *Janata*, which also had Devrao Naik as its editor.[23]

In an August 1928 issue of *Samata*, some activities of the SSS were highlighted, such as a quite characteristic inter-caste dinner, which listed participants and included their castes. There was, of course, Dr Ambedkar (Mahar), the editor D.V. Naik himself (Brahman),[24] C.N. Shivtarkar (Chambhar), Keshav Sitaram Thackeray (Kayastha) and N.V. Khadange (Shimpi, or tailor)—and the list continued, with more Mahar and Brahman diners, accompanied by Marathas, a Matang, a Mali, Satyashodhaks and a Bhandari. A couple of months earlier, an even grander dinner, with 200 guests from different castes, was held at the Tilaks' Gaekwad Wada (now known as Kesari Wada) in Narayan Peth, Pune. Shridharpant Tilak was the host, and himself oversaw the arrangements for this *sahabhojan* (community dinner) held right at the heart of the Maharashtrian orthodoxy. Ambedkar was the guest of honour.

A month prior to the dinner, in April, Shridharpant had taken the shocking step of launching a branch of Ambedkar's SSS right there at the Gaekwad Wada, calling it the 'Anti-Chaturvarnya Samata Sangh'. Orthodox disciples of Lokmanya Tilak threatened Shridharpant with legal action, on top of the suit they had already initiated over the ownership of the profitable newspapers *Kesari* and *Mahratta*. They had even cut the power supply to Gaekwad Wada just prior to Ambedkar's arrival, but Shridharpant instructed everyone to bring lanterns with them, and the dinner turned out to be a success. But this sort of constant harassment that Shridharpant was subjected to for his progressive views took a huge toll on him. Within two months of the dinner, Shridharpant died by suicide. He had sent three suicide notes—one to the Pune collector, one to newspapers and a third to Dr Ambedkar.[25] For months, conservative papers tried to pin Shridharpant's stress and instability on Ambedkar's radical influence, rather than torture by reactionary Brahmans, prompting a grieving Ambedkar to issue furious editorials in response. In one such, Ambedkar wrote beautifully about Shridharpant as a person and his admirable values, remarking that if anyone deserved to be called 'Lokmanya', it was Shridharpant Tilak.

Although by the latter part of 1929, Ambedkar had earned a higher level of respect and recognition by the British leadership for his erudition as well as his social activism, was well on the way to deification by the untouchables for his manifold and indefatigable services to them, and was even garnering ever-increasing notoriety among caste Hindus for his relentless and righteous challenges, he would still remain subject to untouchability in his person. While testifying before the Simon Commission, Ambedkar had explained that he was unable to get a haircut from caste-Hindu barbers due to his status as an untouchable, and it is reported that that very year, while Ambedkar was working on a legal case in Ratnagiri, a *dhobi* refused to wash his suit for fear of pollution. With staggering irony, it came to pass that while Ambedkar was officially inquiring into an alleged case of untouchability being practised in a primary school in Belgaum, Ambedkar himself was prevented from entering the school, lest he pollute it, just as the untouchable student whose family had raised the complaint.

Ambedkar was touring throughout the presidency as a member of the newly formed 'Bombay Depressed Classes and Aboriginal Tribes Committee, 1929-30', more commonly known as the Starte Committee. This had been launched by the Bombay government, upon a resolution in the BLC by P.G. Solanki, in an effort to collect information on the social, educational and economic conditions of the untouchables and aboriginals. The committee did excellent work, culminating in a 1930 report suggesting, among other things, a special officer to look after issues arising in these communities (what we would today call an SC/ST commissioner), scholarships for studying abroad, the need for a moneylenders' act to liberate these communities from this ubiquitous mode of exploitation, a provident fund for labourers and much more. And yet, Ambedkar's personal experience was an unhappy and unfortunate one. Again, due to facing untouchability, Ambedkar met with an accident while travelling. In his autobiographical fragments *Waiting for a Visa*, Ambedkar recalled it in detail.

The year was 1929. The Bombay Government had appointed a Committee to investigate the grievances of the untouchables. I was appointed a member of the Committee. The Committee had to tour all over the province to investigate the allegations of injustice, oppression and tyranny. The Committee split up. I and another member were assigned the two districts of Khandesh. My colleague and myself, after finishing our work, parted company. He went to see some Hindu saint. I left by train to go to Bombay. At Chalisgaon I got down to go to a village on the Dhulia line, to investigate a case of social boycott which had been declared by the caste Hindus against the untouchables of that village.

The untouchables of Chalisgaon came to the station and requested me to stay for the night with them. My original plan was to go straight to Bombay after investigating the case of social boycott. But as they were keen, I agreed to stay overnight. I boarded the train for Dhulia to go to the village, went there and informed myself of the situation prevailing in the village, and then returned by the next train to Chalisgaon.

I found the untouchables of Chalisgaon waiting for me at the station. I was garlanded. The Maharwada, the quarters of the untouchables, was about two miles from the Railway Station, and to reach it one has to cross a river on which there is a culvert. There were many horse carriages at the station plying for hire. The Maharwada was also within walking distance from the station. I expected immediately to be taken to the Maharwada, but there was no movement in that direction, and I could not understand why I was kept waiting.

After an hour or so a *tonga* (one-horse carriage) was brought close to the platform, and I got in. The driver and I were the only two occupants. Others went on foot by a shortcut. The *tonga* had not even gone 200 paces when there was a near collision with a motor car. I was surprised that the driver, hired for driving every day, should have been so inexperienced. The accident was averted only because upon the loud shout of a policeman the driver of the car pulled back.

We somehow managed to come to the culvert on the river. On it there were no walls as there are on a bridge. There was only a row of stones fixed at a distance of five or ten feet. It was paved with stones. The culvert on the river was at right angles to the road we were coming by. A sharp turn has to be taken to come to the culvert from the road. Near the very first side-stone of the culvert, the horse, instead of going straight, took a turn and bolted. The wheel of the *tonga* struck against the side-stone so forcibly that I was bodily lifted up and thrown down on the stone pavement of the culvert, and both the horse and the carriage fell down from the culvert into the river.

So heavy was the fall that I lay down senseless. The Maharwada was just on the other bank of the river. The men who had come to greet me at the station had reached there ahead of me. I was lifted and taken to the Maharwada amidst the cries and lamentations of the men, women and children. As a result of this I received several injuries. My leg was fractured, and I was disabled for several days. I could not understand how all this had happened. The *tonga*s pass and repass the culvert every day, and never had a driver failed to take the *tonga* safely over the culvert.

On enquiry I was told the real facts. The delay at the railway station was due to the fact that the *tongawala*s were not prepared to drive with a passenger who was an untouchable. It was beneath their dignity. The Mahars could not tolerate that I should walk to their quarters; it was not in keeping with their sense of my dignity. A compromise was therefore arrived at. That compromise was to this effect: the owner of the *tonga* would give the *tonga* on hire, but not drive. The Mahars could take the *tonga*, but had to find someone to drive it.

The Mahars thought this to be a happy solution. But they had evidently forgotten that the safety of the passenger was more important than the maintenance of his dignity. If they had thought of this, they would have considered whether they could get a driver who could safely conduct me to my destination. As a matter of fact, none of them could drive, because it was not their trade. They therefore asked someone from amongst themselves to drive. The man took the reins in his hand and started off, thinking that there was nothing in it. But as he got on, he felt his responsibility and became so nervous that he gave up all attempt at control.

To save my dignity, the Mahars of Chalisgaon had put my very life in jeopardy. It was then that I learnt that a Hindu *tongawalla*, no better than a menial, has a dignity by which he can look upon himself as a person who is superior to any untouchable, even though he may be a Barrister-at-law.[26]

As 1929 drew to a close, Ambedkar was forced to spend the final months of the year convalescing, and full of frustration. He had no way to attend to the million things he was now simultaneously engaged in, personally, professionally, politically, socially and legally—including following up on the continuing Mahad case. As soon as he had recovered from the leg injury, different maladies began flaring up, starting especially in 1930 and continuing for the rest of his life. A letter he wrote in 1930 to a friend and colleague paints the picture vividly:

You must have been surprised at my silence. But there was no way but to be silent. My health as you know has been going down and the pressure of work has been increasing. The study of the Chavdar Tank suit was the last straw that has broken the camel's back. I went to Mahad in a broken condition ... and was extremely disappointed when I heard that the case had to be postponed ... All this has taken its toll on me and I am again prostrate with my fainting fits.²⁷

With similar health complaints and frustrations about not being able to get work done, Ambedkar had written to the same friend earlier in 1930:

My associates have gone out of town for a change of air. Therefore, not one of them can come for your meeting. I myself have been lying alone rotting in Bombay. Having to take daily injections makes it impossible for me to stir out.²⁸

As low as Ambedkar seemed at that point, however, little did he know that towards the end of 1930, the Round Table Conferences in London would commence, with him taking centre stage. Ambedkar would thus not only soon stir out, he would find himself stirring up the world.

Bibliography

Agarwal, Sudarshan, ed. *Dr B.R. Ambedkar: The Man and His Message: A Commemorative Volume*. Delhi: Prentice-Hall, 1991.

Ahir, Diwan Chand. *The Legacy of Dr Ambedkar*. Delhi: BR Publishing, 1990.

Ajnat, Surendra. *Letters of Ambedkar*. Jalandhar: Bheem Patrika, 1993.

Ambedkar Age Collective. *Hatred in the Belly: Politics behind the Appropriation of Dr Ambedkar's Writings*. Bangalore: The Shared Mirror Publishing House, 2016.

Ambedkar, B.R. *States and Minorities: What Are Their Rights and How to Secure Them in the Constitution of Free India*. Delhi: Kalpaz Publications, 2017.

Ambedkar, B.R. *Thoughts on Linguistic States*. Jalandhar: Bheem Patrika, 1977.

Ambedkar, B.R. 'Castes in India.' *The Indian Antiquary* XLI (May 1917).

Ambedkar, B.R. *What Congress and Gandhi Have Done to the Untouchables*. Bombay: Thacker and Co., 1945.

Ambedkar, B.R. *Who Were the Shudras? How They Came to Be the Fourth Varna in the Indo-Aryan Society*. Bombay: Thacker and Co., 1946.

Ambedkar, B.R. *The Untouchables: Who Were They and Why They Became Untouchables*. Delhi: Amrit Book Company, 1948.

Ambedkar, B.R. *Conditions Precedent for the Successful Working of Democracy*. Nagpur: YM Panchbhai, 1976.

Ambedkar, B.R. 'Annihilation of Caste.' In *Dr. Babasaheb Ambedkar Writings and Speeches*, Volume 1, edited by Vasant Moon, pp. 23–96. Bombay: Dept. of Education, Government of Maharashtra, 1979.

Ambedkar, B.R. *Dr. Babasaheb Ambedkar Writings and Speeches*, Volume 9, edited by Vasant Moon. Bombay: Dept. of Education, Government of Maharashtra, 2014.

Ambedkar, B.R. BBC interview, 1955. https://www.youtube.com/watch?v=omGcgEstVIE.

Ambedkar, B.R. *Buddha and Karl Marx* (an address to All India Radio, 1954). Chapter 18 in *Dr. Babasaheb Ambedkar Writings and Speeches*, Volume 3, edited by Vasant Moon. Bombay: Dept. of Education, Government of Maharashtra, 1987.

Ambedkar, B.R. *Buddhist Revolution and Counter Revolution in Ancient India*, edited by D.C. Ahir. Delhi: Buddhist World Press, 1996.

Ambedkar, B.R. *Federation versus Freedom*. Chapter 8 in *Dr. Babasaheb Ambedkar Writings and Speeches*, Volume 1, edited by Vasant Moon. Bombay: Dept. of Education, Government of Maharashtra, 1979.

Ambedkar, B.R. *Hindu Social Order* Chapters 2 and 3 in *Dr. Babasaheb Ambedkar Writings and Speeches*, Volume 3, edited by Vasant Moon. Bombay: Dept. of Education, Government of Maharashtra, 1987.

Ambedkar, B.R. *Hindus and Want of Public Conscience*. Chapter 9 in *Dr. Babasaheb Ambedkar Writings and Speeches*, Volume 5, edited by Vasant Moon. Bombay: Dept. of Education, Government of Maharashtra, 1989.

Ambedkar, B.R. *Pakistan, or the Partition of India: The Indian Political What's What!* In *Dr. Babasaheb Ambedkar Writings and Speeches*, Volume 8, edited by Vasant Moon. Bombay: Dept. of Education, Government of Maharashtra, 1990.

Bibliography

Ambedkar, B.R. *Riddles of Hinduism: An Exposition to Enlighten the Masses*. In *Dr. Babasaheb Ambedkar Writings and Speeches*, Volume 4, edited by Vasant Moon. Bombay: Dept. of Education, Government of Maharashtra, 1987.

Ambedkar, B.R. *Riddles of Hinduism: The Annotated Critical Selection*, introduced by Kancha Ilaiah. Delhi: Navayana, 2016.

Ambedkar, B.R. *Selected Works of Dr BR Ambedkar* (Wordpress.com). https://drambedkarbooks.files.wordpress.com/2009/03/selectedwork-of-dr-b-r-ambedkar.pdf.

Ambedkar, B.R. *The Philosophy of Hinduism*. Chapter 1 in *Dr. Babasaheb Ambedkar Writings and Speeches*, Volume 3, edited by Vasant Moon. Bombay: Dept. of Education, Government of Maharashtra, 1987.

Ambedkar, B.R. *Waiting for a Visa*. Chapter 1 of Part V, in *Dr. Babasaheb Ambedkar Writings and Speeches*, Volume 12, edited by Vasant Moon. Bombay: Dept. of Education, Government of Maharashtra, 1993.

Ambedkar, B.R. *The Problem of the Rupee*. In *Dr. Babasaheb Ambedkar Writings and* Speeches, Volume 6, edited by Vasant Moon. Bombay: Dept. of Education, Government of Maharashtra, 1989.

Ambedkar, B.R. *The Evolution of Provincial Finance in British India*. London: PS King & Son, 1925.

Ambedkar, Savita. *Dr. Ambedkar ke Sampark main*. Delhi: Samyak Prakashan, 2014.

Ambedkar, Savita. *Babasaheb: My Life with Dr Ambedkar*. Delhi: Penguin Random House India, 2022.

Anand, S., Srividya Natarajan, Durgabai Vyam, and Subhash Vyam. *Bhimayana: Incidents in the Life of Bhimrao Ramji Ambedkar*. Delhi: Navayana, 2011.

Arya, Sunaina and Aakash Singh Rathore, eds. *Dalit Feminist Theory: A Reader*. London: Routledge, 2019.

Awad, Eknath. *Strike a Blow to Change the World*, translated by Jerry Pinto. Delhi: Speaking Tiger, 2018.

Bahinipati, Priyadarshi, ed. *B.R. Ambedkar: An Enlightened Iconoclast.* Delhi: New Academic Publishers, 2015.

Baisantry, D.K. *Ambedkar: The Total Revolutionary.* Delhi: Segment, 1991.

Bal, Gian Singh. *Understanding Ambedkar.* Delhi: Ajanta Publications, 2000.

Beltz, Johannes and Surendra Jondhale, eds. *Reconstructing the World: B.R. Ambedkar and Buddhism in India.* Delhi: Oxford University Press, 2004.

Bharill, Chandra. *Social and Political Ideas of B.R. Ambedkar.* Jaipur: Aalekh Publishers, 1977.

Cabrera, Luis. *The Humble Cosmopolitan: Rights, Diversity and Trans-state Democracy.* Oxford: Oxford University Press, 2020.

Cháirez-Garza, Jesús Francisco. 'B.R. Ambedkar, Franz Boas and the Rejection of Racial Theories of Untouchability.' *South Asia: Journal of South Asian Studies*, 41:2 (2018): 281-96, DOI: 10.1080/00856401.2018.1431855.

Chakrabarty, Bidyut. *The Socio-Political Ideas of B.R. Ambedkar: Liberal Constitutionalism in a Creative Mould.* Delhi: Routledge, 2019.

Chatterjee, Debi. *Up against Caste: Comparative Study of Ambedkar and Periyar.* Jaipur: Rawat Publications, 2004.

Chaudhary, Poonam. *Situating Ambedkar's Movement.* Delhi: Meena Book Publications, 2018.

Choudhury, Soumyabrata. *Ambedkar and Other Immortals: An Untouchable Research Programme.* Delhi: Navayana, 2018.

Columbia Alumni News. '"Untouchables" Represented By Ambedkar, '15AM, '28Ph.D.', 19 December. New York: Columbia University, 1930.

Columbia University Bulletin of Information: Division of Philosophy, Psychology, and Anthropology Announcement, 1914-1915. New York: Columbia University, 30 May 1914.

Columbia University Bulletin of Information: Division of Philosophy, Psychology, and Anthropology Announcement, 1915-1916. New York: Columbia University, 27 February 1915.

Bibliography

Dangerkery, S.R. 'Dr. B.R. Ambedkar as I knew him,' Milind College of Arts, *Aurangabad College Magazine*, Mahatma Gandhi Birth Centenary Special issue, 1969–70.

Das, Bhagwan. *Thus Spoke Ambedkar: A Stake in the Nation*, Volume 1. Delhi: Navayana, 2011.

Das, Bhagwan. *Thus Spoke Ambedkar: Selected Speeches*, Volume 2. Jalandhar: Bheem Patrika, 1969.

Das, Bhagwan. *In Pursuit of Ambedkar: A Memoir*. Delhi: Navayana, 2010.

Dhupkar, Alka. 'Dr Babasaheb Ambedkar's home in Parel to become memorial, announces CM,' *Mumbai Mirror*, 28 September 2022: https://mumbaimirror.indiatimes.com/mumbai/civic/ambedkars-home-in-parel-to-become-memorial-cm/articleshow/72406825.cms?utm_source=contentofinterest&utm_medium=text&utm_campaign=cppst

Gandhi, M.K. 'Ambedkar's Indictment–II (1936).' In *The Collected Works of Mahatma Gandhi* Vol. LXIII. Ahmedabad: Navajivan Trust, 1963.

Gandhi, M.K. 'Hind Swaraj or Indian Home Rule (1908).' In *The Collected Works of Mahatma Gandhi* Vol. X. Ahmedabad: Navajivan Trust, 1963.

Gandhi, M.K. 'Letter to B.R. Ambedkar (1933).' In Aravinda Malagatti, et al, ed., *What Gandhi Says about Ambedkar*. Mysore: Prasaranga, 2000.

Gandhi, M.K. *Autobiography: The Story of My Experiments with Truth*. Boston: Beacon Press, 2015.

Gandhi, M.K. *Hind Swaraj and Other Writings*, edited by Anthony Parel. Cambridge: Cambridge University Press, 1997.

Geetha, V. and S.V. Rajadurai. *Towards a Non-Brahmin Millennium: From Iyothee Thass to Periyar*. Calcutta: Samya, 2008.

Ghurye, G.S. *Caste and Race in India*. Bombay: Popular Book Depot, 1979.

Goossens, Reuben. 'Peninsular and Oriental Steam Navigation Company: RMS Kaisar-i-Hind.' ssMaritime blog, Remembering the Classic Liners of Yesteryear, available at: http://ssmaritime.com/Kaisar-I-Hind.htm.

Harris, Richard. 'Housing Policy for the Colonial City: The British and Dutch Experience Compared, 1901-1949.' *Urban Geography*, 2009. URBAN GEOGR. 30. 815-837. 10.2747/0272-3638.30.8.815.

Jaffrelot, Christophe. *Dr. Ambedkar and Untouchability: Analyzing and Fighting Caste.* Delhi: Permanent Black, 2005.

Jaffrelot, Christophe, and Narender Kumar, eds. *Dr Ambedkar and Democracy.* Delhi: Oxford University Press, 2019.

Jatava, D.R. *The Critics of Dr. Ambedkar.* Jaipur: Surabhi Publications, 1997.

Jodhka, Surinder S. 'Nation and Village: Images of Rural India in Gandhi, Nehru and Ambedkar.' *Economic and Political Weekly.* Volume 37, No. 32, 2002, pp. 3343–54.

Kadam, K.N. *Dr Babasaheb Ambedkar and the Significance of his Movement: A Chronology.* Bombay: Popular Prakashan, 1991.

Kadam, K.N. *The Meaning of the Ambedkarite Conversion to Buddhism and Other Essays.* Mumbai: Popular Prakashan, 1997.

Kharat, Shankarrao, ed. *Dr. Babasaheb Ambedkaranchi Patre.* Pune: Indrayani Sahitya Prakashan, 2010.

Kausalayayan, Bhadant Ananda. *Had There Been No Ambedkar.* Mumbai: Samyak Prakashan, 2009.

Keer, Dhananjay. *Dr. Babasaheb Ambedkar: Life & Mission.* Bombay: Popular Prakashan, 1954.

Khairmoday, Changdev Bhavanrao. *Dr. Bhimrao Ramji Ambedkar Charitra* (in 12 volumes). Bombay: Dr Ambedkar Education Society, 1966–87.

Kshirsagar, R.K. *Political Thought of Dr Babasaheb Ambedkar.* Delhi: Intellectual Publishing House, 1991.

Kuber, W.N. *Dr Ambedkar: A Critical Study.* Delhi: People's Publishing House, 1973.

Kumar, Aishwary. *Radical Equality: Ambedkar, Gandhi and the Risk of Democracy.* Palo Alto: Stanford University Press, 2015.

Kumbhojkar, Shraddha. 'Politics, caste and the remembrance of the Raj: The Obelisk at Koregaon'. In *Sites of Imperial Memory: Commemorating Colonial Rule in the Nineteenth and Twentieth Centuries*, ed. Dominik

Geppert and Frank Lorenz Müller. Manchester: Manchester University Press, 2015, pp. 39–52.

Kunte, B.G., ed. *Source Material on Dr. Babasaheb Ambedkar and the Movement of Untouchables*, Volume 1. Bombay: Education Department, Government of Maharashtra, 1982.

Lahiri, Shompa. *Indians in Britain: Anglo-Indian Encounters, Race and Identity, 1880-1930*. London: Frank Cass Publishers, 2000.

Latthe, A.B., ed. *Memoirs of His Highness Shri Shahu Chhatrapati Maharaja of Kolhapur*. Bombay: The Times Press, 1924.

Lee, Alexander. *From Hierarchy to Ethnicity: The Politics of Caste in Twentieth-Century India*. Delhi: Cambridge University Press, 2020.

Lees-Milne, James. *The Enigmatic Edwardian: The Life of Reginald, 2nd Viscount Esher*. London: Sidgwick & Jackson, 1986.

Mankar, Vijay. *Dr B.R. Ambedkar: An Intellectual Biography*. Mumbai: Blue World Series, 2016.

Moffitt, Kelly and Jennifer Pellerito. '12 Groundbreaking Asian Columbians You Should Know.' *Columbia News*, 7 May 2021, accessible at:https://news.columbia.edu/news/12-groundbreaking-asian-columbians-you-should-know

Moon, Vasant. *Dr. Baba Saheb Ambedkar*. Delhi: National Book Trust India, 2007.

Mujumdar, Sanjeevani. *Mahamanav, Dr Babasaheb Ambedkar, Jeevan Darshan*. Pune: Symbiosis Society's Dr Babasaheb Ambedkar Museum and Memorial, ND.

Mukherjee, Arun P. 'B.R. Ambedkar, John Dewey, and the Meaning of Democracy'. *New Literary History* 40, no. 2 (2009): 345–70.

Mungekar, Bhalchandra, and Aakash Singh Rathore, eds. *Buddhism and the Contemporary World: An Ambedkarian Perspective*. Delhi: Bookwell, 2007.

Nehru, Motilal. *All Parties Conference, 1928: Report of the Committee Appointed by the Conference to Determine the Principles of the Constitution for India*. Allahabad: All India Congress Committee, 1928.

Nimgade, Namdeo. *In the Tiger's Shadow: The Autobiography of an Ambedkarite*. Delhi: Navayana, 2011.

Omvedt, Gail. 'Ambedkar as a Human Rights Leader.' Ambedkar.org. 15 April 2002/Commentary, Dalit E-Forum, http://ambedkar.org/gail/AmbedkarAs.htm, 1 April 2008.

Omvedt, Gail. 'Undoing the Bondage: Dr. Ambedkar's Theory of Dalit Liberation' in K.C. Yadav, ed., *From Periphery to Centre Stage: Ambedkar, Ambedkarism and Dalit Future*. Delhi: Manohar, 2000.

Omvedt, Gail. *Ambedkar: Towards an Enlightened India*. Delhi: Penguin, 2004.

Omvedt, Gail. *Dalit Visions: The Anti-Caste Movement and the Construction of an Indian Identity*. Delhi: Orient Longman, 2006.

Omvedt, Gail. *Dalits and the Democratic Revolution: Dr. Ambedkar and the Dalit Movement in Colonial India*. London: Sage, 1994.

Omvedt, Gail. *Cultural Revolt in Colonial Society: The Non-Brahman Movement in Western India: 1873-1930*. Bombay: Scientific Socialist Education Trust, 1976.

Pawar, Urmila, and Meenakshi Moon. *We Also Made History: Women in the Ambedkarite Movement*. Delhi: Zubaan, 2008.

Phonsa, Hem Raj. 'Dalit Vision.' Accessible at: http://dalitvision.blogspot.com/2017/02/importance-of-february-month-for-dalit.html

Pol, Prabodhan. 'The Journalistic Legacy of B.R. Ambedkar, the Editor. *The Wire*, 14 April 2018, available at: https://thewire.in/caste/the-journalistic-legacy-of-b-r-ambedkar-the-editor.

Prabhakar, Padhye. *Prakaashaan'tilla Vyakti*. Bombay: J Maa Mahaajana, 1950.

Purandare, Vaibhav. *Savarkar: The True Story of the Father of Hindutva*. Delhi: Juggernaut, 2019.

Pyarelal, Nayyar. 'The Epic Fast (1932).' In Homer A. Jack, ed., *The Gandhi Reader: A Source Book*. Bloomington: Indiana University Press, 1956.

Rajagopalachari, C. *Ambedkar Refuted*. Bombay: Hind Kitabs, 1946.

Rajsekhar, V.T. *Karl Marx and Dr Babasaheb Ambedkar.* Delhi: Dalit Sahitya Akademy, 1988.

Rao, Anupama. *The Caste Question: Dalits and the Politics of Modern India.* Berkeley: University of California Press, 2009.

Rathore, Aakash Singh and Silika Mohapatra, eds. *Indian Political Thought: A Reader.* London: Routledge, 2010.

Rathore, Aakash Singh and Ajay Verma. *B.R. Ambedkar: The Buddha and His Dhamma: A Critical Edition.* Delhi: Oxford University Press, 2011.

Rathore, Aakash Singh. *A Philosophy of Autobiography: Body & Text.* New York, Routledge, 2019.

Rathore, Aakash Singh, ed. *B.R. Ambedkar: The Quest for Justice* (5 Volumes). Delhi: Oxford University Press, 2020.

Rathore, Aakash Singh. *Indian Political Theory: Laying the Groundwork for Svaraj.* New York: Routledge, 2017.

Rathore, Aakash Singh. *Ambedkar's Preamble: A Secret History of the Constitution of India.* Delhi: Penguin Random House India, 2020.

Rathore, Aakash Singh. 'Seen Through Different Glasses: A Controversial Introduction to Annihilation of Caste Reappears as a Book. It Reflects the Elite Left's Opportunistic Appropriation of Ambedkar.' *Outlook,* 14 June 2019, available at: https://www.outlookindia.com/magazine/story/books-seen-through-different-glasses/301791

Rattu, Nanak Chand. *Last Few Years of Dr. Ambedkar.* Delhi: Amrit Publishing House, 1997.

Rattu, Nanak Chand. *Reminiscences and Remembrances of Dr B.R. Ambedkar.* Delhi: Samyak Prakashan, 1995.

Rege, Sharmila and B.R. Ambedkar. *Against the Madness of Manu: B.R. Ambedkar's Writings on Brahmanical Patriarchy.* Delhi: Navayana, 2013.

Rodrigues, Valerian. *The Essential Writings of B.R. Ambedkar.* Delhi: Oxford University Press, 2002.

Rodrigues, Valerian. *Conversations with Ambedkar: 10 Ambedkar Memorial Lectures.* New York: Columbia University Press, 2019.

Round Table India 'Dr Ambedkar Remembers the Poona Pact in an Interview on BBC' (2012). http://roundtableindia.co.in/index.php?option=com_content&view=article&id=3797:drambedkar-remembers-the-poona-pact-in-an-interview-on-the-bbc-&catid=116:dr-ambedkar&Itemid=128

Roy, Arundhati. *The Doctor and the Saint: The Ambedkar-Gandhi Debate: Caste, Race and Annihilation of Caste.* Delhi: Penguin Random House India, 2019.

Sangharakshita. *Ambedkar and Buddhism.* London: Windhorse Publications, 1986.

Saravanamuttu, Manicasothy. *The Sara Saga.* Penang: Areca Books, 2010.

Savarkar, V.D. *Hindutva: Who Is a Hindu.* Bombay: Hindi Sahitya Sadan, 2012.

Shastri, Shankaranand. *My Memories and Experiences of Babasaheb Dr. B.R. Ambedkar.* Delhi: Gautam Book Centre, 1989.

Shourie, Arun. *Worshipping False Gods.* Delhi: HarperCollins, 2000.

Shukla, R. 'Dr. Ambedkar's Courses at Columbia.' South Asia Study Resources Compiled by Frances Pritchett, 2019. http://www.columbia.edu/itc/mealac/pritchett/00ambedkar/timeline/1910s.html

Singh, Janak. *Dr. B.R. Ambedkar: The Messiah of the Downtrodden.* Delhi: Kalpaz Publications, 2010.

Stroud, Scott R. 'Creative Democracy, Communication, and the Uncharted Sources of Bhimrao Ambedkar's Deweyan Pragmatism.' *Education and Culture,* 34 (1) (2018): pp. 61-80.

Stroud, Scott R. 'What Did Bhimrao Ambedkar Learn from John Dewey's Democracy and Education?' *The Pluralist,* 12 (2), 2017: 78–103.

Stroud, Scott R. 'Pragmatism and the Pursuit of Social Justice in India: Bhimrao Ambedkar and the Rhetoric of Religious Reorientation.' *Rhetoric Society Quarterly,* Vol. 46, No. 1 (2016): pp. 5–27, DOI: 10.1080/02773945.2015.1104717, https://www.tandfonline.com/doi/pdf/10.1080/02773945.2015.1104717?needAccess=true.

Stroud, Scott R. *The Evolution of Pragmatism in India: Ambedkar, Dewey, and the Rhetoric of Reconstruction.* Chicago: University of Chicago Press, 2023.

Stroud, Scott R. and Landon D.C. Elkind. 'Exploring the influence of Russell on Ambedkar.' *The Forward Press* blog, 1 August 2017, available at: https://www.forwardpress.in/2017/08/exploring-the-influence-of-russell-on-ambedkar/#_edn2.

Tartakov, Gary Michael. 'Art and Identity: The Rise of a New Buddhist Imagery.' *Art Journal*, Vol. 49, No. 4, New Approaches to South Asian Art (1990): pp. 409–16.

Teltumbde, Anand. *MAHAD: The Making of the First Dalit Revolt.* Delhi: Aakar Publishing, 2016.

Teltumbde, Anand and Suraj Yengde, eds. *The Radical Ambedkar: Critical Reflections.* Delhi: Penguin Random House India, 2018.

Teltumbde, Anand. *Republic of Caste: Thinking Equality in the Time of Neoliberal Hindutva.* Delhi: Navayana, 2018.

Tharoor, Shashi. *Ambedkar: A Life.* Delhi: Aleph, 2022.

Thorat, Sukhadeo. *Ambedkar's Role in Economic Planning and Water Policy.* Delhi: Shipra Publications, 1998.

Vajpeyi, Ananya. *Righteous Republic: The Political Foundations of Modern India.* Cambridge: Harvard University Press, 2012.

Viswanathan, Gauri. *Outside the Fold: Conversion, Modernity, and Belief.* Princeton: Princeton University, 1998.

Vundru, Raja Sekhar. *Ambedkar, Gandhi and Patel: The Making of India's Electoral System.* Hyderabad: Bloomsbury, 2018.

Yadav, K.C., ed. *From Periphery to Centre Stage: Ambedkar, Ambedkarism and Dalit Future.* Delhi: Manohar, 2000.

Yaakkan. *Ambedkar enra payer oru parpanarudaytha? Kazhavapadum payer azhukku.* (Tamil, untranslated. *Does the Name 'Ambedkar' Belong to a Brahmin? Washing Away the Stain of the Name.*) Chennai: Kalagam Press, 2018.

Yengde, Suraj. *Caste Matters.* Delhi: Penguin Random House India, 2019.

Yusufji, Salim. *Ambedkar: Attendant Details*. Delhi: Navayana, 2017.

Zelliot, Eleanor. *Ambedkar's World: The Making of Babasaheb and the Dalit Movement*. Delhi: Navayana, 2013.

Zelliot, Eleanor. *From Untouchable to Dalit: Essays on the Ambedkar Movement*. Delhi: Manohar, 1996.

Zelliot, Eleanor. *Dr. Babasaheb Ambedkar and the Untouchable Movement*. Delhi: Blumoon Books, 2004.

Zene, Cosimo, ed. *The Political Philosophies of Antonio Gramsci and B.R. Ambedkar: Itineraries of Dalits and Subalterns*. London: Routledge, 2013.

Appendix 1

Dr. Bhimrao Ramji Ambedkar Charitra (in twelve volumes)
by Changdev Bhavanrao Khairmoday

C.B. Khairmoday (1904–71) was from Satara. Under the advice of Ambedkar's brother Balaram, he studied at Elphinstone High School. After Ambedkar launched *Bahishkrut Bharat*, untouchable students regularly came to his office to study and to sleep at night, Khairmoday included. Khairmoday helped Ambedkar with his various writing projects, and early on decided that he would chronicle Ambedkar's life, doing so systematically as he was earning his BA degree at Bombay University. He compiled any newspaper articles about Ambedkar that would appear and all the speeches written by him, his letters, reports about his various institutions and so on. The first volume of Khairmoday's biography was published in 1952, and he managed to complete a total of four volumes in his lifetime, covering Ambedkar's life until around 1930. Other people, including his wife, took up the task of bringing out the remaining volumes after Khairmoday's death in 1971.

Khairmoday's biography has proved hugely influential on all subsequent Marathi writings (including later biographies) about Ambedkar, but has never been translated into English. What follows is the complete table of contents* of each of the twelve volumes.

Volume 1

1. Family History
2. Parents
3. Birth
4. Childhood
5. Education – Satara
6. Education – Mumbai
7. Columbia University
8. London University
9. Upon Returning Home
10. Professor
11. Recapitulation – 1
12. Recapitulation – 2
13. Recapitulation – 3
14. Recapitulation – 4
15. Recapitulation – 5
16. Recapitulation – 6
17. Recapitulation – 7
18. London University

Volume 2

1. Dawn
2. The Interim
3. Background (Dalit Social Work Prior to the Ambedkarite Movement)
4. Spark of the Movement

---

*   I would like to thank Rucha Pawar for compiling the Table of Contents.

5. The Motive of Self-Development
6. Ramabai's Sansaar (Family Life)
7. The *Mooknayak* Incident
8. Ambedkar's Family Life
9. Bahishkrut Hitakarini Sabha
10. Charging Forward
11. Legislative Council
12. Nehru's Strategy – in Favour of Muslims
13. Mahar Vatan
14. The Mahar Vatan Bill
15. Untouchables' Booker T. Washington
16. Protest against Increase in Zudi

Appendix

Article from the newspaper *Kesari* – 'Kulkarni Leelamrut' (30/9/1913)
The Manifesto of the Rights of Untouchables (put before the Simon Commission)
Stating the Mahar Vatan Case for the Governor of Bombay

Volume 3

1. Untouchables' Revolt
2. The Mahad Revolution
3. Refuting Critiques – 1
4. Refuting Critiques – 2
5. Refuting Critiques – 3
6. War of Religion, Government and the Depressed Classes
7. Entering Shri Amba Devi Temple – the Satyagraha and Its Conclusion
8. Satyagraha's Discussion
9. Preparing for the Mahad Satyagraha
10. Mahad Satyagraha Begins
11. Mahad Satyagraha Begins

12. Mahad Satyagraha Begins
13. The Burning of Manu Smriti
14. On Raigad Fort
15. After the Raigad Fort Ordeal
16. Complaint Lodged by Savarnas against Ambedkar (Upon Hearing of the Satyagraha)
17. Parvati Satyagraha (in Pune)
18. Nashik Satyagraha (Kala Ram Temple)

Volume 4

1. Untouchables' First Political Assembly
2. Round Table Conference
3. Round Table Conference: Memorandum of the Political Rights of Untouchables
4. Round Table Conference: Minority Subcommittee
5. Round Table Conference: Conflict between Gandhi and Ambedkar in the Second Conference
6. Round Table Conference: Reactions to the Gandhi-Ambedkar Debate
7. Round Table Conference: Federal Structure Committee
8. Round Table Conference: The Raja-Munje Pact
9. Round Table Conference: Charge Sheet Pressed against Gandhiji and Congress by the Depressed Classes
10. Round Table Conference: The Franchise Committee

Reference Literature

Volume 5

1. The Poona Pact – Background
2. The Poona Pact – Gandhi's Hunger Strike
3. The Poona Pact – Signatures
4. After the Poona Pact

Appendix 1

5. Joint Parliamentary Committee Work: Indian Minister's Testimony – 1
6. Joint Parliamentary Committee Work: Indian Minister's Testimony – 2
7. Joint Parliamentary Committee Work: Indian Minister's Testimony – 3
8. Joint Parliamentary Committee Work: Indian Minister's Witness – 4
9. Social Reform Progress – 1
10. Social Reform Progress – 2
11. Social Reform Progress – 3
12. Social Reform Progress – 4
13. Social Reform Progress – 5
14. Social Reform Progress – 6
15. Social Reform Progress – 7

References: Books

References: Newspaper Articles and Reports

Literature Based on Dr. Ambedkar – Comments

Volume 6

1. Ramabai's Demise
2. Conversion Movement – 1
3. Conversion Movement – 2
4. Conversion Movement – 3
5. Conversion Movement – 4
6. Conversion Movement – 5
7. Conversion Movement – The Depressed Classes' Share
8. Dr. Munje – Ambedkar Correspondence
9. Conversion Movement – 6
10. Conversion – Support and Criticism
11. Other Movements – 1

12. Other Movements – 2
13. Other Movements – 3
14. Shankar Laxman Gokhale's Open Letter to Dr. Ambedkar (Yeola Dalit Conference)

Appendix

Caste and Conversion

Volume 7

1. Independent Labour Party
2. The Depressed Classes – Conversion and Political Rights
3. Legislative Assembly Work – 1
4. The Untouchables' Railway Workers' Union
5. Legislative Assembly – 2

Volume 8

1. 92 *Kalami Rajya* (Government of India Act, 1935)
2. Dr. Ambedkar – Political Significance
3. Cripps Mission Plan – 1
4. Cripps Mission Plan – 2
5. Viceroy's Cabinet of Ministers – 1
6. Viceroy's Cabinet of Ministers – 2
7. Viceroy's Cabinet of Ministers – 3
8. The Untouchables' Military Occupation
9. Gandhi's Negotiation
10. The Successful Tour of the South – 1
11. The Successful Tour of the South – 2

References

Volume 9

1. Two Shimla Conferences
2. Cabinet Mission Plan

3. Satyagraha against Congress Rule
4. The Rise of Independence
5. In the Constitutional Committee
6. Contribution to the Constitutional Committee
7. Contribution to the Constitutional Committee (continued)
8. Constitution Committee's Credit

Volume 10

N.R. Phatak's letter to Khairmoday

1. After Independence (National Flag)
2. After Independence (The Question of Refugees)
3. *Sanyukta* (Joint) Maharashtra Movement
4. Hindu Code Bill
5. Resignation from the Cabinet and the Statement
6. Responses to the Resignation
7. Contesting the Election – 1
8. Contesting the Election – 2
9. Campaigning for Election – 1
10. Campaigning for Election – 2
11. Evaluating the Failure

References

Volume 11

Preface by N.R. Pathak

1. Speeches in the Rajya Sabha
2. Speeches on Democracy
3. Formation of Andhra Pradesh
4. Practicing Untouchability – Crime and Law
5. International Policy

6. Scheduled Caste, Scheduled Tribe Report
7. Amendments (Events)

Volume 12

1. Representation
2. Editor's Note
3. Biographer's Note
4. Prof. N.R. Pathak's Praise for Biographer

A Few Incidents:

Taking up Buddhist Diksha - 1
Taking up Buddhist Diksha – 2
Public Opinion on Dhamma Diksha
Parinirvan Yatra – Delhi
Accounts of Homage

References

Appendix 2

The Resolutions of the Mahad Conference (20 March 1927)

One (to the savarna Hindus):

If savarna Hindus desire that the bahishkrut emancipation movement should not create antagonism between themselves and the bahishkrut people, then this conference recommends the following suggestions to them:

1. When the bahishkrut classes try to exercise their rights of citizenship by making use of public water sources, savarna Hindus resort to stopping all transactions with them and declare social boycott against them. Instead, savarna Hindus should actively help the bahishkrut people in their endeavours.
2. Savarna Hindus should accept bahishkrut people as domestic servants.

3. Savarna Hindus should promote inter-caste marriages as a method to abolish caste.
4. They should accept poor bahishkrut students on daily terms for meals or arrange for their food and help them.
5. They should not rely on the bahishkrut people to drag away dead animals and should arrange for this themselves.

Two (to the government):

1. In the Bombay Legislative Council, Shri S.K. Bole has brought out a resolution regarding the opening of public wells and tanks to the untouchables. The government should implement it and display notices to that effect at those places. If necessary, they should impose Criminal Procedure Code §144 and arrange for anticipatory bail for local leaders helping the untouchables exercise their rights.
2. This conference appeals to the government to make arrangement for removal of the extreme inconvenience that the untouchables have to go through to get drinking water in many villages.
3. The government should allot forest lands to the bahishkrut people for their economic development.
4. The government should pay attention to the following things to ameliorate the sufferings and raise the economic status of the extremely backward bahishkrut people:
    a) Provide government service to unqualified persons from the untouchable classes wherever possible.
    b) Recruit untouchables into the military.
    c) Take untouchable candidates in the navy.
    d) Second-year trained teachers should be given the post of supervisor in the education department.
    e) Literate untouchables should be given suitable positions in the local police force.
    f) Untouchable people should be recruited into the police department.

5. The method of paying *balute* from villagers for government service should be stopped and in its place a kind of cess should be levied on them as in other provinces such as the Central Provinces. Village servants should be given a monthly salary from this cess.
6. The custom of bahishkrut people consuming the meat of dead animals should be prohibited by law because it causes serious damage to their health and lowers their social status.
7. The government should apply force in respect of education and prohibition.
8. The conference expresses sadness that the deputy collectorship did not go to Shri M.K. Jadhav.
9. There is money available in the earlier fund raised by Platoon No. 111 contributed by the employees from Mahad taluka. This money should be utilized to start a boarding for the students belonging to the untouchable class of this taluka.
10. The following things should be implemented for the progress of the boycotted classes whose condition has been pathetic in respect of education:
    a) A committee should be appointed to enquire into how to achieve progress in their education.
    b) A boarding should be opened in every district.
    c) A grant of Rs 10 per month per student should be given to boardings run by private institutions.
    d) A school should be opened in villages with more than thirty boys/girls.
    e) Scholarships should be given.

Three (to the untouchables):

11. This conference requests the bahishkrut *panchas* to implement the following with respect to the marriage of children:
    a) They should stop the custom of marrying boys younger than twenty years and girls younger than fifteen years.

b) Wherever schools are available, they should make it compulsory for parents to educate their children. Those who violate this should be made liable for punishment.
c) They should not execute remarriage without proper enquiry into both the bride and groom.
d) In remarriages a tax of Rs 7 should be collected. There should not be any other tax, except for the clothes and ornaments for the couple and meals for the panchas.

12. Untouchable people should give up menial vocations like Maharki and adopt independent professions like farming.
13. They should start cooperative banks necessary for farming.
14. This conference makes an earnest request to bahishkrut people to establish cooperatives to escape the trap of moneylenders and to face difficulties in times of famine and flood.

Four:

This conference condoles the inhumane assassination of Swami Shraddhanandji and feels that the Hindu castes should annihilate caste as he preached.

Appendix 3

This is the first editorial written by Dr Ambedkar for Issue Number 1 of *Bahishkrut Bharat* (3 April 1927). Translated by Dr B.R. Kamble.

We Are on the Scene Again

This writer had started a fortnightly newspaper called *Mooknayak* on 31st January 1920. There he had stated in the first issue itself that there is no more effective means than the newspaper to voice against the injustice done to the untouchables by the Caste Hindus and also to suggest the ways and means for their progress and total liberation from their slavery imposed on them by the high-Caste Hindus from ages past. But when we throw our glance to the newspapers that are brought out in Bombay Presidency we are constrained to say that they do no other work than safeguarding the interest of their respective caste only. They do not bother for the interests of other castes; not only this but even at times they go against the interests of others in their view points.

We would like to tell such newspapers that if any one caste remains backward or is kept backward its effect will definitely have to be endured by the rest of the castes. Society is like a boat; if a sailor, because of his mischief or to make fun of other sailors strikes a hole in the boat sooner or later he too has to sink along with others. Thus, it is doubtless that those who wish to harm other castes sooner or later will have to suffer its effects. Hence, we tell the newspapers who have their selfish motive that while harming others they will sow the seeds of harming themselves. Fortunately for us there are some newspapers which accept these viewpoints in their publications. The Papers like *Din Mitra, Jagruti, Deccan Rayat, Vijayi Maratha, Dnyan Prakash, Indu Prakash, Subodh Patrika,* etc, often write about the problems of Untouchables. But it is also certain that these newspapers are born to devote themselves to the problems of Non-Brahman castes whose number is very large and hence it is not possible for them to devote themselves to the Untouchables, who have enormous problems of their own. Under these circumstances, anybody can feel that to discuss the Untouchables' enormous problems there is need of a separate paper devoted to the cause of these underdogs. This paper is born to meet this need. To discuss the problems of the Untouchables papers like *Somavamshiya Mitra, Hindu Nagarika,* and *Vithal Vidhvamshak* were born but soon shut down. But here we end by assuring that if our subscribers encourage us by subscribing to the paper regularly, *Mooknayak* will not fail in showing our people the right path and their experience will show them that our assurance was not wrong.

But the writer who had given this assurance to the readers of *Mooknayak* could not keep his promise because of unavoidable circumstances in his life mission. After some experience of running the *Mooknayak* its founder immediately realised that he must find a profession which will keep him free for social service and at the same time earn his livelihood to keep him free from his economic problems. In pursuance of this he had to go to England to complete his Barrister course which he had kept incomplete when he returned to India in his first phase of learning in America and in England. While returning to England he had handed over the charge of running *Mooknayak* to a young man who had received training in running the newspaper.

While handing that paper over it was hoped that when the present writer returns from England he will have an opportunity to see that *Mooknayak* had prospered. But his hope proved simply futile because he came to know just before he started returning from England that *Mooknayak* continues no more. It will be a futile exercise to ponder over the causes of the end of *Mooknayak*. Here, we only think that it will not be out of place if we explain the old issues carrying them further in our new newspaper under a new name.

When the present writer had started *Mooknayak* some six years back the background was that the new reformed system of government was to be implemented in India. In the circumstances of new ensuing political reforms while explaining the need of the newspaper the present writer had stated that 'If an observer looks to the physical and social scene in India he will undoubtedly find out that India is a home of glaring inequality'.

The inequality in Hinduism is incomparable and hateful. The interrelation between the Hindu communities is definitely not befitting to the character of Hinduism. The communities that are incorporated in Hindu society are inspired by the social idea of high and low in their social status. Hindu society is a multistoried building. However, every story is a closed compartment without any passage of entrance to others. Since there is no passage for communication between the stories the man who is born in a lower story must die there, however worthy he might be; he has no entry into the upper story. As for a man in an upper story, however unworthy he might be, no one dares to pull him down to a lower story. In short it can be said that the social status of man in Hindu society is not based on his merit or demerit. Moreover, since inter-dining and inter-caste marriage are prohibited by custom and social usage, each caste has remained separated from the other castes – this has prevented the castes from promoting oneness or a sense of brotherhood among them. Not only this but even their day-to-day dealings are not without restrictions. Dealing between castes is only from outside the threshold of their house, and some castes are untouchables whose touch pollutes the upper castes. Because of the idea of pollution, untouchables rarely come into contact with the so called high-caste people in Hindu society. The prohibition of inter-dining and inter-caste marriage has marred the growth of fellow feeling among the castes and the practice of touchability-untouchability has added strength to the caste practice, so much so that the untouchable castes—though they are called Hindus—have remained outside the mainstream of Hindu society and its framework. Under this system the Hindus can form themselves into three classes; namely, the Brahmans, Non-Brahmans, and the Untouchables. If we look at the effects of this social inequality it can be seen that it has affected each caste differently. The Brahmans, the highest caste among the Hindus, regard themselves as Bhudevas, gods on earth. The Brahmans think that the existing social inequality is very much beneficial to them as it is enjoined by the Shastras that all other castes are born to serve them. Hence by extracting services from all other castes they are enjoying the fruits by their self-created rights. If they have done any work it is the work of writing the Dharma Shastras. But these Dharma Shastras are full of inconsistencies, a mixture of high thinking and the meanest possible social practices. These scripture writers, while teaching in their writing that all movable and immovable things are different forms of god, support glaring inequality in their thought and practice. It is not a sign of their being in their senses. Right or wrong, unfortunately, these Shastras have tremendous impact on the minds of the masses. There is no denying the fact that these innocent Hindu masses are worshipping their enemies as their gods. We need not go too far to find out why the innocent masses have fettered themselves with a harmful religious idea. This happened because Brahmans constantly preached to the people that the preservation of religious knowledge, and preaching that knowledge to the masses, is the sole right of the Brahmans.

It is true that in the absence of power and for want of education Non-Brahmans have remained backward. But the ways and means of earning their living such as agriculture, trade and commerce and involvement in government services are open to them. But the social inequality that has been imposed on untouchables makes their social disabilities immense. In the combination of physical and mental weakness, poverty and ignorance, the untouchable communities are drowned in deep sorrow. The deep-rooted sense of slavery among them is retracing their steps backward. Education alone is the remedy over their mental weakness, because of which they think that the condition in which they are placed for years together is their fate and there is no escape. Education is available for purchase but due to their grinding poverty Untouchables are unable to purchase it, and if someone is able to purchase it, it is not easily available because due to the Caste Hindus' practice of untouchability it is not that easy for untouchables to seek entry into schools. The untouchables have remained poor by and large because all professions of earning are not open to them. They are very rarely found in trade, commerce, and in government services. Such is their miserable plight. We do not know whether our people are aware that so long as there are people in Hindu society who think that there is nothing wrong in degrading some people as untouchables the progress of existing untouchable communities in India is not possible. Similarly the so-called untouchables have also realised that the upper caste Hindu leaders have tried to create a wrong impression about their position to the British Government, which depends upon high-caste Hindus for governance. In this country of caste distinctions and caste hatred the untouchables want their separate electorates to elect their own representatives to legislatures and the caste Hindus have opposed their demands, and hence the untouchables have complained to the government against the Caste Hindus. In short the untouchables have understood the tactics of the caste Hindus who, by acquiring political power from the British, wish to perpetuate their caste supremacy over the untouchables. This is a good sign of awakening among the untouchables.

These views were expressed before the Reform Act of 1919 was implemented. Now the Act has come into force. The power that was in the hands of the British Government has fallen into the hands of upper caste Indians in some proportion. Without bothering for the representation of the untouchable communities, the British Government has handed the power over to the Caste Hindus as the owner of cattle does in handing his cattle over to the butcher. The condition of the untouchables six years before has now deteriorated from bad to worst. Hence the right minded among the untouchable communities will definitely admit that to stop the injustice being done to the untouchables and bring out their problems and their existing condition before the world there is no better remedy than a newspaper entirely wedded to their cause. Not only this but it is likely that there is going to be another Reform Act in 1930, and by that whatever power the British Government has retained now may also fall into the hands of Indians. If this happens and if the untouchables do not get adequate representation for themselves, they will see their fate doomed once and for all. The mental outlook of the upper Caste Hindus towards untouchables and their problems is not impartial, broad or pure. It is the considered opinion of this writer that if the untouchables are to avoid this coming tragedy then they must launch their movements and start their agitations from right now. May God bless us for our success!

Appendix 4

Final Order of the Bombay High Court Re: Mahad Tank (17 March 1937)
APPEAL NO. 462 OF 1933 FROM APPELLATE DECREE

Narhari Damodar Vaidya; and the others
(Original Plaintiffs Nos. 2 to 6)…………………......Appellants.

Dr Bhimrao Ramji Ambedkar, Member
of Joint Parliamentary Committee, London;
and others (Original Defendants)…………………Respondents.

    Second Appeal against the decision of S.M. Kaikini, Esquire, Second Assistant Judge at Thana in Appeal No. 32 of 1931.
    Mr V.B. Virkar for the Appellants, Counsel Mr S.V. Gupte, with Mr B.G. Modak for Respondent No. 1.
    17th March 1937
    Coram:- Broomfield and N.J. Wadia J.
    Oral Judgement (Per Broomfield J.):-

Appendix 4

The appellants, on behalf of the caste Hindus of the town of Mahad, sued the respondents, who represented the so-called 'Untouchables' for a declaration that the Choudhari Tank near the town belongs to them and that they alone have a right to use it and the respondents are not entitled to use it, and for an injunction against the respondents not to use it. The claim to ownership is not now persisted in and it is conceded that, as found by the trial court, the tank belonged to the Government under the provisions of Section 37 of the Land Revenue Code and has now vested in the Municipality of Mahad under Section 50 of the District Municipalities Act. It is also conceded now that the caste Hindus are not entitled to use the tank exclusively by as against all the world, since Mohamedans may, and do use it. It is contended nevertheless that the appellants have the right to use it themselves and to exclude the 'Untouchables' from the use of it, and this right is said to be based on immemorial custom.

The trial Judge found that the plaintiffs have proved a longstanding custom (he does not describe it as immemorial) of using the tank water to the exclusion of the 'Untouchables'. He held however, that the custom conferred no legal right upon the plaintiffs because 'mere use of a public tank by one-class and non-use by another would not clothe the user with any legal rights or rights of ownership'. On appeal the Assistant Judge confirmed the finding that the caste Hindus have not proved that they have any legal right to exclude the 'Untouchables'. He has relied to some extent on a judgment of Sir Sadashiv Ayar in *Mariappa v. Vaithilinga*, a case not reported apparently in the authorised *reports* but to be found in 1913 Mad. W. N. 247 and 18 Indian cases 979; but his main reason seems to be that he held that the custom is not shown to be immemorial.

The Chowdhari tank is a small lake or a large pool; between four and five acres in extent, on the outskirts of the town. It is surrounded on all sides by municipal roads beyond which are houses occupied by caste Hindus (and very few Mohamedans), and the owners of these houses also own in many cases strips of land on the edge of the tank, ghats or flights of steps to get to the water and the masonry embankments along the sides. There are no houses of 'Untouchables' anywhere near. It is not known how old the tank is, except that it is admittedly not less than 250 years old. There is no evidence as to its origin. It is not even clear that it is artificial. The Trial Judge took the view that it was "a natural excavation in the bed of the earth, of course repaired and remodelled by human agency." If it is so and the point was not disputed in the argument before us it is probably many centuries old. The water-supply comes from the monsoon and a few natural springs. The population of the town Mahad is between seven and eight thousand, of whom less then 400/- are 'Untouchables'. The Municipality was established in 1865, but there is no evidence available, at any rate on the record of this case, as to the early history of the town or as to the time when the side was first inhabited.

The Plaintiffs have examined a number of witnesses, many of them old inhabitants, whose evidence may be said to have established that within the period of living memory the tank has been used exclusively by the caste Hindus (and a few Mohamedans) and has never been used by the 'Untouchables'. It is in fact admitted that the latter never used it, before the year 1927, when a campaign against the doctrines of 'untouchability' was carried out by defendant N.I., and some of the 'Untouchables' went and drank water as a mark of protest. They were assaulted and beaten by the caste Hindus and there were criminal prosecutions which led to the present suit. As there is no record of any attempt having been made by the 'Untouchables' to use the tank before that there is no evidence of any positive acts of exclusion. What is provided is user by the one party and absence of user by the other. This was, undoubtedly not any accidental causes, but to the mutual acceptance of the doctrine of 'Untouchability' which until recent years was not openly challenged.

The learned Assistant Judge comments on the fact that there is no evidence of the exclusion of the 'Untouchables' in pre-British times, nothing to show that the exclusion or exclusive user was in force in the days of the Maratha rule or the Musalman rule. It is of course not always necessary to produce evidence going back beyond the memory of living persons. On proof of enjoyment for a period even less than that the courts have frequently felt justified in holding, in the absence of evidence to the contrary, that a custom has existed from time immemorial. Nor, of course, is it necessary in a case of this kind to have evidence of positive acts of exclusion of one party by the other. There could be no such evidence as long as the enjoyment of the caste Hindus was not challenged, and it would not be likely to be challenged as long as the doctrine of 'untouchability' prevailed and was accepted. But a custom proved to have existed during the period of living memory can only be presumed to have existed from before the period of legal memory in cases where conditions may be assumed to have been permanent and stable. Is it reasonable to infer that what has happened during the period covered by the evidence also has happened from time immemorial? This is where the plaintiffs' case in our opinion breaks down. As long as conditions were at all similar, as long as the houses of the caste Hindus have surrounded the tank (which is not necessarily very long as the tank is on the outskirts of the town and the land around it was not likely to be occupied until after considerable expansion of the original settlement), it may be safely presumed that the practice was the same as at present. It would not be safe to presume, however, that conditions have been similar for a period long enough to establish the alleged custom. The Konkan has had a chequered history, even in comparatively modern times, and to suppose that the caste Hindus have been in a position to exercise exclusive control over this large natural reservoir, situated as it is, from time immemorial, would be contrary to reasonable probability.

In this connection some of the observations of Sir Sadashiv Ayar in *Mariappa v. Vaithilinga* are very instructive. He cites a saying of Manu's:

'waters are pure as long as a cow goes to quench her thirst in and they have a good scent, colour and taste', and he points out that the Shastric writings 'make a distinction between rivers, tanks and other receptacles which are more easily contaminated and where purification by time, atmospheric conditions and movement of the water is much more difficult'. The learned Judge suggests that the dictates of the Hindu religion would not require any elaborate precautions against the pollution of water in a large open tank, and he was dealing with a tank in a village site considerably smaller than the Choudhari Tank at Mahad. The doctrine of 'Untouchability' therefore does not appear to go far enough to lend very much support to the appellants' case and it is doubtful whether any attempt would be made to secure exclusive use of the water until such time as the tank came to be surrounded by the houses of the caste Hindus.

This is the only case to which our attention has been drawn dealing with a claim to exclude 'Untouchables' from the use of a watering place of this description. The temple-entry cases, e.g. *Anandrav v. Shankar*, (1883) I.L.R., 7 Bom 323, and *Sankaralinga v. Rajeswara*, (1908) I.L.R., 31 Mad 236, P.C., are not really on all fours. In such cases long practice acquiesced in by the other castes and communities may naturally give rise to a presumption of dedication to the exclusive use of the higher castes, and may throw upon the 'Untouchables' the burden of proving that they are among the people for whose worship a particular temple exists. No such presumption of a lawful origin of the custom can be said to arise here.

We therefore agree with the learned Assistant Judge that the appellants have not established the immemorial custom which they allege. Had they succeeded on this point it might have been necessary to consider whether the custom were unreasonable or contrary to public policy (though strictly speaking, that was not pleaded in the lower courts). It would certainly have been necessary to consider the legal effect of the vesting of the Choudhari Tank in the Municipality, and the question whether in any case the appellants could be granted any relief in this suit in which the legal owner is not a party. But as it is not necessary to decide these questions in the view we take of the case, and as they have not been very fully or effectively argued, we prefer to express no opinion.

Appeal dismissed with costs.

The Seal of the High Court at Bombay.

By order of the Court
Sd/-
R.S. Bavdekar Registrar

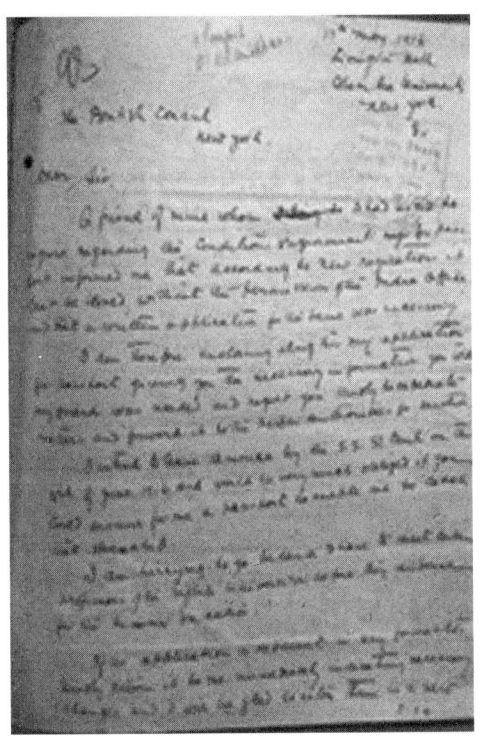

Ambedkar's 1916 letter requesting travel documents for his voyage from New York to London

Sir,

As the sources and materials for the completion of my thesis are to be found only in the British Museum and other libraries in England the Baroda State has permitted me, at its expense, to stay in London for one year and complete my research. Hence the application for passport. I intend to leave Bombay about the 1st of June 1916 and hope you will kindly arrange to issue me a passport at your earliest convenience.

Thanking you in anticipation I am

Yours faithfully,

B. R. Ambedkar

contd

application

Thanking you very much dear

Yours faithfully

B. R. Ambedkar

P.S. If you think that it will take some time to get the reply you may ask for a cable reply and charge it to me.

contd

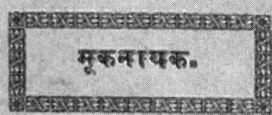

Mooknayak (Leader of the Voiceless), the inaugural issue of 31 January 1920, with the quatrain of Tukaram along the masthead

TELEPHONE: 01-836 8484 EXT. 115
TELEGRAMS: HICOMIND, LONDON, W.C.2.

भारत का हाइ कमीशन
लन्दन
THE HIGH COMMISSION OF INDIA,
LIBRARY
INDIA HOUSE,
ALDWYCH,
LONDON, W.C.2.

OUR REFERENCE: LIBY/052/79 LSE

9th April, 1979

Dear Sir,

    We have received an enquiry from India addressed to our High Commissioner, who has asked me to find out the answer, if this is possible:-

    The date on which London University conferred the degree of D.Sc. on Dr. B.R. Ambedkar. We know that the thesis was entitled 'The Problem of the Rupee' and that the degree was finally granted in June 1923. There was much controversy about this particular thesis as it was revolutionary in character for that period of time, and Dr. Ambedkar was asked to write some of the work again, although I believe that in the end it was submitted as originally prepared. Dr. Ambedkar was at the London School of Economics.

    If the exact date could be given we would be most grateful.

Yours faithfully,

N. Travis (Mrs)
Librarian

The Administrative Officer,
London School of Economics & Political Science,
Houghton Street,
Aldwych, W.C.2.

In 1979 the government of India attempted to discover whether and why Ambedkar's doctoral thesis had at first been rejected by LSE

P. S. KING & SON, LTD,
PUBLISHERS.

DIRECTORS:—
A. W. WATERLOW KING, J.R.
HORACE H. KING, M.A.
WALTER REES.
ROLLA H. SIMPER.

TELEGRAMS;
PARLIAMENTARY, LONDON.
TELEPHONE;
VICTORIA 4324.

ORCHARD HOUSE,
2 & 4, GREAT SMITH STREET,
WESTMINSTER, S.W.1.

5th. June, 1924.

Prof. E. R. A. Seligman,
Columbia University,
New York, U.S.A.

Dear Sir,

It is some time since we had the pleasure of corresponding with you, and we write to you now in regard to a typescript which has been submitted to us by B. R. Ambedkar, M.Sc. You may remember that we published his book, "The Problem of the Rupee" with a Prefatory Note by Edwin Cannan, Professor of Political Economy in the University of London.

Mr. Ambedkar writes us now from India that he has ready for publication another typescript covering the subject of the distribution of ~~references~~ between the Central and Provincial Governments in India, and he informs us that you are writing a Preface to it.

We have not yet seen the typescript, but we think we shall be inclined to publish it, for we have an appreciation of the Author's work, and if you were writing a Preface as the Author suggests it would be sufficient guarantee for us that the typescript was worth printing.

Next time you are in England we hope you will find an opportunity of calling on us here or letting us know your address for our Mr. King would very much like to have the pleasure of meeting you again.

Yours faithfully,

A. W. Waterlow King

A 1924 letter from Ambedkar's publisher, PS King & Son in Westminster, to his Columbia University supervisor, Professor Edwin Seligman

TABLE OF CONTENTS.

Introduction.
    Definition and Outline of the Subject.

Part I.
    Provincial Budget - its origin.
    Chapter 1.
        The Imperial System and its Breakdown.
    Chapter 2.
        Imperialism v. Federalism.
    Chapter 3.
        The Compromise. - Imperial Finance without Imperial management.

Part II.
    Provincial Budget - its development.
    Chapter 1.
        Budget by Assignments.
    Chapter 2.
        Budget by Assigned Revenues.
    Chapter 3.
        Budget by Shared Revenues.

Part III.
    Provincial Budget. Its Mechanism.
    Chapter 1.
        The limitations of Provincial Finance.
    Chapter 2.
        The nature of Provincial Finance.

This is the full table of contents for Ambedkar's LSE master's thesis, long believed missing but recently found in the Senate House Library, London. It is titled 'Provincial Decentralization of Imperial Finance in British India', and ultimately formed the first half of his Columbia University doctoral dissertation, similarly titled 'The Evolution of Provincial Finance in British India'

महाड सत्याग्रहास जाणाऱ्या लोकांस

जाहीर खबर.

ता. २५-१२-२७ पासून महाड येथें सुरू होणाऱ्या सत्याग्रहास जाणाऱ्या मंडळींस विनंतिपूर्वक कळविण्यांत येतें कीं, त्यांनीं आपल्या-बरोबर ताट, तांब्या, कांबळी व तीन दिवस पुरेल इतकी भोजनाची सामुग्री जरूर आणावी. आम्ही तेथें भोजनाची व्यवस्था करणार आहोंत तरीपण प्रत्येकानें आपापली तयारी ठेवावी. डॉ. आंबेडकर व इतर सत्याग्रह कमिटीचे लोक मुंबईहून ता. २४-१२-२७ रोजीं आग-बोटीनें निघणार आहेत. तर ज्यांना त्यांच्याबरोबर येणें असेल त्यांनीं ता. १५-१२-२७ पूर्वी आपल्या जाण्यायेण्याच्या खर्चांकरितां ५ रुपये बहिष्कृत हितकारिणी सभेच्या ऑफिसांत आणून दिल्यास त्यांच्या-करितां स्वतंत्र बोटीची व्यवस्था करण्यांत येणार आहे. तरी ही सोय ज्यांना पसंत असेल त्यांनीं ताबडतोब आपलीं नांवें बहिष्कृत हितकारिणी सभेच्या ऑफिसांत नोंदवावीं व सेक्रेटरीकडे ५ रुपये देऊन पावती घ्यावी. व ज्यांना कमिटीच्या मंडळींबरोबर यावयाचें नसेल त्यांनीं दासगांवला उतरण्याची खबरदारी घ्यावी.

महाड येथें सत्याग्रहाच्यावेळीं अलोट गर्दी होणार आहे. म्हणून त्यावेळीं गर्दीमध्यें आपला मनुष्य अचुक ओळखता यावा या करितां सत्याग्रहांत भाग घेणाऱ्या स्वयंसेवकानें बहिष्कृत हितकारिणी सभेच्या नांवाचें पदक छातीवर लाविलें पाहिजे. ज्यांच्या छातीवर सभेच्या नांवाचें पदक नसेल त्यांच्या संरक्षणाची किंवा इतर कसल्याही प्रकारची जबाबदारी सत्याग्रह कमिटी आपल्यावर घेणार नाहीं. सद-रहू पदकाची किंमत फक्त दोन आणे ठेवण्यांत आली आहे. व तें बहिष्कृत हितकारिणी सभेच्या ऑफिसांत विकत मिळेल.

आपला,
सिताराम नामदेव शिवतरकर,
सेक्रेटरी सत्याग्रह कमिटी.

A public notice regarding the Mahad Satyagraha by S.N. Shivtarkar, in his capacity as secretary of the Satyagraha Committee. (A full translation appears on the following page.)

PUBLIC NOTICE

Those who are going for the Satyagraha at Mahad, starting on 25 December 1927 are earnestly requested that they should bring a plate, a tumbler, a blanket and food for three days along with them. We are going to make arrangements for meals there. But still everyone must be prepared for himself. Dr Ambedkar and other members of the Satyagraha committee will leave Mumbai on 24 December by a boat. Those who wish to come with them, must deposit Rs 5/- towards transport expenses in the office of the Bahishkrut Hitkarini Sabha before 15 December 1927 so that a separate boat could be arranged for them. Those who like this arrangement should immediately register their names in the office of the Bahishkrut Hitkarini Sabha and pay Rs 5 to the secretary and obtain a receipt. Those who do not want to travel with the committee members should ensure they alight at Dasgaon.

There is going to be a huge crowd at Mahad during the Satyagraha. Therefore, in order to recognize our people in the crowd, all participants in the Satyagraha should wear the badge of Bahishkrut Hitkarini Sabha on their chest. The committee will not take responsibility for the security or any other thing of those who do not bear the badge. This badge is priced nominally at just 2 annas and shall be available in the office of the Bahishkrut Hitkarini Sabha.

Yours sincerely,
Sitaram Namdev Shivtarkar
Secretary, Satyagraha Committee

Notes

Preface

1. Savita Ambedkar's autobiography is a striking exception, offering an intimate portrayal of Ambedkar—indeed, which is rather too graphic when it comes to describing his medical problems. But that book, strictly speaking, is the autobiography of Savita Ambedkar and not a biography of Dr Ambedkar, despite the fact that the recent English translation is titled *Babasaheb* (Penguin, 2022). The Marathi original is *Dr. Ambedkaranchya Sahwasat*, or *In Companionship with Dr. Ambedkar*.
2. Shashi Tharoor, *Ambedkar: A Life* (Delhi: Aleph, 2022), p. iv, italics added.
3. Savita Ambedkar in *Babasaheb: My Life with Dr Ambedkar*, p. 17.
4. Hagiography also taints Savita Ambedkar's autobiography; indeed, the passage cited here continues thus: 'Whoever saw him for the first time would immediately understand why foreigners referred to him as a German prince. His awesome personality combined with his enormous scholarship left an indelible impression upon the observer' (*Babasaheb: My Life with Dr Ambedkar*, p. 18). The second line about the 'indelible impression' can be corroborated through a great number of sources—his personality and scholarship did usually tend to make an impression. But the first line about foreigners referring to him as a German prince … well, let's just cite one foreigner's assessment—that of his thesis supervisor in London, who liked Ambedkar a great deal: '[H]is character is rather Scotch-American, though in appearance he is a fat Indian'

(Available in the archives of the London School of Economics as 'Ambedkar's Student File', accessible at: https://www.lse.ac.uk/library/assets/documents/Ambedkars-LSE-student-file.pdf.).

5   Arun Shourie, *Worshipping False Gods* (Delhi: HarperCollins India, 2000).
6   Changdev Bhavanrao Khairmoday, *Dr Bhimrao Ramji Ambedkar Charitra* (in twelve volumes) (Bombay: Dr Ambedkar Education Society, 1966–1987). The late Aniket Jaaware had long been in the process of translating the complete set. After his death, it appears that many of his talented former students have taken up the task, under the guidance of his widow, Urmila Bhirdikar, a well-known and accomplished translator.
7   You will more often see the spelling 'Khairmode', but that is actually a misspelling. For the stationery that he himself used for correspondence always had embossed upon it the spelling 'Khairmoday'. As a general hermeneutical guide, then, we can know which later biographer actually fact-checked Khairmoday's own Ambedkar biography by observing how they spelt his name. If they spelt it how he spelt it in his own internal documents, Khairmoday, then they must have scrutinized his sources. However, if they spelt it as it is popularly misspelt, Khairmode, then we may infer that they did no fact-checking, meaning that Khairmoday's errors will reappear in biographies that rely upon him as their source.
8   Dhananjay Keer, *Dr Ambedkar: Life & Mission* (Bombay: Popular Prakashan, 1954).
9   In my own earlier writings, I had myself relied upon these standard biographies. This is now a cause of regret, as I have discovered inaccurate claims that I had previously made as a consequence. The embarrassment of this is at least compensated by being able to correct those—and so many other—errors throughout the two volumes of this biography.
10 Sharmila Rege writes, 'We know from the twelve-volume Marathi biography of Ambedkar written by C.B. Khairmode that Ambedkar intended to write an autobiography in English and also a biography of Gandhi. [T]hree notebooks marked for three parts of the proposed autobiography were found in Ambedkar's study after his death.' Sharmila Rege and B.R. Ambedkar, *Against the Madness of Manu: B.R. Ambedkar's Writings on Brahmanical Patriarchy* (Delhi: Navayana, 2013). Nanak Chand Rattu corroborates this, stating that he himself persuaded Ambedkar to dictate his life story to him as he typed it out. Rattu was Khairmoday's source for the claim that Rege relied upon. As for the autobiography of Ambedkar, all we have of it today are portions of *Waiting for a Visa* and his unpublished autobiographical preface for *The Buddha and His Dhamma*, published in Aakash Singh Rathore and Ajay Verma, *B.R. Ambedkar: The Buddha and His Dhamma: A Critical Edition* (Delhi: Oxford University Press, 2011).

11 'Ambedkar's Student File', from LSE archives, accessible at: https://www.lse.ac.uk/library/assets/documents/Ambedkars-LSE-student-file.pdf
12 One finds this in both official and unofficial Columbia sources. For example, in the Columbia University Library's Notable Columbians archive—just to mention one minor error—we find sentences like, '[I]n 1950 he resigned from his position as the country's first minister of law when Nehru's cabinet refused to pass the Women's Rights Bill.' It was, of course, in 1951, and over the Hindu Code Bill. See: https://guides.library.columbia.edu/uarchives/notables. And unofficially, there is Prof. Emerita Frances W. Pritchett's widely-viewed website, absolutely packed with Keer's erroneous claims, though it is otherwise very useful. More recently Anupama Rao, from Columbia University's Barnard College, has undertaken the task of organizing the archives, clearing the way for correcting old errors and hopefully also making new discoveries. As for the obvious and important question as to why the faculty members from prestigious universities like LSE and Columbia had so long neglected to double-check these 'authoritative' sources or conduct original research to verify the many specious claims made about their much-celebrated alumnus, that is a far more complicated and sensitive question—possibly related to their social location or caste privilege, or to the academic politics of appropriation. But we will have to forego all of that here, as it falls much beyond the scope of Ambedkar's own life. But see, for example: Aakash Singh Rathore, 'Seen Through Different Glasses: A controversial introduction to Annihilation of Caste reappears as a book. It reflects the elite Left's opportunistic appropriation of Ambedkar', *Outlook*, 14 June 2019, available at: https://www.outlookindia.com/magazine/story/books-seen-through-different-glasses/301791; as also, the editors' introduction in Aakash Singh Rathore and Ajay Verma (eds), *B.R. Ambedkar: The Buddha and His Dhamma: A Critical Edition*, where the thorny issue of the appropriation of Ambedkar is discussed.
13 Dhananjay Keer, *Dr Ambedkar: Life & Mission*, p. 107.
14 From *Prabuddha Bharat*, Year 1, Issue 15, 2 June 1956, cited (with a slightly altered translation) by Savita Ambedkar in *Babasaheb: My Life with Dr Ambedkar*, p. 231.
15 Vaibhav Purandare, *Savarkar: The True Story of the Father of Hindutva* (Delhi: Juggernaut Books, 2019), pp. xvii–xviii, and p. 210.
16 See the original letter from Ambedkar to Savarkar, dated 18 February 1933, included here. Keer claims that Ambedkar wrote: 'If the untouchables are to be part and parcel of Hindu society, then it is not enough to remove untouchability; for that matter you must destroy chaturvarnya. I am glad that you are one of the very few who have realized this.' Vaibhav Purandare, *Savarkar: The True Story of the Father of Hindutva* (Delhi: Juggernaut Books,

2019), p. 210. Ambedkar's words are, effectively, the exact opposite of what Keer and thus Purandare have misrepresented him as saying.

17 According to Savita Ambedkar, one of these three occasions was the day after Ambedkar had suffered a heart attack: 'While we were still at Mirabel Hotel, the celebrated biographer Dhananjay Keer came over, tracking Saheb down. Doctor Saheb's nasal tubes had just been removed and he was lying on the bed. Keer was in the process of writing Doctor Saheb's biography ... After making inquiries about his health, Keer began talking about the biography ... Saheb began talking animatedly, which got me worried. I signaled to Keer to wind up the conversation, to which he complied.' *Babasaheb: My Life with Dr Ambedkar*, p. 194–95.

18 Nanak Chand Rattu, *Reminiscences and Remembrances of Dr B.R. Ambedkar* (Delhi: Samyak Prakashan, 1995), p. viii.

19 Changdev Bhavanrao Khairmoday, *Dr Bhimrao Ramji Ambedkar Charitra*, Vol. 2 (Bombay: Dr Ambedkar Education Society, 1968), p. 81.

20 Including Savita Ambedkar's autobiography, which contains common errors of dating and of fact. For example, in the opening pages, she writes: 'Within a short span of six years he acquired an M.A., Ph.D., D.Sc., LL.D, DLitt, Bar-at-Law and a host of other degrees.' Leaving aside the honorary degrees (LLD and DLitt) that came much later in the 1950s, even the MA, PhD, DSc and Bar-at-Law were not acquired in a span of six years, but rather in fourteen years. Ambedkar had, however, acquired an MA and an MSc, degrees she entirely neglects to mention, within a period of eight years.

21 Ashok Gopal's new biography of Ambedkar, *A Part Apart: The Life and Thought of Babasaheb Ambedkar* (Delhi: Navayana, 2023), is a fresh biography with new research, and thus very welcome. It differs from this one, however, in several important respects. For example, as its subtitle indicates (*The Life and Thought of Babasaheb Ambedkar*), it is half intellectual biography, offering an interpretation of Babasaheb's voluminous writings, an endeavour that does not occupy me in this book. This is because so many other intellectual biographies already exist and shall continue to appear now that Ambedkar studies has become a full-blown academic enterprise. Another divergence indicated by Gopal's title, *A Part Apart*, is that it presents Ambedkar polemically, focusing upon setting him apart, in the common vein of identity politics. In my view, however, Ambedkar's tribulations and triumphs also carry universal significance. He was every inch a Dalit, and his greatness emerged in and through being this so self-consciously. This identity was undoubtedly a constraint, but it should not be used as a means of reduction. Ambedkar made himself into, and he fully remains, a world-historical figure from whom any and every person can and should learn, and could emulate, as we each—irrespective of caste, creed and country—strive to grow into better versions of ourselves. My biography focuses more on personality and less on polemics. Finally, moving from

title to content, Gopal's biography is also largely reliant upon Khairmoday's biography (suspiciously cited with the spelling 'Khairmode'), and seems to repeat a great many of its unsupported claims, mistaken dates and the like.
22 A 15 March 1948 letter from Ambedkar to Sharada Kabir, cited in Savita Ambedkar, *Babasaheb: My Life with Dr Ambedkar*, pp. 74–75.

Chapter One: From Bhiva Ambadawekar to Bhimrao Ambedkar (1891–1912)

1 Nanak Chand Rattu, *Reminiscences and Remembrances of Dr B.R. Ambedkar* (Delhi: Samyak Prakashan, 1995), p. 55.
2 Nanak Chand Rattu, *Reminiscences and Remembrances of Dr B.R. Ambedkar*, p. 73. The reader might ask: Why did Ambedkar prefer the 15th over the 14th for their wedding day? The practical reason was that there would be countless visitors on the 14th, thus interrupting the simple ceremony that they had planned. But the more interesting reason was that in 1948, 15 April was a Thursday, and Ambedkar regarded Thursdays as auspicious: 'I fixed 15th because it is a Thursday and Thursday for me is a very *shubh din* … I prefer Thursday, which my experience shows to be my *shubh din*.' Coincidentally, 6 December 1956, the day Dr Ambedkar died, was also a Thursday. Cited in Savita Ambedkar, *Babasaheb: My Life with Dr Ambedkar*, pp. 80, 84–85.
3 Compare Dhananjay Keer, *Dr Ambedkar* (pp. 459–60) with Savita Ambedkar, *Babasaheb* (pp. 211–12), which have conflicting interpretations of these dates—perhaps because of what Ambedkar had told Savita Ambedkar about his birth year in the letter.
4 The original evidence seems to indicate that Ambedkar actually had only four siblings, with these latter two sisters also having died at childbirth or very young. Chandra Bharill (*Social and Political Ideas of B.R. Ambedkar*, [Jaipur: Aalekh Publishers, 1977], p. 3) also claims that nine of the fourteen children had died, and that Ambedkar had only two brothers and two sisters.
5 The Tamil researcher Yaakkan, however, argues that Ramji in fact occasionally used the name 'Ambedkar' himself. Yaakkan, *Ambedkar enra payer oru parpanarudaytha? Kazhavapadum payer azhukku* (Tamil, untranslated. *Does the Name 'Ambedkar' Belong to a Brahman? Washing Away the Stain of the Name*) (Chennai: Kalagam Press, 2018).
6 Ambedkar's biographer Khairmoday has stated that Dr Ambedkar told him most of these details himself, and other details appeared in the newspaper *Navyug* on 13 April 1947. See Khairmoday, *Dr Bhimrao Ramji Ambedkar Charitra*, Vol. I, pp. 49, 52–53, where he writes:
[Ambedkar:] We had a Brahman master by the name 'Ambedkar'. He would not teach us much. But he loved me a lot. During our lunch break, to eat, I used to have to go to my house which was far away from school. This, Ambedkar Master did not

like. But just for that time, because I would be free to roam around outside, I used to have a lot of fun going home during lunch break to get some bread. But our master came up with an idea. He would pack and bring some bread and vegetables, and every day, without fail, during lunch break, he would call me and give me some bread and vegetables from his own assorted meal. Of course, so that there would be no physical contact, he would drop the bread and vegetables into my hands from above. I feel proud when I say that the sweetness of that bread and vegetables given out of love is unfading ...

When in Camp School Satara, Bhiva did not have the slightest clue about what it meant to study. Whatever was taught in school, that is all he would study ... On this, Ambedkar recalled:

Our Ambedkar Master was something else. When the school bell would ring, he would come to class, and would hand over the entire class to one older boy named Rahimtulla, and would carelessly just leave. Ambedkar Sir would not teach much in school. That is why students would not have much homework ...

Babasaheb did not complain that Ambedkar Sir did not impart proper discipline to study at the right age. On the contrary, this teacher would treat him with great care and affection, as I have already mentioned. Ambedkar Master was his first teacher. About him, Ambedkar said words of great respect. He said, 'When I left to go abroad for the Round-Table Conference, at that time he had sent me a very loving letter. I still have it in my possession. In the future, if it ever comes to mind to write an autobiography, I will publish it in that.' (*Navyug*, 13 April 1947)

This teacher had come to meet Babasaheb in 1927. At the time, Babasaheb's office was on the ground floor of a school building behind Damodar Hall. As soon as the teacher entered the office, Babasaheb immediately got up and stood, and in an emotionally moved tone uttered the word 'Master' and bent down in veneration. Wiping his eyes, the teacher said to his eminent student, 'May you live forever, son,' giving him this blessing. I witnessed this incident with my own eyes. Looking closely at Babasaheb's great library, Master was nodding. Babasaheb got a suit of clothes made for Ambedkar Master, and gave him 25 paise as *gurudakshina*.

7   Mhow is now called Dr Ambedkar Nagar and is located in Madhya Pradesh.
8   Diwan Chand Ahir, *The Legacy of Dr Ambedkar* (Delhi: BR Publishing Corporation, 1990), p. 173.
9   There is no corroboration for this from the early years, but I have included it because, interestingly, Ambedkar's love for planting saplings, and of botany and horticulture more generally, has been attested to by several people in his later years. Namdeo Nimgade, in his autobiography *In the Tiger's Shadow: The Autobiography of an Ambedkarite* (Delhi: Navayana, 2011), has recounted Dr Ambedkar's careful cultivation of his garden at his Delhi bungalow, as well as his frequent visits to the Agricultural Research Institute to walk through

the gardens and collect plant specimens. Savita Ambedkar has also mentioned her husband's planting of saplings throughout the Milind College campus: 'He would always be occupied in beautifying the Nagasena Vana premises in Milind College. He had mandated that whoever came visiting would plant a tree. He had got hundreds of saplings of various kinds planted under his own supervision.' *Babasaheb: My Life with Dr Ambedkar*, p. 126.

10 B.R. Ambedkar, *Waiting for a Visa*, in: *Dr. Babasaheb Ambedkar Writings and Speeches (BAWS)*, Vol. 12 (1993), p. 670.

11 Ambedkar's autobiographical fragments, *Waiting for a Visa*, offer other reminiscences of casteism from his early childhood and beyond. From the early childhood period now being discussed, see 'On the Way to Goregaon', the remarkably poignant first chapter of *Waiting for a Visa*.

12 Ambedkar began working with a Sanskrit tutor in 1927 with the aim of reading the *Manusmriti*, but his effort was not systematic until the early 1950s, starting while drafting the Hindu Code Bill. Savita Ambedkar has nicely captured the context out of which his structured lessons would finally arise: 'Doctor Saheb would be reading and writing ceaselessly. He worked on the Hindu Code Bill with the same intensity with which he had earlier worked on the Constitution. For this purpose, he was required to study the Smritis, the Shastras, the Vedas and the Puranas. There was the relentless reading of hundreds of books, other writings, and the making of notes ... Saheb had appointed a few Sanskrit scholars for translating the commentaries and shlokas in the religious books. The room was literally full to the brim with translations and commentaries on religious books. The Hindu Code Bill was being sculpted with Saheb sitting in conference with Hindu religious pundits, resolving doubts, holding discussions and arguments and finding ways out.' Savita Ambedkar, *Babasaheb: My Life with Dr Ambedkar*, pp. 150, 128.

13 As we learn from a letter that Ambedkar wrote to his fiancée, Sharada Kabir, on 19 February 1948, after she herself began calling him 'Raja': 'Another mysterious thing is the pet name you have given me. It was the very name by which I was called by my fellow students when I was studying in the Elphinstone High School. I am wondering what suggested it to you? You are welcome to use it.' Savita Ambedkar, *Babasaheb: My Life with Dr Ambedkar*, p. 62.

14 Richard Harris, 'Housing Policy for the Colonial City: The British and Dutch Experience Compared, 1901-1949', *Urban Geography*, 2009.

15 As Ambedkar stated decades later while moving a bill in the Bombay Legislative Council to amend the Bombay Police Act: 'If the House would allow me to say so, I am very familiar with the kind of evil to which [the Home Minister] has referred. I have spent a very great part of my life in what I may call the underworld of Bombay City. I have lived from 1911 to 1933 in the Improvement Trust chawls, among labourers and the lower classes, and I know perfectly well, more than the Commissioner of Police or

the Honourable the Home Minister, how these poor people are molested by what are called mavalis and dadas, how utterly impossible it is for these victims to obtain any redress, because they themselves, for fear of further molestation, would not go to a court of law and seek to get a conviction …' *BAWS*, Vol. 2, p. 139. Also see: Alka Dhupkar, 'Dr Babasaheb Ambedkar's home in Parel to become memorial, announces CM', *Mumbai Mirror*, 28 September 2022.

16 Hem Raj Phonsa, in the blog Dalit Vision, offers rivalling details about Ramabai as well as about the marriage, in line with Khairmoday, but with far greater specificity: 'She was the second daughter of Bhiku Walangkar, a resident of Walang village near Dapoli in Konkan … He worked as a porter at Dapoli. He used to carry fish loads on his head from the seaside to the bazaar. His earnings were so meager that he could hardly make both ends meet. Ramabhai was born on 7th February 1898. Her childhood name was Ramibhai and she had two sisters, Gorabhai and Meerabhai, and a brother named Shanker Dhutrey, also called Shanker Walangkar, who worked in a press. These unfortunate children lost first their mother and after some time their father too in childhood, so were brought up by their uncle in Bombay …

'The marriage pandal was an open shed of the Byculla Fish market in Bombay, after the market was closed. At night the bridegroom and his relatives were lodged in one spacious corner of the open shed, with the bride and her relatives in another corner. The small stones in the market served as benches, where a small gutter of dirty water flowed underneath their feet. They vacated in the early morning before sunrise to enable the merchants to carry on with their daily business. Ramibhai was renamed Ramabhai after the marriage.' Accessible at: http://dalitvision.blogspot.com/2017/02/importance-of-february-month-for-dalit.html

17 Not Rs 50, as Jaffrelot erroneously writes. Christophe Jaffrelot, *Dr. Ambedkar and Untouchability: Analyzing and Fighting Caste* (Delhi: Permanent Black, 2005), p. 27. With respect to Ambedkar's access to the Maharajah, the Ambedkar chronicler and collector Vijay Surwade has a wonderful account of their meeting, with the most charming and minute details, in a forthcoming book, tentatively titled *Ambedkar in Baroda*.

Chapter Two: The Alma Mater (1913–16)

1 Keer is the source of this oft-repeated claim, which I have been unable to corroborate, and which is elsewhere contradicted.
2 According to Nanak Chand Rattu, on a certain occasion, Mahadev Desai, Mahatma Gandhi's personal secretary, asked Ambedkar about his childhood. During that exchange, Ambedkar told Desai that while in Baroda, he lived in the Dalit area, where military men lived (hence not in the Arya Samaj office). See *Reminiscences and Remembrances of Dr B.R. Ambedkar*, pp. 55–56.

3   B.G. Kunte, ed., *Source Material on Dr. Babasaheb Ambedkar and the Movement of Untouchables*, Volume 1 (Bombay: Education Department, Government of Maharashtra, 1982), p. 1.
4   Vijay Mankar, *Dr B.R. Ambedkar: An Intellectual Biography* (Bombay: Blue World Series, 2016), on p. 443 mistakenly calls Gangadhara the second son.
5   From the unpublished preface to *The Buddha and His Dhamma*, in: Aakash Singh Rathore and Ajay Verma, *B.R. Ambedkar: The Buddha and His Dhamma: A Critical Edition* (Delhi: Oxford University Press, 2011).
6   Cited by Eleanor Zelliot, *Ambedkar's World: The Making of Babasaheb and the Dalit Movement* (Delhi: Navayana Publishing, 2013), p. 109, from *The Indian Review* (December 1909).
7   Sanjeevani Mujumdar, *Mahamanav, Dr Babasaheb Ambedkar, Jeevan Darshan* (Pune: Symbiosis Society's Dr Babasaheb Ambedkar Museum and Memorial, ND), p. 15.
8   'Columbia's Hall of Babel', *The New York Times*, 10 July 1921, available at: http://www.columbia.edu/itc/mealac/pritchett/00ambedkar/timeline/txt_cosmopolitanclub_1921.pdf
9   Naval Bhathena's real name, his major and years of study, and the fact that he never managed to complete his degree can all be reasonably inferred from Columbia University's 1916–17 *Directory of Students*, which is available online in digital form at: https://babel.hathitrust.org/cgi/pt?id=nnc2.ark:/13960/t50g4c458&view=1up&seq=514
10 It is interesting that only one of these four professors was an economist (i.e., Seligman, who was the head of the economics faculty). *Columbia Alumni News*, 19 December 1930, p. 12.
11 For this, see especially the brilliant work by Scott R. Stroud, *The Evolution of Pragmatism in India: Ambedkar, Dewey, and the Rhetoric of Reconstruction* (Chicago: University of Chicago Press, 2023).
12 Savita Ambedkar, *Dr. Ambedkar Ke Sampark Main* (Delhi: Samyak Prakashan, 2014), p. 44.
13 Diwan Chand Ahir, *The Legacy of Dr Ambedkar* (Delhi: BR Publishing Corporation, 1990), p. 8.
14 Available at: https://blogs.lse.ac.uk/lsehistory/2016/01/29/no-more-worlds-here-for-him-to-conquer-br-ambedkar-at-lse/
15 This oft-repeated instance, with varying words used, originates from Khairmoday, *Dr Bhimrao Ramji Ambedkar Charitra*, Vol. 1, p. 71.

Chapter Three: An Indian in New York

1   As cited in Salim Yusufji, *Ambedkar: Attendant Details* (Delhi: Navayana Publishing, 2017), p. 50.

2 Accessible at: https://timtsengdotnet.files.wordpress.com/2013/12/mabel-lee-the-meaning-of-woman-suffrage-1914.pdf

3 Kelly Moffitt and Jennifer Pellerito, '12 Groundbreaking Asian Columbians You Should Know', *Columbia News*, 7 May 2021, accessible at: https://news.columbia.edu/news/12-groundbreaking-asian-columbians-you-should-know

4 This does not mean to suggest that Ambedkar did not assiduously continue to acquire books on socialism—he did indeed. Dozens of heavily marked-up books can be found in his personal library covering the history of socialism, socialist ethics and politics, socialist labour movements and so on. V. Geetha has listed over a dozen that Ambedkar studied closely in the late 1940s alone. They include: Howard Selsam, *Socialism and Ethics*, 1943; Francis Williams, *The Triple Challenge: The Future of Socialist Britain*, 1948; Norman MacKenzie, *Socialism: A Short History*, 1949; William Dale Morris, *The Christian Origins of Social Revolt*, 1949; Jack Lindsay, *Marxism and Contemporary Science*, 1949; and numerous others. See: https://thewire.in/caste/unpacking-library-babasaheb-ambedkar-world-books

5 In 1924, while recommending a new programme structure for Bombay University, Ambedkar submitted the following:

> The duration of studies for post-graduate degrees should be four years (I am speaking only for social sciences). There should be two stages of two years each. At the end of the first stage the candidate should be entitled to the M.A. degree. He should specialize in one subject only which should be the subject of his major interest. The test should consist of a written examination accompanied by an essay of some 75 typewritten pages showing his familiarity with the art of using original sources and commenting upon them. At the end of the second stage the candidate should be entitled to the Ph.D. degree. There the test would include an oral examination and a thesis of a respectable size fit for publication. The thesis will embody the investigations of the candidate in a particular field lying within the scope of the subject he had taken at the M.A. as being of major interest to him. Besides this the candidate will present himself for an oral examination in two subjects to be known as subjects of minor interest which will be allied to the subjects of his major interest. This arrangement will allow specialization with a broad base.

This is nearly identical to his programme at Columbia University. Ambedkar went through the initial stage of two years, specializing in economics, sitting a written exam at the end and submitting a seventy-five-page research paper submission ('Ancient Indian Commerce'), and his later MA thesis ('Administration and Finance of the East India Company'), thus entitling him to the MA degree. Two 'subjects of minor interest' (sociology and history) were added to the major.

6 B.R. Ambedkar, *BAWS*, Vol. 12, p. 3, where Ambedkar cites extensively from Franz Cumont's *Oriental Religions in Roman Paganism*.
7 B.R. Ambedkar, *BAWS*, 12: 53.
8 B.R. Ambedkar, *BAWS*, 12: 72.
9 B.R. Ambedkar, B.R. Ambedkar, *BAWS*, 12: 56.
10 B.R. Ambedkar, *BAWS*, 6: 48.
11 Gail Omvedt (*Ambedkar: Towards an Enlightened India* [Delhi: Penguin, 2004], p. 8) writes: '[Ambedkar] was awarded his M.A. in 1915 and submitted his dissertation for his Ph.D. in 1916.' Vijay Mankar (*Dr B.R. Ambedkar: An Intellectual Biography* [Mumbai: Blue World Series, 2016], p. 6) writes: '*The National Dividend of India – A Historical and Analytical Study* earned him the Ph.D. in 1916, but conferred on 8.6.1927 as per rules of publication.' At the Dr Babasaheb Ambedkar Museum and Memorial in Pune one finds a display reading: 'Later [Ambedkar] presented the thesis *The National Dividend of India—A Historical and Analytical Study* to the same University for the degree of Ph.D. (1916).' Janak Singh (*Dr. B.R. Ambedkar: The Messiah of the Downtrodden* [Delhi: Kalpaz Books, 2010], p. 51) writes: 'Ambedkar's thesis, *The National Dividend of India—A Historical and Analytical Study*, for which he was awarded a Ph.D. degree by Columbia University, New York, in 1917 ....and continues: 'In his earlier M.A. dissertation "Ancient Indian Commerce".' Shashi Tharoor (*Ambedkar: A Life* [Delhi: Aleph, 2022], p. 12) also writes that Ambedkar's MA thesis was 'Commerce in Ancient India' and that his PhD was awarded in 1916 for 'The National Dividend'. This kind of confusion is ubiquitous. Some biographies claim that Ambedkar earned two MAs at Columbia in addition to the PhD, again, prior to leaving New York. All of these errors seem to originate in both Keer, for English readers, and Khairmoday, for Marathi readers, who both write incorrectly about the titles of Ambedkar's theses, the degrees earned and the dates.
12 Despite all of the confusion regarding 'The National Dividend of India' (see the previous note), we know that this was the tentative original title for Ambedkar's Columbia University doctoral dissertation because this is what he himself indicated in his December 1917 application for a professorship at Sydenham College, Bombay.
13 Jesús Francisco Cháirez-Garza, 'B.R. Ambedkar, Franz Boas and the Rejection of Racial Theories of Untouchability', *South Asia: Journal of South Asian Studies*, 41:2, 2018, pp. 281–96.
14 B.R. Ambedkar, *Annihilation of Caste*, preface to the third edition (Bombay: Government of Maharashtra Education Department, 1944).

Chapter Four: London Calling (1916–17)

1 There is a great deal of confusion in the literature about the duration of the scholarship that Ambedkar had received, as well as the period of its extension.

For example, William Gould (in *Ambedkar in London*) writes that Ambedkar's scholarship 'ran from June 1914 to June 1917 (following an extension of one year)', p. 16. But this cannot be correct, since Ambedkar had reached New York a year before this, in July 1913 (as Gould himself acknowledges on the following page, without noticing the discrepancy). Gould seems to be relying upon the exhibition at the Dr Babasaheb Ambedkar Museum and Memorial in Pune, replicated at the Ambedkar House Museum, London, which displays contradictory information on this subject. Other biographers, such as Eleanor Zelliot, relying on Khairmoday, state that the initial grant was for three years and that Ambedkar received a one-year extension, which he used for London. The records are themselves confusing: the extant 5 April 1913 Hujur Order puts the initial length of the scholarship at 'two years'; in Ambedkar's 1916 passport application, also extant, he states that he had received 'an extension of one year' for studying in London. Thus, there is one full year of scholarship that is unaccounted for. I am able to set this record straight. Ambedkar received an initial scholarship of two years. He then received a one-year extension. And then he received, once again, a one-year extension. It is with this second extension that he was able to study in London. Interestingly, the Baroda state archival records also show that Ambedkar requested, and received, an increase in the amount of his scholarship at the time of the second extension, given that London was more expensive than New York. All of these details will come out in Vijay Surwade's forthcoming book tentatively titled *Ambedkar in Baroda*. However, earlier biographers do not seem to have been much bothered by this mystery. Gail Omvedt fancifully writes: '[Ambedkar's] Baroda scholarship had expired and when the Diwan refused an extension of two years, he appealed to the maharaja himself. Without waiting for a reply, he left for London, landing without any money in his pocket, travelling ticketless on the train and convincing the people with whom he was to stay to pay for the carriage that brought his luggage. Two days later a letter arrived awarding him a one-year extension.' (pp. 8–9). As we shall soon see, Ambedkar's arrival in the UK could not have played out precisely like this.

2 Khairmoday, *Dr Bhimrao Ramji Ambedkar Charitra*, Vol. 1, p. 80.
3 Nehru Memorial Museum and Library, Ambedkar Papers: Reel 2.
4 India Office Records file, 'Journey to England from the USA of British subject Bhimrao, alias Brimvran Ambedkar', 1916, shelfmark IOR/L/PJ/6/1443, File 2349.
5 India Office Records, File 2349.
6 Ibid.
7 These biographers are relying on Keer, p. 31.
8 India Office Records, File 2349.
9 Ibid.

10 The Open University's blog, 'Making Britain: Discover how South Asians shaped the nation, 1870-1950', entry on 21 Cromwell Road, available at: https://www.open.ac.uk/researchprojects/makingbritain/content/21-cromwell-road

11 The NIA had been thoroughly infiltrated with British spies, and the caretaker of the NIA housing at Cromwell Road, a woman named Ms Beck, was widely believed to be the handler for the Indian informants. The spying was so extreme that even the academic papers of Indian students were secretly vetted by the Bureau of Information. By 1914, several Indian student groups were fed up, collectively calling 'for the total and immediate abolition of the Department as injurious to their interests' (Shompa Lahiri, *Indians in Britain: Anglo-Indian Encounters, Race and Identity*, 1880-1930 [London: Frank Cass Publishers, 2000], p. 171). Ambedkar remained at 21 Cromwell Road for only about two weeks.

12 Nehru Memorial Museum and Library, Ambedkar Papers: Reel 2. C.S. MacTaggart to Percy Anstey, 14 May 1918, cited by Jayasankar Krishnamurty, 'Ambedkar's Educational Odyssey, 1913–1927', *Journal of Social Inclusion Studies*, 5(2), February 2020, available at: https://www.researchgate.net/publication/339148161_Ambedkar's_Educational_Odyssey_1913-1927

13 The University of London's 18 December 1916 Senate Resolution regarding Ambedkar's exemption from the BSc examination reads: '[T]hat Bhivram Ramji Ambedkar be registered as an internal student as from October 1916 and admitted as a candidate for the M.Sc. (Econ.) degree.' LSE archives, 'Ambedkar's Student File', accessible at: https://www.lse.ac.uk/library/assets/documents/Ambedkars-LSE-student-file.pdf

14 It is also further evidence, as against the many biographers who mistakenly claim that Ambedkar had received his Columbia University PhD before leaving New York (Janak Singh, K.N. Kadam, etc.), that he clearly had not.

15 Michael Cox, 'Goldsworthy Lowes Dickinson, LSE and the origins of International Relations', the LSE blog: available at: https://blogs.lse.ac.uk/lsehistory/2018/12/12/goldsworthy-lowes-dickinson-lse-and-the-origins-of-international-relations/

16 We can hope that it is due to this temporary merging of locations that the Indian government's own Ministry of Law and Justice, which, of course, Dr Ambedkar had led as the first law minister, incorrectly states in its short biography of Ambedkar that he had taken his law degree from Lincoln's Inn. More likely, however, it is just apathy. See: https://doj.gov.in/page/about-dr-b-r-ambedkar

17 See Scott R. Stroud, 'What Did Bhimrao Ambedkar Learn from John Dewey's *Democracy and Education?*', *The Pluralist*, Vol. 12, No. 2, 2017, pp. 78–103.

18 Published in London by George Allen and Unwin Ltd, 1916, and reprinted in 1917.

19 Vijay Mankar, for example, and K.N. Kadam, in *Dr. Babasaheb Ambedkar and the Significance of His Movement: A Chronology* (Bombay: Popular Prakashan, 1991). Keer, however, does not make this claim.
20 Scott Stroud and Landon D.C. Elkind, 'Exploring the Influence of Russell on Ambedkar', Forward Press, 1 August 2017, available at: https://www.forwardpress.in/2017/08/exploring-the-influence-of-russell-on-ambedkar/#_edn2
21 James Lees-Milne, *The Enigmatic Edwardian: The Life of Reginald, 2nd Viscount Esher* (London: Sidgwick & Jackson, 1986), p. 146.
22 University of London Senate Resolution dated 18 July 1917, available at: https://www.lse.ac.uk/library/assets/documents/Ambedkars-LSE-student-file.pdf

Chapter Five: Sleepless in Baroda (1917–20)

1 Reuben Goossens, 'Peninsular and Oriental Steam Navigation Company: RMS Kaisar-i-Hind', ssMaritime blog, Remembering the Classic Liners of Yesteryear, available at: http://ssmaritime.com/Kaisar-I-Hind.htm
2 'The Old P&O Steam Navigation Company, circa 1835-1972', entry on 'The SS Salsette of 1908', available at: http://www.pandosnco.co.uk/salsette.html
3 Diwan Chand Ahir, *The Legacy of Dr Ambedkar* (Delhi: BR Publishing Corporation, 1990), p. 138.
4 This is Prabhakar Padhye's version of the event (from his book *Prakaashaan'tilla Vyakti*, p. 51), which differs from that of Keer and others.
5 Bhadant Ananda Kausalayayan Mahathera (in *Had There Been No Ambedkar*, p. 37) reports this amount as Rs 600, which makes sense, given that Ambedkar's own transport cost was around £100 (that is, roughly Rs 1,200 at that time). Thus, the insurance claim paid out around half of the passenger ticket price.
6 The work is widely available, including in *Dr. Babasaheb Ambedkar Writings and Speeches*, Government of Maharashtra Education Department, Vol. 12, edited by Vasant Moon (Bombay: Education Department, Government of Maharashtra, 1993), Part I, pp. 661–91.
7 See another account in Bhagwan Das, *Thus Spoke Ambedkar*, sourced from *Janata*, 23 May 1930. Keer and Khairmoday also have differing accounts.
8 K.A. Keluskar, article in *Janata* (Khas Ank), 1933, also reported in both Keer and Khairmoday.
9 Gail Omvedt, *Ambedkar: Towards an Enlightened India*, p. 10. But we must also keep in mind that Ambedkar himself, in 1921, states that he had been employed at the finance and accounts department in Baroda all the way up till March 1918. See: https://drambedkarbooks.files.wordpress.com/2015/01/ambedkar-in-germany-3.jpg

Chapter Six: Struggle, Sydenham, Southborough and Shahu Maharaj

1. This is if we understand the phrase 'keeping terms' to indicate a requirement to follow the mandated syllabus term by term, or semester by semester, and then completing the required examinations. Steven Gasztowicz KC, himself a lawyer trained at Gray's Inn, has provided a very different definition of 'keeping terms'. He argues that 'keeping terms' actually referred to minimum sessions of required dining at the Inn. Specifically, a minimum of eating at the Inn for three days during each of the twelve semesters. But if Gasztowicz were correct, then Ambedkar would never have been called to the bar in 1922, as he had been absent from the inn for numerous consecutive semesters—indeed for three full years—unable to meet the minimum dining requirements that Gasztowicz claims were mandatory. Gasztowicz writes, possibly with some inaccuracy: 'Missing one of the dinners would have meant their call to the Bar having to be deferred by a term, until the required number of "Terms" had been kept—in other words, another three dinners eaten in Hall.' This does not seem to have happened to Ambedkar. He was able to pass all of the requisite examinations once back in London, and was called to the Bar within twelve semesters of enrolling at the inn. However, my chronology assumes that there were only two, or at the most three, terms per year. If there were, in fact, four terms per year, taking a total of only three years to complete the twelve terms prerequisite to being called to the Bar, Gasztowicz would be completely correct. See 'Ambedkar as Lawyer: From London to India in the 1920s', in William Gould, Santosh Dass and Christophe Jaffrelot, eds, *Ambedkar in London* (London: Hurst and Co, 2022), pp. 68–70.
2. B.R. Ambedkar, 'Mr Russell and the Reconstruction of Society', in *BAWS*, Vol. 1 (Bombay: Government of Maharashtra, 2014), p. 486.
3. Cited in Eleanor Zelliot, *Ambedkar's World: The Making of Babasaheb and the Dalit Movement* (Delhi: Navayana Publishing, 2013), p. 71.
4. N.M. Joshi secured a small office for Ambedkar in the Hararwalla Building in Parel, which he would later regularly use for social service and trade union activities.
5. Eleanor Zelliot, *Ambedkar's World*, p. 114, citing *Evidence Taken before the Reforms Committee*, Vol. 1 (Calcutta: Government of India, 1919), pp. 278–79.
6. Eleanor Zelliot, *Ambedkar's World*, p. 114.
7. In 1899, a Brahman priest had denied the Maharajah the right to Vedic rituals, reifying his status as a Shudra, rather than a Kshatriya. This launched a decade-long public debate, known as the Vedokta controversy, which helped lay the foundations for the non-Brahman movement, bringing Mahatma Phule's work into an even wider theatre of meaning. It also served to radicalize the Maharajah himself. See Gail Omvedt, *Cultural Revolt in Colonial Society:*

The Non-Brahman Movement in Western India: 1873-1930 (Bombay: Scientific Socialist Education Trust, 1976), pp. 124–36.
8   See, for example, Keer, pp. 42–43 (followed verbatim by Shashi Tharoor in *Ambedkar: A Life*), as well as Eleanor Zelliot, *Ambedkar's World*, p. 75.
9   DNA web team, 'Babasaheb Ambedkar, Shahu Maharaj Shared Bond: Pune Researcher', DNA, 24 April 2011, accessible at: https://www.dnaindia.com/mumbai/report-babasaheb-ambedkar-shahu-maharaj-shared-bond-pune-researcher-1535567
10 Ibid.
11 Ibid.
12 Translation by Prabodhan Pol, slightly amended. See '100 Years of Mooknayak, Ambedkar's First Newspaper That Changed Dalit Politics Forever', The Wire, 31 January 2020, available at: https://thewire.in/media/mooknayak-ambedkar-newspaper

Chapter Seven: A Loud Voice for the Voiceless (1920)

1   As mentioned by Prabodhan Pol, 'The Journalistic Legacy of B.R. Ambedkar, the Editor', The Wire, 14 April 2018, available at: https://thewire.in/caste/the-journalistic-legacy-of-b-r-ambedkar-the-editor
2   Savita Ambedkar, *Babasaheb: My Life with Dr Ambedkar*, p. 67.
3   Translation of extracts partly taken from *The Hindu*, 'In a tower without a staircase: An extract from the inaugural issue of B.R Ambedkar's journal, "Mooknayak"', 1 February 2020, available at: https://www.thehindu.com/books/in-a-tower-without-a-staircase-an-extract-from-the-inaugural-issue-of-br-ambedkars-journal-mooknayak/article30700662.ece, and partly taken from the website Round Table India, 'B.R. Ambedkar: From the pages of Mook Nayak', available at: https://www.roundtableindia.co.in/from-the-pages-of-mook-nayak/
4   Contrary to what is stated in the biographies of Khairmoday, Eleanor Zelliot, Christophe Jaffrelot, Gail Omvedt and Shashi Tharoor, who all erroneously claim that Shahu Maharaj funded Ambedkar's trip to London.
5   A.B. Latthe (ed.), *The Memoirs of His Highness Shri Shahu Chhatrapati Maharaja of Kolhapur* (Bombay: The Times Press, 1924).
6   Cited in Surendra Ajnat, *Letters of Ambedkar* (Jalandhar: Bheem Patrika Publications, 1993), p. 22. This letter is also partially cited by Christophe Jaffrelot, *Dr. Ambedkar and Untouchability: Analyzing and Fighting Caste* (Delhi: Permanent Black, 2005), p. 29, from the source material at the Nehru Memorial Museum and Library. However, Jaffrelot mistakenly believes that Shahu Maharaj is writing not to Sir Alfred Pease but to a professor at the London School of Economics. Shashi Tharoor, relying on Jaffrelot, makes the same mistake in *Ambedkar: A Life* (Aleph, 2022, p. 21).

7 The letters exchanged between Ambedkar and Shahu Maharaj testify not only to their fondness for each other but also to the fact that Ambedkar was executing the task in London that Shahu had hoped he would. For example, in a letter dated 3 February 1921, Ambedkar recounted his recent meeting with Edwin Montagu, the secretary of state for India. He noted: 'I take every opportunity possible to put every important English man I meet into a right frame of mind regarding the inter-relations of social and political problems in India.' The letter is available at: https://www.thebeacon.in/2018/12/30/potrait-of-a-scholar-and-activist/#_edn2

8 Sanjeevani Mujumdar, Mahamanav, *Dr Babasaheb Ambedkar, Jeevan Darshan* (Pune: Symbiosis Society's Dr Babasaheb Ambedkar Museum and Memorial, ND), p. 23.

Chapter Eight: Lunchless in London (1920–22)

1 Letter of 3 August 1920, from the Seligman papers, Rare Book and Manuscript Library, Columbia University.

2 Round Table India, 'B.R. Ambedkar: From the pages of Mook Nayak', available at: https://www.roundtableindia.co.in/from-the-pages-of-mook-nayak/

3 The trade union leader and founder of the Social Service League of Bombay, N.M. Joshi (after whom the street that the building is located on is now named), had this office space allotted to Ambedkar for trade union and social service activities—possibly explaining why the Baroda bureaucrats had written to Joshi to complain about Ambedkar!

4 Prabhakar Padhye, *Prakaashaan'tilla Vyakti* (Bombay: J Maa Mahaajana, 1950), p. 30, available at: https://archive.org/details/in.ernet.dli.2015.364911/page/n49/mode/2up?view=theater

5 The common complaint was that Mair came between the director and the staff. Beatrice Webb, wife of Sidney Webb and co-founder of LSE, wrote in a 1928 letter: 'It is, I am pretty certain, a platonic relationship—but in spite of their mature age it is far too romantic to be comfortable for the institution over which they preside as Director and Secretary.' Sue Donnelly, 'A controversial appointment – Jessy Mair, School Secretary, 1920-1939', LSE blog, 3 December 2019, available at: https://blogs.lse.ac.uk/lsehistory/2019/12/03/a-controversial-appointment-jessy-mair-school-secretary-1920-1939/

6 University of London, Senate House Library blog, 'Herbert Somerton Foxwell and the Goldsmiths' Library: A Brief History', ND, available at: https://london.ac.uk/senate-house-library/our-collections/special-collections/printed-special-collections/goldsmiths/foxwell

7 There is no set of books published under the title 'Annual Reports' for the East India Company. It may have been, perhaps, *The minutes and memoranda of the general committees and offices of the East India Company*, 1700-1858, that Ambedkar had sought to acquire, as the dates match. However, no such set of books can be found among Ambedkar's various book collections and libraries. The mentioned collection is available with the India Office Records (IOR/D) of the British Library in London. See: https://www.amdigital.co.uk/images/product-downloads/flyer/East_india_Company.pdf

8 Maren Bellwinkel-Schempp, 'Ambedkar Studies at Heidelberg', available at: https://drambedkarbooks.com/2015/01/18/dr-ambedkar-in-germany/

9 As Ambedkar suggested to Bhathena, he was in a hurry to purchase the German marks because he believed that the devalued currency would soon rise again and thus be more expensive for him to acquire. He actually miscalculated this quite badly, since the marks continued to radically deflate in value. 'As the first repayments were made to the Allies in the early 1920s, the value of the German mark sank drastically, and a period of hyperinflation began. In early 1922, 160 German marks was equivalent to one US dollar. By November of 1923, the currency would depreciate to 4,200,000,000,000 marks to one US dollar.' Had Ambedkar held off by a year, he would not have even needed Rs 2 from Naval, let alone Rs 2,000! For the information about German marks, see: Nick Goodell, '1920s Hyperinflation in Germany and Bank Notes', Spurlock Museum of World Cultures blog, 6 August 2018, available at: https://www.spurlock.illinois.edu/blog/p/1920s-hyperinflation-in/283#:~:text=As%20the%20first%20repayments%20were,marks%20to%20one%20US%20dollar

10 As William Gould reports after consulting the Camden archives and marriage registrations, there is 'no evidence of a person by the name Fanny Fitzgerald living at 10KHR [i.e., 10 King Henry's Road] in the twenty years either side of his time in London. In April 1917, just a few years before Ambedkar's arrival, Gaston Amedee Proust took over the property as the rate payer, and he passed away on 17 June 1918. In October 1918, his wife, a Mrs Frances Proust (née Brooks) took over as ratepayer and continued to live at the property until April 1941.' *Ambedkar in London*, p. 23.

11 William Gould, citing records in the national archives. *Ambedkar in London*, p. 23.

12 Psalm 16:11 of the King James Version. Ambedkar's dedication appears in the front matter of: *What Congress and Gandhi Have Done to the Untouchables* (Bombay: Thacker and Co, 1945). We will discuss the long and poignant dedication more fully in the next volume of this biography.

13 Cited at: https://raattai.wordpress.com/2016/05/29/ambedkars-family/

14 Sanjeevani Mujumdar, *Mahamanav, Dr Babasaheb Ambedkar, Jeevan Darshan* (Pune: Symbiosis Society's Dr Babasaheb Ambedkar Museum and Memorial, ND), p. 24.

15 Savita Ambedkar, *Babasaheb: My Life with Dr Ambedkar*, p. 21. Savita added, 'The letters of Saheb's colleagues, friends, followers and workers demonstrate one thing forcefully: they would all inquire very solicitously about his health. Add to that Saheb's reference to his health in almost every one of his own letters. It is clear that from 1934 onwards, he was always down with one ailment or the other. He was later struck by serious afflictions like neuritis, diabetes, rheumatism, breathing problems and heart ailments. I have already established this by producing Dr Ambedkar's letters to his friends and colleagues.' (p. 279)

Chapter Nine: Mr Ambedkar, to Ambedkar Bar-at-Law, to Dr Ambedkar (1922–23)

1 Edwin R.A. Seligman's private papers, letter dated 23 September 1920 from Seligman to Ambedkar, Rare Book and Manuscript Library, Columbia University. Once again, we have definitive evidence here that Ambedkar had not received his Columbia University PhD by this time.
2 Edwin R.A. Seligman's private papers, letter dated 16 February 1922 from Ambedkar to Seligman, Rare Book and Manuscript Library, Columbia University.
3 Sanjeevani Mujumdar, Mahamanav, *Dr Babasaheb Ambedkar, Jeevan Darshan* (Pune: Symbiosis Society's Dr Babasaheb Ambedkar Museum and Memorial, ND), p. 25.
4 Cited by Steven Gasztowicz KC, 'Ambedkar as Lawyer: From London to India in the 1920s', in: William Gould, Santosh Dass and Christophe Jaffrelot, eds, *Ambedkar in London*, p. 97.
5 Dhananjay Keer, *Dr Ambedkar: Life & Mission*, p. 49.
6 Including, most recently, Ashok Gopal, in his biography *A Part Apart.*.
7 Letter dated 23 April 1979, LSE archive, 'Ambedkar's Student File', accessible at: https://www.lse.ac.uk/library/assets/documents/Ambedkars-LSE-student-file.pdf
8 Shashi Tharoor repeats this false claim of Keer in his biography *Ambedkar: A Life*, p. 24.
9 *The Hindu*, 'The LSE and India', Sunday Magazine, 23 November 2003, available at: https://www.thehindu.com/todays-paper/tp-features/tp-sundaymagazine/the-lse-and-india/article28524830.ece
10 B.R. Ambedkar, *The Problem of the Rupee*, in *BAWS*, Vol. 6, 1989, p. 330.
11 Edwin Cannan, 'Foreword', in B.R. Ambedkar, *The Problem of the Rupee*, p. 331.
12 Cited in: Janak Singh, *Dr. B.R. Ambedkar: The Messiah of the Downtrodden*, p. 32.
13 Rohit De, 'Lawyering as Politics', in: Suraj Yengde and Anand Teltumbde, *The Radical in Ambedkar* (Delhi: Penguin Random House, 2018), p. 137.

14 Sanjeevani Mujumdar, *Mahamanav, Dr Babasaheb Ambedkar, Jeevan Darshan* (Pune: Symbiosis Society's Dr Babasaheb Ambedkar Museum and Memorial), ND, p. 27.
15 Manicasothy Saravanamuttu, *The Sara Saga* (Penang: Areca Books, 2010), p. 43.

Chapter Ten: A Barrister in Bombay (1924–26)

1 Later in the 1930s, Ambedkar, suffering financially from the boycott of his legal practice that had been informally imposed by caste-Hindu lawyers as well as Congress-party sympathizers, sought a high court judgeship, raising the issue with no less than the viceroy of India, Lord Linlithgow. In an exchange of letters among Linlithgow, the governor of Bombay Sir Roger Lumley and the secretary of state for India Leo Amery, the three discussed the reasons for and against offering Ambedkar a high court judgeship—finally deciding to leave it up to the chief justice of the Bombay High Court. See: India Office Records, Private Papers of Lord Linlithgow. IOR/L/PO/17, 1941.
2 Nanak Chand Rattu, *Reminiscences and Remembrances of Dr B.R. Ambedkar*, p. 77.
3 'Ambedkar's connection with Hyderabad recalled', *The Hindu*, 13 January 2015, accessible at: https://www.thehindu.com/news/cities/Hyderabad/ambedkars-connection-with-hyderabad-recalled/article6783123.ece
4 Rohit De, 'Lawyering as Politics', in: Suraj Yengde and Anand Teltumbde, *The Radical in Ambedkar*, p. 137.
5 Savita Ambedkar, *Babasaheb: My Life with Dr Ambedkar*, p. 86.
6 In his excellent essay, Rohit De accidentally refers to the author of the book, Dinkarrao Jawalkar, as the publisher, and the publisher of the book, Keshavrao Jedhe, as the author.
7 Surendra Ajnat, *Letters of Ambedkar*, p. 21.
8 Khairmoday reports that when Javalkar and Jedhe initially came to consult Ambedkar about their case, he had already read their book. He called it 'a good book written in bad taste'. He suggested that Javalkar better learn from the Brahmans rather than simply rail against them: 'Brahmans have transformed themselves in social and religious terms and they will continue to do so. Only cursing Brahmans the way you non-Brahmans and Marathas are now doing is not going to solve anything. The Brahmans have already initiated widow-remarriage and inter-caste marriage, why haven't the Marathas done the same? Brahmans will continue to evolve over time, because they have an insatiable desire both for knowledge and for capital. They have always sought to protect their interests, which is how they managed to dominate all the other castes. Remember this: Brahmans have brains inside their brains!' Khairmoday, *Dr Bhimrao Ramji Ambedkar Charitra*, Vol. 2, pp. 198–99.

Notes

9. The original books of Jamshed R. Batliboi have been digitized and preserved online, accessible at: https://dspace.gipe.ac.in/xmlui/bitstream/handle/10973/41008/GIPE-009443-Contents.pdf?sequence=2&isAllowed=y
10. Savita Ambedkar, *Babasaheb: My Life with Dr Ambedkar*, p. 124.
11. Accessible at: https://archive.org/details/in.ernet.dli.2015.113677/page/n3/mode/2up
12. These adverts, fliers and pamphlets produced by Jamshed R. Batliboi are accessible at:https://dspace.gipe.ac.in/xmlui/bitstream/handle/10973/41008/GIPE-009443-Contents.pdf?sequence=2&isAllowed=y
13. B.R. Ambedkar, *BAWS*, Vol. 2, pp. 311–12.
14. That sociology and history were Ambedkar's two minors at Columbia University is established by the 1915–16 Register of Students, p. 369, in the Columbia University archives. A digital text is available at: https://babel.hathitrust.org/cgi/pt?id=nnc2.ark:/13960/t14m9w579&view=1up&seq=389&q1=ambedkar
15. B.R. Ambedkar, *BAWS*, Vol. 2, p. 312. This is not the first time that Ambedkar has railed against the people of Bombay for ignoring the need for a proper library. Recall his similarly strongly worded letter to the *Bombay Chronicle* from a decade back, upon hearing of the death of Sir Pherozeshah Mehta: 'It is unfortunate that we have not as yet realized the value of the library as an institution in the growth and advancement of a society. But this is not the place to dilate upon its virtues. That an enlightened public as that of Bombay should have suffered so long to be without an up-to-date public library is nothing short of disgrace and the earlier we make amends for it the better!' (Cited in Salim Yusufji, *Ambedkar: Attendant Details* [Delhi: Navayana, 2017], p. 50.)
16. Indeed, as we see from a letter addressed to Edwin R.A. Seligman by the publisher, dated 5 June 1924, Seligman's foreword to Ambedkar's book was deemed the equivalent to a positive peer review of Ambedkar's manuscript.
17. B.R. Ambedkar, *Evolution of Provincial Finance in British India* (London: PS King, 1925), p. vii.
18. No university would have cared, and indeed, a majority of doctoral dissertations probably contain significant amounts of material from their author's earlier master's theses; nevertheless, Ambedkar was very principled on this issue. Even his own wife, Savita Ambedkar, was unaware of his MSc degree as she boasted about his academic accomplishments: '[H]e acquired an M.A., Ph.D., D.Sc., LL.D, DLitt, Bar-at-Law and a host of other degrees.' This list included the honorary degrees bestowed upon Dr Ambedkar in the 1950s, but not the MSc he had laboured over, half starving in the process.
19. 'Report of the Royal Commission on Indian Currency and Finance', *Federal Reserve Bulletin*, September 1926, pp. 657–64, available at:https://fraser.stlouisfed.org/files/docs/publications/FRB/pages/1925-1929/27416_1925-1929.pdf

20 It is increasingly common nowadays to attribute the idea of the formation of the RBI to Ambedkar, on account of his testimony before the Royal Commission on Indian currency and finance. However, Ambedkar's testimony *in itself* does not bear this out. Perhaps he worked towards this end behind the scenes, but I have not been able to find any evidence of it. The frequently heard claim about the formation of the RBI, that 'its need, working style and its outlook was presented by Dr Ambedkar in front of the Hilton Young Commission', is not borne out by the actual transcript of that testimony (the quotation is from 'Formation of Reserve Bank of India – Dr Ambedkar's Role', from the Ambedkar Today blog, available at: https://www.ambedkaritetoday.com/2019/04/dr-ambedkars-role-in-formation-of-reserve-bank-of-india.html; however, the claim is ubiquitous). But it is true that Ambedkar's *The Problem of the Rupee* was constantly referred to by most of the members of the commission, and one of the primary problems that Ambedkar identified within that work was the proper control of the innumerable independent banks in India, along with the main issue of the stabilization of the currency—both of which are the tasks of a central bank. For example, Ambedkar wrote: 'Banks other than Presidency banks have been entirely immune from any legislative control whatsoever, except in so far as they are made amenable to the provisions of the Indian Companies Act ... The control of these banks is one of the important problems of banking legislation in India.' (B.R. Ambedkar, *The Problem of the Rupee*, in *BAWS*, Vol. 6, p. 54.) Nevertheless, the commission questioned Ambedkar far more on the issue of stabilization than on the issue of banking reform.

21 *Report of the Royal Commission on Indian Currency and Finance*, Vol. IV, Minutes of Evidence, pp. 313–22, 'Evidence before the Royal Commission on Indian Currency and Finance on 15th December', Paragraph 6163, available at: http://www.ambedkar.org/ambcd/31.%20Evidence%20Before%20the%20Royal%20Commission%20on%20Indian15.12.25.htm#_msoanchor_1

22 *Report of the Royal Commission on Indian Currency and Finance*, Vol. IV, Minutes of Evidence, pp. 313–22, paragraphs 6166–79.

Chapter Eleven: 'Educate, Agitate, Organize'

1 Eleanor Zelliot, *Ambedkar's World: The Making of Babasaheb and the Dalit Movement* (Delhi: Navayana Publishing, 2013), p. 235, footnotes 69 and 70.
2 Eleanor Zelliot, *Ambedkar's World*, p. 235, footnote 70.
3 Ibid.
4 Eleanor Zelliot, *Ambedkar's World*, p. 94.
5 B.G. Kunte, ed., *Source Material on Dr. Babasaheb Ambedkar and the Movement of Untouchables*, Vol. 1, p. 7.
6 Christophe Jaffrelot, *Dr. Ambedkar and Untouchability*, p. 46.

7   Christophe Jaffrelot, *Dr. Ambedkar and Untouchability*, pp. 46–49.
8   Anand Teltumbde points out that Antonio Gramsci, the Italian Marxist revolutionary who was born the same year as Ambedkar, also used the slogan as the motto for his communist newspaper *L'Ordine Nuovo*: 'Educate yourselves because we'll need your intelligence. Agitate because we'll need all your enthusiasm. Organize yourselves because we'll need all your strength.' See: Anand Teltumbde, *MAHAD: The Making of the First Dalit Revolt* (Delhi: Aakar Publishing, 2016), p. 101.
9   Christophe Jaffrelot, *Dr. Ambedkar and Untouchability*, p. 51.
10 I am referring to Ambedkar's unfinished work, *Revolution and Counter-Revolution in Ancient India*, about which I have written, in relation to egalitarian values, in *Ambedkar's Preamble: A Secret History of the Constitution of India* (Penguin, 2020), Chapter 3, on equality. As for debunking the Eurocentric belief that egalitarianism arose as a uniquely Western value, I have addressed this comprehensively, in relation to Ambedkar's own thought and work, in my earlier book *Indian Political Theory: Laying the Groundwork for Svaraj* (Routledge, 2017), Chapter 8, on tradition, hybridity and equality.
11 Eleanor Zelliot, *Ambedkar's World*, pp. 77–78, citing Khairmoday, *Dr Bhimrao Ramji Ambedkar Charitra*, Vol. 2, pp. 117–18.
12 Ibid.
13 Interestingly, on the occasion in Mahad, where Ambedkar burnt the *Manusmriti*, in the pandal beside which the pyre was dug hung a portrait of Gandhi, as inspiration for the protests under way. Anand Teltumbde, *MAHAD: The Making of the First Dalit Revolt*, p. 204.
14 The topic is mused on by Sir Roger Lumley, governor of Bombay, in an exchange of letters with Viceroy Linlithgow: 'If Ambedkar were removed from the political scene … his whole movement for the uplift of the scheduled castes would fairly soon collapse. He has no lieutenant who could carry on in his place. It is he alone who holds his Party and his movement together, and no one else has a quarter of his intelligence or could command any allegiance. They would soon start quarreling amongst themselves, and the Congress would step in and bring a section over to them, and the other would collapse … [Ambedkar] mentioned two people [who could succeed him], one of whom, Mr Bole, M.L.A., you met at Ganeshkhind; but he, although probably the best of them, could not, I am sure, ever take Ambedkar's place.' See: India Office Records, Private Papers of Lord Linlithgow. IOR/L/PO/17, 1941, p. 2.
15 Savita Ambedkar (*Babasaheb: My Life with Dr Ambedkar*, pp. 170–71) describes the events surrounding which the photo was taken: 'It was for the first time since Saheb had resigned from his post as law minister that we were going to Mumbai. We alighted at the Bori Bunder railway station on Sunday, 18 November 1951 … The Scheduled Castes Federation and the Socialist

Party had organized a joint function to welcome us. We had travelled to Mumbai by the Punjab Mail. As soon as the train entered Bori Bunder station, the mammoth gathering broke out into slogans of "Dr Ambedkar zindabad" [long live Dr Ambedkar] and "Dr Ambedkar ki jai" [victory to Dr Ambedkar] … Since it was a very small and formal function, chairs had been placed for just the two of us. Rao Bahadur S.K. Bole had been a senior colleague of Saheb from the very beginning; since arrangements for only two chairs had been made at the place of the meeting, Saheb called Rao Bahadur Bole to him and got his eighty-five-year-old senior colleague to sit on his lap. This event provoked a burst of laughter from Saheb, Bole himself and me. The rest of the crowd broke out laughing too. The photojournalists caught this rare moment perfectly with their cameras. Every one of the newspapers published this picture the next day along with details of this funny incident.'

16 Eleanor Zelliot, *Ambedkar's World*, p. 120.
17 Surendra Ajnat, *Letters of Ambedkar*, p. 48.
18 C.B. Khairmoday, *Dr Bhimrao Ramji Ambedkar Charitra,* Vol. 2, pp. 115–18, provides a great deal of detail about the birth, ill health and death of Rajratna, as well as Ambedkar's close relationship with him. This is an excerpt: 'No Hindu nurse was willing to work in a chawl for a Mahar family, so they found a Christian nurse. She used to see Ramabai and Rajratna twice a week and give them medicine and tonics. When Ambedkar came back from the court, he would change his clothes and then sit playing with the boy, or carry him on his shoulders and chat with people in the chawl. His way of playing with the child was unique. Other people call their children *Dada, Raja, Babu* and so on while playing with them, but Ambedkar would say things like, "You are a lion cub; you descended from warriors; you are the royal son of the emperor; you must do great things!"… Rajratna contracted double pneumonia in July 1926. Ambedkar, Ramabai, Lakshmibai and Shankarrao used to stay up all night and take care of him. On July 18, he began to feel better, so on July 19 Ambedkar went to the High Court. But Rajratna's illness suddenly worsened, and Shankarrao ran to the High Court to call Ambedkar home. Ambedkar came home at 4:30pm, and then he broke down …'
19 Cited in C.B. Khairmoday, *Dr Bhimrao Ramji Ambedkar Charitra,* Vol. 2, p. 104, and D. Keer, *Dr Ambedkar: Life & Mission*, pp. 66–67.

Chapter Twelve: From Bhima Koregaon to the Mahad Conference (1927)

1 Translated by the author, who was present on the occasion.
2 Shraddha Kumbhojkar, 'Politics, caste and the remembrance of the Raj: The Obelisk at Koregaon', In: *Sites of Imperial Memory: Commemorating Colonial*

Rule in the Nineteenth and Twentieth Centuries, ed. Dominik Geppert and Frank Lorenz Müller (Manchester: Manchester University Press, 2015), pp. 39–52.

3 Inscription on the 1822 Koregaon monument plaque.

4 Mahars were forbidden from serving in the Peshwa military forces, in a reversal of Shivaji's prior policy. There were prohibitions against them moving freely in public, and they were punished atrociously for violating caste norms. Under Peshwa rule, punishments became caste-based as in the *Manusmriti*, and there are numerous tales of Peshwa atrocity against the Mahars. For example, it is commonly told that in this period, untouchables were made to tie brooms behind their backs to wipe away their polluting footprints and pots around their necks to ensure that their sweat or spit did not pollute the ground.

5 Sir Mehta seems to have been rather widely disliked, not least of all for his hostile attitude towards the Congress. As a member named W.S. Mukadam stated: 'Now, Sir, for these two days, old and new members of this House—so many of them—have criticised the Honourable Finance Member. I wholeheartedly do not join with all of them, because, Sir, I have compared the present Finance Member with his predecessors, and I find that the Indian Finance Member is in no way second to his predecessors … At the same time, I never expected from the Honourable Sir Chunilal Mehta that he would dare to ridicule the Congress mandate and belittle the Swaraj party. I expected from him, Sir, as a sportsman that he is, a word of admiration for the discipline of the Swaraj party. But instead of that admiration, I do not know with what view, as he is now in the seventh heaven, with what idea he has tried to whip the members of the Swaraj party of the last year, and tried to ridicule the Congress mandate and also the non-co-operation movement.' Bombay Legislative Council Debates (from 18 February 1927), Vol. XIX of Dhananjayarao Gadgil Library of Gokhale Institute of Politics and Economics (GIPE), p. 179. Accessible at: https://dspace.gipe.ac.in/xmlui/handle/10973/37154

6 Bombay Legislative Council Debates (From 18 February 1927), Vol. XIX, of Dhananjayarao Gadgil Library of Gokhale Institute of Politics and Economics (GIPE), p. 168. Accessible at: https://dspace.gipe.ac.in/xmlui/handle/10973/37154

7 It appears that Ambedkar ultimately managed to get Jadhav the deputy collector's position, and that later there was a celebration by the untouchables to felicitate Jadhav. A resolution at the Mahad conference in March 1927 confirms that Jadhav had not been granted the position by that time: 'The conference expresses sadness that the Deputy Collectorship did not go to Shri M.K. Jadhav [see Appendix 2].' Khairmoday suggests that Ambedkar went outside the BLC process and directly appealed to the governor of Bombay. Moreover, Kadam notes that 'M.K. Jadhav was felicitated at Baramati, on his appointment as District Deputy Collector' in March 1928. (K.N. Kadam,

Dr Babasaheb Ambedkar and the Significance of his Movement: A Chronology [Bombay: Popular Prakashan, 1991], p. 89). This means that Ambedkar worked on this for the better part of a year before he finally succeeded. As he would later say, 'You know how much trouble I had to get him in.' (*BAWS*, Vol. 2, p. 516.)

8 For example, BLC members Moulvi Rafiuddin Ahmad ('I would be only too pleased to see Dr. Ambedkar in a position which would enable him to help the education of the depressed classes'), N.A. Bechar ('My honourable friend Dr. Ambedkar spoke so convincingly yesterday') and W.S. Mukadam ('I congratulate my honourable friend Dr. Ambedkar on making out a case for more boarding schools'). Member S.K. Bole even used the person of Ambedkar himself as evidence of the correctness of Ambedkar's impassioned speech on the need for more expenditure on education: 'The backward and depressed classes are backward in education because no equal facilities are given to them. We are backward, not because we have no brains. If we are given equal opportunities and equal facilities, then I say that even depressed classes can produce men of the eminence of my honourable friend, Dr. Ambedkar.' See: Bombay Legislative Council Debates (From 18 February 1927), Vol. XIX, of Dhananjayarao Gadgil Library of Gokhale Institute of Politics and Economics (GIPE), p. 1015 and passim. Accessible at: https://dspace.gipe.ac.in/xmlui/handle/10973/37154

9 Bombay Legislative Council Debates (from 18 July 1927), Vol. XX, of GIPE. Accessible at: https://dspace.gipe.ac.in/xmlui/handle/10973/37155

10 R.B. More, 'The Satyagraha of Chavadar Tank', reprinted in Anand Teltumbde, *MAHAD: The Making of the First Dalit Revolt*, p. 258.

11 Cited in, Savita Ambedkar, *Babasaheb: My Life with Dr Ambedkar*, p. 20.

12 Anand Teltumbde, *MAHAD: The Making of the First Dalit Revolt*, p. 167.

13 'Dr. B. R. AMBEDKAR: Will Government be pleased to state: (a) whether it is a fact that the Gaonkaris of the villages of (i) Ralerass, (ii) Pangaon, (iii) Pangri … in the district of Sholapur have been acting in conspiracy to stop the Rayots and shop-keepers of their respective villages from having any dealings with the Mahars of their villages and have assaulted the Mahars of their villages and have in some cases outraged the modesty of the Mahar women and have gone to the length of throwing filth in the water-sources used by the Mahars because the Mahars in these villages have in their efforts at self-improvement given up the carrying of the carcasses of dead animals; (b) what steps they propose to take to protect the Mahars from such tyranny?' Bombay Legislative Council Debates (from 18 July 1927), Vol. XX, of GIPE, p. 52.

14 R.B. More, 'The Satyagraha of Chavadar Tank', p. 265. However, as per Teltumbde, the home department's figure is 2,500–3,000, and the DSP, Kolaba, reports 3,000.

15 The episode was described in anodyne fashion by Judge Vaidya during the interim injunction: '[I]n consequence of this contamination, the touchable classes could not take water from the tank for over 24/25 hours, until the water was purified, at great cost, by performing ceremonies laid down by the Hindu Shastras.' Referenced in Narhari Damodar Vaidya vs Bhimrao Ramji Ambedkar (1937), 39 BOMLR 1295, 173 Ind Cas 910.

Chapter Thirteen: From Doctorsaheb to Babasaheb

1 Round Table India, '"We Are on the Scene Again": Dr. Babasaheb Ambedkar', 28 October 2021, available at: https://www.roundtableindia.co.in/dr-babasaheb-ambedkar/
2 B.R. Ambedkar, 'The religious battle of Mahad and the responsibility of Savarna Hindus', cited in Anand Teltumbde, *MAHAD: The Making of the First Dalit Revolt* (Aakar, 2016), p. 142.
3 Ibid, p. 143.
4 Ibid, p. 144.
5 Ibid, pp. 146–47.
6 Ibid, pp. 148–49.
7 Ibid, pp. 150–51.
8 Ibid, pp. 151–52.
9 Ibid, p. 154.
10 Ibid, pp. 154–55.
11 Ibid, p. 156.
12 Ibid.
13 Ibid, pp. 157–58.
14 Ibid, p. 159.
15 As witnessed by a certain Professor Helekar, a Bombay lawyer, who one day happened to stalk Ambedkar: 'While walking along Sandhurst Road I saw Dr Ambedkar near the lane where the Manoranjan Press used to be at the time. The Doctor had some books in his hand, purchased from the Press. My curiosity arose as to what books this great man had come to purchase there. The simple man boarded a tram near the Prarthna Samaj Junction. I took a seat behind him and peeped into the book. He was then reading a Marathi book on Buddhism by Dharmanand Kosambi.' In Nanak Chand Rattu, *Reminiscences and Remembrances of Dr B.R. Ambedkar*, p. 135.
16 The report is rather suspect, as it appears only in Keer (p. 96), notorious for attempting to ally Ambedkar and Savarkar. Had Ambedkar actually used the term, it would, of course, have been the standard device of a legal orator, providing retorts to every objection his opponent had raised, legal, social, cultural, etc.
17 In fact, the main organizer, Mahar leader G.A. Gawai, claimed in a later interview with Eleanor Zelliot that there had never been any temple-entry

satyagraha at all! Eleanor Zelliot, *Ambedkar's World: The Making of Babasaheb and the Dalit Movement*, p. 83.
18 Bombay Legislative Council Debates (from 18 July 1927),Vol. XX, of GIPE, p. 31. Accessible at: https://dspace.gipe.ac.in/xmlui/handle/10973/37155
19 B.R. Ambedkar, *BAWS*,Vol. 2, p. 48.
20 Ibid, p. 62.
21 Ibid, pp. 49–50.
22 In his biography, *Dr. Ambedkar and Untouchability: Analyzing and Fighting Caste*, Christophe Jaffrelot erroneously claims that Ambedkar had not been able to go to Amravati because of his brother's death (p. 50).
23 Bhadant Ananda Kausalayayan Mahathera, *Had There Been No Ambedkar*, p. 52.
24 Vijay Mankar, *Dr B.R. Ambedkar*, p. 21.

Chapter Fourteen: Mahad Reloaded: The Satyagraha

1 Cited in Anand Teltumbde, *MAHAD: The Making of the First Dalit Revolt* (Delhi: Aakar Publishing, 2016), pp. 164–65.
2 See the 'About' link of the Samata Sainik Dal website: https://ssdindia.org/about/
3 Cited in Anand Teltumbde, *MAHAD*, pp. 175-6.
4 Cited in Anand Teltumbde, *MAHAD*, p. 345.
5 Dhananjay Keer, *Dr Ambedkar: Life & Mission*, p. 91.
6 Anand Teltumbde, *MAHAD*, p. 340.
7 Ibid, p. 348.
8 Ibid.
9 Anupama Rao has pointed out that since the Samata Sainik Dal was formed largely for security and protection, their uniforms were designed to evoke the Mahar military past. This included khaki shorts, a khaki topi and khaki chaps, along with a red shirt. She writes, 'Drawing upon images of militarized masculinity as well as the status and respect that Mahars derived from a military past, the Samata Sainik Dal provoked a completely different set of associations—combat, armed resistance, virility—from those attached to nonviolent protest.' Anupama Rao, *The Caste Question: Dalits and the Politics of Modern India* (Berkeley: University of California Press, 2009), pp. 100–01.
10 The Maharashtra government, Gazetteer's Department, 'Trade Routes', available at: https://gazetteers.maharashtra.gov.in/cultural.maharashtra.gov.in/english/gazetteer/Kolaba%20District/trade_routes.html#6.
11 Cited in Anand Teltumbde, *MAHAD*, pp. 206–07, 210, 212–13, 214, 216.
12 Anand Teltumbde, *MAHAD*, p. 226.
13 Ibid, p. 227.
14 Ibid, p. 234.

15 Shankaranand Shastri, *My Memories and Experiences of Babasaheb Dr B.R. Ambedkar* (Delhi: Gautam Book Centre, 1989), pp. 140–50.

Chapter Fifteen: Between Mahad and the Round Table Conference (1928–29)

1 C.B. Khairmoday, *Dr Bhimrao Ramji Ambedkar Charitra*, Vol. 3, p. 138.
2 Savita Ambedkar claims that she and Dr Ambedkar secretly converted to Buddhism in a private ceremony sometime in 1951. *Babasaheb: My Life with Dr Ambedkar*, p. 11.
3 Keer recounts the saga of two consecutive Ganpati festivals (September 1928 and 1929), where the efforts of Ambedkar's new Social Equality League (Samaj Samata Sangh), actually formed at the time of the same festival in 1927, intervened so that untouchables were permitted to enter the area where the idol would be—in these cases, violence was averted. D. Keer, *Dr Ambedkar: Life & Mission*, pp. 119 and 132.
4 Rohit De, 'Lawyering as Politics', in: Suraj Yengde and Anand Teltumbde, *The Radical in Ambedkar*, p. 407.
5 Ibid, p. 143.
6 Sir Chunilal Mehta was the finance member at the time (1926–28), having taken over from an Englishman, Sir Henry S. Lawrence (1921–26). Sir Mehta had earlier been the revenue member (1923–25) and was subject to a healthy dose of criticism from Ambedkar when he held that portfolio as well. It is not clear why Ambedkar disliked Mehta as much as he did, other than that his policies were far from people-centric and he seemed never to sanction funds for the benefit of the untouchables. As mentioned earlier in Chapter Twelve, Mehta was not popular among Congress members either.
7 B.R. Ambedkar, *BAWS*, Vol. 2, pp. 6-7.
8 Ibid, p. 471.
9 Dr Ambedkar's editorial in the *Bahishkrut Bharat* of 16 August 1929 gives his own account of these events. We should note that the Bombay Legislative Council records themselves indicate that Ambedkar was present in the BLC for at least two further days in 1929 (5 and 9 October), and for at least six days in 1930. Nevertheless, he was indeed mostly absent. Keer, *Dr Ambedkar: Life & Mission*, pp. 111–14, also offers a detailed account of the Watan Bill saga. Keer's account is characteristically rather more damning of the behaviour of the Muslim members of the BLC.
10 B.R. Ambedkar, *BAWS*, Vol. 2, p. 87.
11 The thrust of Ambedkar's remedy entailed voluntary cooperative farming and government-subsidized advanced agricultural technology, whereas the government went the opposite direction and crafted a plan for the few large wealthier farms to buy out the numerous small holdings of poorer farmers.

Ambedkar thought that this capitalist approach would end up producing more urban proletariat, instead of encouraging independent livelihoods, available to untouchables, in the rural areas.

12 B.R. Ambedkar, *BAWS*, Vol. 2, p. 133.
13 Ambedkar publicly excoriated this report in a speech in Nagpur in 1930. It might be interesting to note here, however, that in the late 1940s, Ambedkar appears to have forgotten about it altogether. During the Constituent Assembly Debates, Ambedkar criticized the Indian National Congress for never having demanded basic rights in the past. In response, another member interrupted Ambedkar to query whether he was aware of the 1928 Nehru Committee Report. Ambedkar appeared not to have understood the reference and carried on with his speech. But all of this, of course, will come much later in our story.
14 Motilal Nehru, *All Parties Conference, 1928: Report of the Committee Appointed by the Conference to Determine the Principles of the Constitution for India* (Allahabad: All India Congress Committee, 1928), pp. 59–60, available at: https://indianculture.gov.in/rarebooks/all-parties-conference-1928-report-committee-appointed-conference-determine-principles-1
15 Keer wrongly claims that Dr Ambedkar closed down the BHS on 14 June 1928 upon launching the DCES. See: D. Keer, *Dr Ambedkar: Life & Mission*, p. 124.
16 B.R. Ambedkar, *BAWS*, Vol. 2, p. 315.
17 Ibid, p. 317. Italics are in the original.
18 *Bahishkrut Bharat* of 31 May 1929.
19 B.R. Ambedkar, *BAWS*, Vol. 2, p. 473.
20 There are innumerable articles in journals and newspapers, and many books, that delve into various aspects of this complicated question. One book that is particularly perspicacious is Anand Teltumbde's *Republic of Caste: Thinking Equality in the Time of Neoliberal Hindutva* (Delhi: Navayana, 2018), particularly Chapter 2 for the theoretical background of the problem.
21 The specific design of the SSS for pushing savarna Hindus to 'walk the talk' about their commitment to reforming Hinduism was made clear in a note that Ambedkar wrote in *Bahishkrut Bharat* announcing its formation: 'In principle, the Samaj Samata Sangh is not antithetical to Hinduism. Our honest opinion is that if anyone can revive Hinduism today, it can only be the Sangh. And, therefore, we request every Hindu to contribute to our cause and fulfil their responsibility towards the upliftment of Hinduism.'
22 About Ambedkar's relationship with Tulsa, Khairmoday writes: 'Of all his sisters, Ambedkar was especially fond of Tulsa. Since childhood, Tulsa had borne the brunt of many things for Ambedkar. Till she passed her B.A. exam, he frequently lived at her place. Tulsa's husband, Dharmaji Katekar, used to work as a gate-keeper at a railway workshop. He had a room in the workshop's chawl with thin metal walls, in front of the David mill. Ambedkar would stay

there for many days, study there, and go to high school and college from there.' C.B. Khairmoday, *Dr Bhimrao Ramji Ambedkar Charita*, Vol. 2, p. 269.

23 Naik, consistently supportive of Ambedkar throughout, had a rather love-hate relationship with Vinayak Damodar Savarkar, who had written a letter of support for the SSS, which Naik published in *Samata*. After Naik published, in the next issue, healthy criticism of Savarkar, accusing him of hypocrisy, Savarkar wrote a letter in response to Naik, which the latter once again published in *Samata*. Savarkar wrote: 'I believe that it is absolutely critical to annihilate caste from Indian society. Caste in any hereditary form is unacceptable and harmful to the strength of the nation. Inter-marriages and inter-dining must take place within Hindu society ... One may criticise me for holding on to my Hinduness—that critique I can understand. But to call me a supporter of caste is unjustified.' In an editorial in the same issue, Naik commented: 'Does Barrister Savarkar truly belong to us from his "heart", the way in which his "brain" seems to belong to us? This is the question about which our readers must think carefully. Personally, I do not think Barrister Savarkar belongs to us by heart ... I would like to remind Savarkar, who himself proclaimed that the place of religion is the heart—my dear sir, the place of "equality" is also the heart and not the brain ... I would very much like him to become truly our man, rather than sitting in the camps of Brahmanism.' *Samata*, 24 August 1928, pp. 4–6.

24 Naik was also the editor of the journal *Brahman-Brahmanetar* (or 'Brahman-Non-Brahman'), which has led authors in the secondary literature to incorrectly assume that he was a Maratha from the non-Brahman movement.

25 Devrao Naik published Shridharpant Tilak's letter to Ambedkar (dated 25 May 1928) in the 29 June 1928 issue of *Samata*.

26 *Waiting for a Visa* is widely available, including in: *Dr. Babasaheb Ambedkar Writings and Speeches*, Vol. 12, edited by Vasant Moon (Bombay: Government of Maharashtra Education Department, 1993), Part I, pp. 661–91.

27 Letter to Bhaurao Gaikwad from December 1930, as cited in Savita Ambedkar, *Babasaheb: My Life with Dr Ambedkar*, p. 22.

28 Letter to Bhaurao Gaikwad from May 1930, as cited in Savita Ambedkar, *Babasaheb: My Life with Dr Ambedkar*, p. 23.

Index

activism, 24–25, 89, 92, 100, 111, *see also* social activism
Adarekar, Govind Ramji, 175
address, x; Bombay business, 71; Brook Green, Hammersmith, 76; home, 70–71; London, 37, 71
'Administration and Finance of the East India Company,' Ambedkar, 28
Ahmad, Rafiuddin, 243n8
Akhil Bharatiya Bahishkrut Samaj Parishad (All-India Conference of the Excluded), 56
Ambadawe (Ambawade), 3, 154
Ambedkar: A Life, Tharoor, xi
Ambedkar/Bhimrao Ramji / Ambedkar Bhivram Ramji 8–10, 16–18, 21, 73, 87, 92, 97,115; accident of, 177–180; as 'Babasaheb,' 146; Barrister-at-Law, 38, 75, 79, 87, 91, 95; biographers, 91, 97, 110, (*see also under separate entries*); birth of, 1–2, 4; career of, xv, (*see also* legal career/practice); and celebration on accomplishments of, 7; CV for University of Bonn, 75; on death of his children, 116; drinking water from Chavdar tank, 129, (*see also* Chavdar tank); on false Mahatma (Gandhi), xx; first editorial of, 58, 60, 65, 70, 107, 132; and Frances, 77, 108; and high court judgeship, 237n1; as 'Indian in question,' 35; journalism of, 58; as law minister, resignation of, 92, 241n15; legal work as activism, 100; letters between Shahu Maharaj and, 234n7; letter to Savarkar, xv, 221n13; letter to Seligman, 69; letter to Shahu Maharaja, 68, 79; Lumley on, 240n14; monetary policy and, 106; murder attempts

on, 160–161, 165; as Parwari, 11; on Phule, xx; planting saplings, 224n9; Savita on, xii; and Rai, 21; reading habit of, 7, 22; Seligman on, 19; two PhDs by, 97; worked/labouring as, 5, 8, 50; as young Bhima (Bhiva/Raja), ix, 1–9, 7, 19, 22–23, 29, 34, 70, 113

Ambedkar, K.K., teacher of Babasaheb, 3, 223-224n6

Ambedkar House/Museum in London, ix, xix, 77

Amravati, 143–144, 146; temple-entry campaign, 143–144

'Ancient Indian Commerce,' thesis by Ambedkar, 26–27, 99

annihilation of caste, 30, 110, 155–156

'Annihilation of Caste,' Ambedkar, 30

Anstey, Percy, 36, 51–52

Anti-Chaturvarnya Samata Sangh, 176

Asnodkar, 72

Attlee, Clement, 172–174

backward classes, 67, 122, 145

Bahishkrut Bharat - fortnightly, 58, 66, 131–132, 134, 137, 144, 147, 149, 151, 166, 173–175; as editor of, 66, 132, 175; first editorials, 134; 'The Religious Battle of Mahad and the Responsibility of the British Government,' 134, 137–138; 'The Religious Battle of Mahad and the Responsibility of Savarna Hindus' in, 134–135; 'The Religious Battle of Mahad and the Responsibility of the Untouchables' in, 134, 140

Bahishkrut Hitakarini Sabha (BHS), 107–111, 125, 132, 147–149, 170–172, 174–175

Baloo, Palwankar, 53

baluta system, 144, 167

Baroda Legislative Council, 14

Baroda State, xiii, 9–11, 13–14, 33–34, 41, 43, 46–49, 53, 75, 103; Accountant General's office, 43; administrative service, 10–11; agreement with, 10, 14–15, 43; harassment by bureaucrats, 52; obligation to, 49; Parsee inn incident, 43–47, 49; scholarship from, 9, 13–14, 32, 38, 43, 177, (*see also* Shahu Maharajah); tragedy in, 47

Batliboi, Jamshed R., 96–98, 132, 166

Batliboi's Accountancy Training Institute (BATI), 97; lecturer at, 96

Bhagawad Gita, 151

Bhakti movement, 164

Bhathena, Nowrosji M. (Naval), 16, 50, 66, 76, 96, 235n9

Bhatkar, Pandhurang, 60

Bhima Koregaon/ battle of Koregaon, 117–119, 121, 123, 127, 142; commemoration-related protests, 126; *vijay stambha*, 117–118

Bhosale, Shahu Chhatrapati Maharaj. *See* Shahu Maharaj

Bhuleshwar satyagraha, 165

biographers, xi, xix, 35, 39, 72, 84, 146, 160, 233n4; factual errors by, xix

biographies, x–xi, xiii, xv, xvii, xix–xx; Ambedkar on, xx; of Ambedkar, xii–xiii, (*see also* hagiography) misinformation/inaccurate claims, xiv, xvii, xix, 220n6

Birla, G.D., 104

Boas, Franz, 29–30

Bole, S.K., 7, 113–114, 175; resolution, 113–114, 121, 123, 128, 130, 144;

sitting on lap of Ambedkar, 114, 241n15
Bombay Improvement Trust (BIT), 8; Chawl, 125, 225n15
Bombay Depressed Classes and Aboriginal Tribes Committee (Starte Committee), 177
Bombay Hereditary Offices Act, 1874, 167–168
Bombay High Court, 97, 123, 166; and judgeship at, 92
Bombay Law Journal, editorial committee of, 91
Bombay Legislative Council (BLC), 2, 7–8, 113–115, 119, 121–122, 126–128, 132, 144, 150, 167, 170–171, 177; at budget of, 166–167; introducing 'Bill No. XII of 1928, 167–168; resolution of depressed classes, 144
Bombay Textile Labour Union, 172–173
Bombay University Act Amendment Bill, 144–145
Bombay University, 9, 50, 98–99, 144; course recommendation to, 227n5; as examiner at, 98
Bombay, 5–6, 10–12, 15–16, 23–24, 36–37, 39, 41–51, 53–55, 65–66, 69–71, 74–76, 87–92, 95, 107–109, 119, 124–126, 128–129, 143–144, 146–147, 164–165; as business address, 71; Dabak Chawl, Lower Parel, 6; libraries in, 23
Bonn University, 75–76, 84
books, 9, 36, 38, 41, 74–75, 77, 87–89, 99, 101–102, 104, 126, 128, 163, (*see also* libraries); collecting, 23,
39, 97–98, 164; as company, 44; of Marx, 26; obsession with, 6
Bradley, F.H., 17
Brahmanism, 95, 135, 137
Brahmans, 149, 237n8
bravery, 4, 142
British Army, 118; Mahars and, 127
British East India Company, and Peshwas, 118
British imperialism, 27–28
British Museum, 34, 72–73
British Resident at Baroda, identity of, 34
Brutus's words in Julius Caesar, 7
bubonic plague epidemic, 8
Buddhism, 26, 111; conversion to, 163; Kosambi's book on, 143
Buddhism: A Study of the Buddhist Norm, Davids, 26
Bureau of Information for Indian Students, London, 35

Camden, 77
Cannan, Edwin, 33–34, 36, 40, 51, 78, 84, 86–87, 102: on Ambedkar, 51–52; as MSc thesis supervisor, 74; as supervisor, 82
Cannan, Edward, 51
casteism, 5–6, 10, 64, 123, 174
castes, 17, 21–22, 30, 61, 64, 91–92, 96, 118, 155–156, 170, 172, 174, 176; Ambedkar on, 30; Brahmans, 62–63, 67, 93, 109, 113, 123, 149, 151, 156, 163, 165, 174, 176; Chambhars, 53, 108, 129, 159–160, 165, 176; Hindus, 5, 55, 62, 64, 112, 124, 132–134, 148, 166, 177–178; inter-relationship, 61; order of, 61; outcastes, 63, 65, 107, (*see also*

untouchables); upper, 62, 64, 110, 123, 135, 137
"Castes in India", Ambedkar, 30, 54, 127
Chandraseniya Kayastha Prabhu (CKP), 124
chaturvarnya/chaturvarna system (caste system), xvi, 156, 221n13 see also casteism; castes
Chavdar Tale Satyagraha, Mahad, 122
Chavdar tank, 122–123, 128–130, 137–138, 147, 150–152, 155, 157–159, 180; court injunction, 157; purification of, 130, 136–137, 147; suit against fetching water from, 152
Chiplunkar, Vishnushastri, Javalkar on, 94–95
Chitre, Bhai Anant Vinayak, 124, 126, 128, 154
Chokhamela: dedicating book to, 163; temple to, 164
Christianity, 46, 135–136
Clarke, Baron George Sydenham, 39
Columbia Alumni News, 16
Columbia University, xv, xx, 16, 18, 25–26, 29, 31–34, 36–39, 42, 49–50, 69, 71, 80–82, 98–99, 101–103, 115; bestowing PhD, 146; enrolling at, 15; library of, 22–23
communal representation, 54, 145
communists, 172–173
conferences, 56–57, 111–113, 123–127, 144, 148, 150, 154–160
consciousness, 24, 114, 142
conversion, 46, 112, 135, 140–141; to Buddhism, 163
Cosmopolitan Club, 15–16
Crawford Lake Satyagraha, 125

Dalits: consciousness, 58; movement, 113, 174
Dalvi, Dattoba, 55, 79, 166
Davids, Rhys (Mrs), 26
De, Rohit, 93, 95
Declaration of Rights, 170
deification, 162, 177
Democracy and Education, Dewey, 39
depressed classes, 54–55, 57, 108–109, 112, 114, 120–122, 135, 144–145, 148, 169–170, 172–173; conference in Ratnagari, 174; hostels and institutions, 109; meet in Trimbak, 164; rights, 54; self-representation of, 57, 109
'Depressed Classes, The,' 13
Depressed Classes Education Society (DCES), 170–171, 174
Deshache Dushman (Enemies of the Country), Javalkar, 93–94
Dewey, John, 16–17, 25–26, 29–30, 39, 50, 55
Dickinson, Goldsworthy Lowes, 37
direct action, 114, 122, 125, 131, 140, 142, 165
discriminations, 5–6, 124, 172
dissertation, 29, 32, 37–39, 80, 82–83, 87, 89, 102; "Ancient Indian Commerce", 228n11; for Columbia PhD, 71, 75; for Columbia University "The National Dividend", 42; DSc, 97; on financial history of India, 33; on imperial finance in India, 32; lost at sea, 30, 32, 42, 49, 75, 81–82, 86–87, 102; 'The National Dividend of India,' for PhD, 29; 'The Problem of the Rupee,' 82–83, 87–88, 97, 102–104, 239n20; resubmission of,

86–87, 97; on the stabilization of the Indian exchange, 82
Dnyaneshwar, 164
Dover-Calais crossing, 41
Dr Ambedkar Diamond Jubilee Celebration Committee, 2
Dr Ambedkar Seva Dal, 148, 153
Dr. Babasaheb Ambedkar Life & Mission, Keer, xiii
Dr Babasaheb Ambedkar Museum and Memorial, Pune, xix, 228-229n1
Dr Babasaheb Ambedkar Writings and Speeches (BAWS), xix
Dr Bhimrao Ramji Ambedkar Charitra, Khairmoday, xii
drinking water, forbidden of, 6
DuBois, W.E.B., 24
Duleepsinhji, 90

education, 121; Bar-at-Law degree, 103; commercialization of, 121–122; courses attended, 17–21, 25, 29, 33, 37–38, 73, 75, 96–97; of decline to list MSc, 115; girls and women, 24, 127, 160; MSc thesis, 'Provincial Decentralization of Imperial Finance in British India,' 71, 75, 82, 101–103; qualification, BA, MA, MSc, DSc and PhD, Bar-at-Law, xv, 9, 32, 36–37, 42, 71, 73, 83, 87, 92, 96–97, 102–103, 115, 222n17, 238n17; MSc thesis, 101–103; report to constitution commission, 170
Elkind, Landon, 39
Elphinstone High School, 6
England, arrival in, 15, 19, 29, 33–34, 66–67, 78, 81, 133; landlady in Hammersmith, 71–72, 76

Essay on the Civilisations of India, China and Japan, An, Dickinson, 38
Evolution of Provincial Finance in British India, The, Ambedkar, 20, 71, 99, 101–102, 134

family; Anandrao (elder brother), 3, 5–7, 49; Anand Teltumbde (grandson-in-law), 126, 247n220; as army men, 4; Balaram (eldest brother), 3, 5, 43, 123, 126, 146; Bhimabai Murbadkar (mother), 2,5; brothers, 1, 3–4, 8; father, 1, 4, 9–12, 24, 48, 88, 127, 164, (*see also* Sakpal, Ramji Maloji); Ganga (sister), 3; Gangadhar (son), 68, 79; Indu (daughter), 66; Jijabai (stepmother), 5, 48–49; Laxmibai (sister-in-law), 49, 175; Manjula (sister), 3, 5, 7; Meerabai (paternal aunt), 5; Mukund (nephew), 49, 68, 79; parents, 88, 102; Rajratna (son), 175, 241n18; Ramabai (elder sister), 3, 9, 11, 49, 52; Ramabai/Ramu (wife and earlier as Ramibhai), 8, 43, 49, 66, 68, 79, 111, 116, 131, 146, 175, 225-226n16; Ramesh (son), 11; Savita/ Sharada Kabir, (second wife), 16, 93, 96, (*see also under separate entry*); siblings of, 223n4; sisters, 1, 3–5, 11; Tulsa (sister), 3, 5, 7, 175, 247–248n22; Yashwant (son), 5, 9, 49, 68, 79
Federal Court of India in Delhi, 90
first editorials, 58, 60, 65, 70, 107, 132
Fitzgerald, Frances 'Fanny' (Frances Proust), 41, 108, 112, 155; letter to Ambedkar, 77–78; William Gould on, 235n10

Index

Foxwell, Herbert Somerton, 69, 73; personal library of, 74; to Seligman, 74
Franchise Committee, *see* Southborough Committee
French Revolution, 155
fundraising, 150–151

Gadgil, N.V., 165
Gadkari, Ram Ganesh, 75
Gaikwad, Maharajah Sayajirao, 12–13, 24, 52–53, 103
Gaikwad, Sambhaji, 125
Gandharpale Buddhist caves, 160
Gandhi, Mahatma, 77, 112–113, 129, 137, 151; harijanization, 111
Ganveer, Ratnakar, 59
Gasztowicz KC, Steven, on definition of 'keeping terms,' 232n1
gender consciousness, 24
Gholap, Dnyandeo D., 60, 66, 80
Girni Kamgar Union, 172–173
Goldenweiser, Alexander, 29
Gopal, Ashok, 222n18
Government Law College, Bombay, law professor at, 95, 166
Gray's Inn, 38, 40, 42, 50, 71, 75, 89; Order Books of, 83
Gulamgiri (or 'Slavery'), Phule, 24

hagiography, xii, 219n4, problem of, xviii
Harlem Renaissance, 24
high-caste: elites, 136; Hindus, 136
High Court of Bombay, 89
Hind Swaraj, Gandhi, 60
Hindu Code Bill, 6; Savita on, 224-225n12
Hinduism, 64, 111–112, 136–137, 141, 156, 163–164

Hindu-Muslim unity, 112
Hindus, 44, 46–47, 61–62, 127, 136, 140–141, 143–144, 156, 163–164, 166, 172; practice of violent inequality, 135
Hindutva, 144
Hobhouse, Leonard, 38
hostels, 144; winning government grant for, 171
human rights, 138, 156
humiliation, 4, 6, 48–49, *see also* discriminations

Independent Labour Party, political party, 148
Indian Antiquary, The, Ambedkar, 30
Indian Currency and Finance, Keynes, 20
Indian Gymkhana, 89–90
Indian Home Rule League of America, 21
Indian National Congress (INC), 169
India Office in London, xix
Indian Statutory Commission, 169
injustices, 28, 64, 70, 132–133, 139, 141, 178
inter-caste: alliances, 174; dinner, 176; D.V. Naikand, 175; marriages, 155–156, 174–175
In the Tiger's Shadow, Nimgade, 224n9
Irwin, Lord, 109
Islam, 27, 135–136, 141

Jacobi, H., 75–76, 85
Jadhav, M.K., 121, deputy collectorship and, 242-243n7
Jadhav, N.T., 108
Jaffrelot, Christophe, xi, xix, 110; Eurocentric framework on Ambedkar, 111
Jallianwala Bagh massacre, 60

Index

Janata newspaper, 47; Devrao Naik as editor of, 175
Javalkar, Dinkarrao, 94–95, 149–150, 157
Jedhe, K.M., 94, 149–150, 157, 165: acquittal of, 95
Jeram, Shivlal, 14
Joshi, Narayan Malhar, 53, 234n3
Joshi, R.M., 51
Judicial Committee of the Privy Council (JCPC) 90

Kabir, 4, 59, 93, 162, 164
Kadam, G.B., 124
Keer, Dhananjay, biographer xiii–xvii, xix, 72, 84–85, 91: Ambedkar on, xvii; anti-Muslim bias of, xvii; misinformation in biography by, xv–xviii; Rattu on, xvii
Keluskar, Krishnaji Arjun (Dada Keluskar), 7, 9, 26, 47, 100
Kesari, newspaper, 94
Keynes, John Maynard, 20, 74, 86–87
Khadange, N.V., 176
Khairmoday ((Khairmode), C.B., biographer, xii–xv, xviii–xix, 72, 77, 84, 125, 146, 160, 220n5; death of, xviii
Khairmoday, Dwarkabai, xviii
Kher, B.G., 91, 109
Kosambi, Dharmanand, 143

Laski, Harold J., 84–85
Lee, Mabel Ping-Hua, 25
legal career/practice, 89, 91, 93, 85, 97, 111; appealing for brothel owner, 95
liberty, 12, 16, 147
libraries, 23, 26, 45, 74, 82, 99, 109–110, 125; Ambedkar on, 238n15; in London, 34, 75; Goldsmiths' Library, 73–74; India Office, 33; Kress Library of Business and Economics at Harvard University, 74; Nehru Memorial Museum and, xx, 233; New York Public Library, 23; Senate House Library in London, xx
Life of the Buddha, Keluskar, 7
Little and Company, 94
London, 19–20, 32–40, 70; Baroda state scholarship for study in 13; bookshops, 75; returning to India from 116;
London Chamber of Commerce, 96
London School of Economics and Political Science (LSE), xiv–xv, xx, 33, 70; enrolled in, 36
Lumley, Roger Sir, 240n14

Mackinder, Halford, 37
Mahad: agitation, 123, 131, 135, 149; litigation, 166
Mahad Conference, 117, 121–122, 124–125, 127, 129, 134, 140, 148–149
Mahad satyagraha, 95, 122, 150–152, 154, 157, 160, 162, 166, 174–175; female delegates, 160
Maharajah of Baroda, 122–126, 129–131, 134–135, 137, 139–141, 147–148, 150–155, 159–160, 162, 164, 173, 180, *see also* Shahu, Maharajah
Mahars, 11, 53, 94, 117–118, 123, 126–127, 160, 168, 179–180; army and, 127; assaults on, 243n13; atrocity against, 242n4; hockey club, 110; movement, 55; soldiers, 142
Mahar Samaj Seva Sangh, Bombay, 175

Mahratta, newspaper, 94
Mair, Jessy, xiv, 73; Beatrice Webb on, 234n5
Malik, H.S., 90
Mangaon Conference, 56–57
Manusmriti, burning of, 113, 149, 156–157, 160, 174
Manuvaadi faculty, 6
Marathas, 27, 54, 56, 109, 176
Marathi, 57–60, 68, 72, 75, 88, 93, 125, 157
Marx, 26
Marxist, 25, 30
mass agitation, 112, 135, *see also* Mahad agitation
maternity benefits bill, 168
McCulloch, J.R., 75
'Meaning of Woman Suffrage, The,' Lee, 25
Mehta, Chunilal, Sir, 120, 166
Mehta, Pherozeshah, death of, 23–24
Mhow, 4, 224n7
monetary policy, 82, 104
'moneylenders' act, 177
Mookerjee, Rajendra Nath, Sir, 103
Mooknayak (Leader of the Voiceless), Marathi newspaper, 57, 60, 66, 68, 70, 76, 80, 86, 107, 123, 132–133; first editorial in, 70; subscription of, 65
More, R.B., 123, 125–126, 148, 154
Muller, Wm., 74
Mumba Devi temple, Bombay, 165
Munshi, K.M., 144–145
Muslim League, 169

Nagpur Conference, 56–57
Naidu, Sarojini, 35

Naik, Devrao Vishnu, 175–176; bestowing sacred thread upon untouchables, 174
National Indian Association (NIA), ix, 35–36; and spying, 230n11
nationalism, 27
National Negro Committee (later NAACP, National Association for Advancement of Coloured People), 24
Nehru, Jawaharlal on Laski, 85
Nehru Committee Report, 169–170
newspapers, 35, 64–66, 94, 107, 131–133, 143, 165, 176
New York, x, xiii, xix, 13, 19, 21–24, 26, 31–32, 34–35, 38, 70, 74–75, 101–102
Nicholson, Joseph Shield, 74
Nimgade, Namdeo, 224n9
Nizam of Hyderabad, 89, 93
non-Brahmans, 63, 67, 149; movement, 56, 94, 149
Non-Cooperation Movement, 60
non-violence, 129, 151
Northbrook Indian Society, ix

Omvedt, Gail, xi, xix
orthodox Hindus, 151, 174; and allies, 151; attacking satyagrahis, 165; filing suit against taking water from Chavdar lake, 152

Panthers, xx
Padhye, Prabhakar, 72, 92, 100
Paranjpye, R.P., 100, 109
Parsees/ Parsis, 44–47, 61, 109
A Part Apart: The Life and Thought of Babasaheb Ambedkar, Gopal 222n18
Parvati temple satyagraha, Pune, 165

Parwari, Mahars in military as, 11
Patil, Appasaheb, 56
Pawar, Dattoba, letter to, 116
Pease, Alfred, Sir., 67
Pendharkar, Baburao, charity play of, 151
Peshwa rule, 118
Phule, Jyotirao, Mahatma, 88, 94
Prabuddha Bharat, weekly, 58
priestly profession, 156
Principles of Social Reconstruction, Russell, 39; review to, 50
Proust, Gaston Albert, 77
Provincial Depressed Classes Conference, Barshi, 108
public appearance, 53
Purandare, Vaibhav, xvi–xvii
purification, 130, 136–137, 143, 147, 152

Rai, Lala Lajpat, 21, 169
Raigad fort, 160–161
Rajbhoj, P.N., 129, 160, 165
Ramasamy, E.V (Periyar), 169
Ramsay, T.B.W., 89–90
Rattu, Nanak Chand, 220n7, xvii; on wedding day of Ambedkar, 221-222n2
Reform Acts in 1919, 133; 1930, 133
Rege, Sharmila 220n7
religion, 4, 44, 63, 135, 163; divisions based on, 61
'Repayment of debts,' 53
'Report on the Constitution of the Government of Bombay Presidency, A.,' 171–172
Republic of Caste, Anand Teltumbde, 247n220
resistance, 56, 141–142
resolution, 65, 108, 114, 144, 148, 156, 158, 177
Revolution and Counter-Revolution in Ancient India (unfinished book of Ambedkar), 240n10
Riddles in Hinduism, Ambedkar, 135
Robinson, James Harvey, 16–18
Rockefeller Jr, 15
Round Table Conference in London, 3, 53, 162, 173, 181
Royal Commission on Indian Currency and Finance, 'Statement of Evidence' to, 103, 239n20
Royce, Josiah, 17
Russell, Bertrand, 55

sacred texts, for attack on, 113, *see also Manusmriti*, burning of
Sahasrabudhe, Bapusaheb (Gangadhar Nilkanth), 125, 128, 154, 157
Sakpal/Sankpal, Ramji Maloji (Ambadawekar) father, 3, 5, 7–10, death of, 11; education of, 4; moving to Bombay, 6; positions of, 4
Samata: fortnightly (later as *Janata*), 58, 66, 175–176, *see also Janata* newspaper
Samata Sainik Dal (SSD/Equality Army), 148, 153, 159, 163, 245n9
Sandesh, weekly, 94
Saravanamuttu, Manicasothy, 90
Satara, 4–5, 16
satyagraha, 110, 112, 147, 153, 157, 159, 165–166; committee, 150, 153, 158, 165; conference, 122, 154; at Mahad, 122, 150; temple-entry, 164
Satyashodhak Samaj, 149–150

Savarkar, V.D., xv–xviii; Ambedkar on, xvi; biography by Keer, xv; Naik on, 248n23; Purandare on biography on, xvi
Savarna Hindus, 129, 134–137, 139, 151, 153, 158, 165, 174
Savita Ambedkar (or Sharada Kabir as second wife *see also under* family), xx, on Ambedkar and Keer 221n14; autobiography of, xii, 219n1; on Hindu Code Bill, 224-225n12, *see also* Hindu Code Bill
Scheduled Castes Federation, 2
scholarship/stipend, 9, 14, 32, 38, 43, 177, 228-229n1; (*see also* Baroda State); Dada Keluskar and, 9; itemized list of expenses, 14; to study at Columbia University, 13
school, 3, 7, 16, 24, 63, 124, 144, 160, 164, 177, (*see also* education); separate seatings in, 5–6
Schopenhauer, 17
'science of finance,' 20, 29, 102
Seager, Henry Rogers, 33: on Ambedkar to Cannan, 33
self-help, 57, 108, 111
Seligman, E., 16–17, 19–21, 25, 28–29, 32–33, 69, 71, 73–74, 81, 102; on Ambedkar to Webb, 33; as Columbia supervisor, 102; letter to, 81–82
Setalvad, Chimanlal Harilal, Sir, 109
Seva Dal, 160
Shahu Maharajah, 49, 55–57, 67, 79, 94; Akkatai as daughter of 56; to Ambedkar, 57; on Brahmans, 67; death of, 83; letter to, 83, 94; to Pease, 67; on Tilak, 94

Shastras, 62, *see also Manusmriti*; sacred texts
Shastri, Shankaranand, 165
Shaw, George Bernard, 110
Shivtarkar, Sitaram Namdeo, 53, 74–75, 79, 108, 126, 128, 143, 148, 150, 153–154, 160
Shourie, Arun, xii
Shotwell, James, 16–19
Shridharpant. *See* Tilak, Shridhar Balwant (Shridharpant)
Shudra varna, book on genealogy of, 56
Siddharth College, Mumbai University, xiii, xx, 96; Savita on, 96
Simkhovitch, Mary Kingsbury, 25
Simkhovitch, Vladimir, 25; courses of, 30
Simon, John, 169
Simon Commission, 167, 169, 171–172, 177; statements by Ambedkar to, 169–171
Small Holders' Relief Bill, 168–169
'Small Holdings in India and Their Remedies,' Ambedkar, 50–51
Smith, Adam, 20
social: activism, 100, 177; battle, 167; boycott, 56, 178; reform, 25, 108, 144; service, 92, 131, 133; work, 89, 100, 125, 132, 146, 162–163, 174
Social Equality League (Samaj Samata Sangh/SSS), 149, 174–176, 247n21, 248n23; formation of, 246n3
Social Service League (SSL), 108, 124–125, 131, 149, 165
Solanki, P.G., 120, 172, 175, 177
Southborough, Lord, 54
Southborough Committee, 54–55, 60
spirituality, 117, 163

Spratt, Philip, Ambedkar appealing for, 93
SS *Ancona* to New York City, 15
SS *Kaisar-i-Hind*, 41–42
SS *New York* to Liverpool, 34
SS *Salsette*, 41–42; sank with works and dissertation of Ambedkar, 42
SS *Sardinia*, to England, 15
State of Baroda. *See* Baroda State
'Statement concerning the state of education of the depressed classes in the Bombay Presidency,' 170
Statement of Evidence, 103–104
Stroud, Scott, 39
Students' Union, 84–86
studies/studying: in Germany, 76; in London, 19–20, 49; Sanskrit, 76; United States, 13, 15, 25, 32, 38, *see also* education
Sukha, Vithabai, 95
Sung, Shahir Rajendra Kamble, 117
Supreme Court of India, 90
Swaraj, 64
Sydenham College in Bombay, 36, 39, 49, 51–55, 66, 69, 75, 100

temple-entry campaign, 143–144; in Bombay, 165
temple purification, 143, *see also* Chavdar Tank; purification
Thakre, Keshav Sitaram, 176
Thakurdas, Purshottamdas Sir, 104–105
Thakurdwar temple visit, 143
Tharoor, Shashi, xi–xii, xix
thesis, 27–29, 40, 42, 51–52, 56, 71, 75, 78, 82, 84, 87, 98–99, 102–103; annual reports of EIC for, 74; as 'National Dividend,' 82; 'The Evolution of Provincial Finance in British India', 71; 'Provincial Decentralization of Imperial Finance in British India,' for MSc (Econ) 78; 'The Stabilization of the Indian Exchange,' 81, *see also* dissertation
Tilak, Bal Gangadhar 'Lokmanya,' 60, 95, 174; statue for, 94
Tilak, Shridhar Balwant (Shridharpant), 174; death by suicide, 176
Tipnis, Surbanana, 128, 130
Tolstoy, Leo xx
Tukaram, Sant, 57, 124, 164

United States, 13, 15, 25, 32, 38
University of London, 33, 75, 84–85, 102; administration, 78; awarding DSc to Ambedkar, 87
University Reforms Committee, 98–100
untouchability, 21, 44, 63–64, 137, 141–143, 150, 156, 163, 177; abolition of, 155–156; as blot on Hinduism, 137; demanding eradication of, 141, 150, 156, 174; Gandhi on, 112; stigma of, 63; unlawful custom of, 138
untouchables, 12, 42–43, 54–57, 62–65, 108, 110–113, 123, 125–130, 132–139, 141–144, 146–151, 157–158, 164–165, 167, 169–170, 172, 174–175, 177–178; army ban on recruitment of, 128; literacy among, 128; rioters on, 139

Vaikom, satyagraha at, 112
Vakil, Chandulal Nagindas, 50–51

varnashrama order, 156
Vedokta controversy, 232-233n7
violence, 50, 129, 135, 137, 143, 148, 151
voluntary cooperative farming, 247n11
voyage back to India, 40–41

Waiting for a Visa, Ambedkar, 5, 31, 43, 177, 224n10
War-time regulations, 34
Washington, Booker T., 24
watan system, 167–168

Web, Beatrice, 33
Webb, Sidney, 33, 69, 74, 234n5
'A Wise Girl,' play, 7
women, 23, 25, 62, 127, 160, 179; in Parvati temple satyagraha, 165
Works of David Ricardo, The, J.R. McCulloch, 75
Worshipping False Gods, Shourie, xii

Young, Edward Hilton, 103

Zelliot, Eleanor, xi, xix

About the Author

Aakash Singh Rathore is a philosopher of international repute and the author of nine books, including *Ambedkar's Preamble: A Secret History of the Constitution of India* (2020). He has also edited over a dozen books, including *B.R. Ambedkar: The Buddha and His Dhamma: A Critical Edition* (2011) and, more recently, *B.R. Ambedkar: The Quest for Justice* (a box set of five volumes, 2021). His *Hegel's India* was shortlisted for the Non-Fiction Book of the Year at the Tata Literature Live! Book Awards 2017.

Professor Rathore has taught politics, philosophy and law at Jawaharlal Nehru University, Delhi University, University of Pennsylvania and Rutgers University. He is international fellow at ETHOS, Rome, and was previously fellow at the Indian Institute of Advanced Study, Shimla.

Professor Rathore serves as the series editor for the fifteen-volume *Rethinking India* book series and was the co-editor (with Ashis Nandy) of its first volume, *Vision for a Nation*. Beyond the pen, Professor Rathore is a top-ranking triathlete and has completed six Ironman races on five continents. He tweets @ASR_Metta and is @aakash_ironman on Instagram.

30 Years *of*
HarperCollins *Publishers* India

At HarperCollins, we believe in telling the best stories and finding the widest possible readership for our books in every format possible. We started publishing 30 years ago; a great deal has changed since then, but what has remained constant is the passion with which our authors write their books, the love with which readers receive them, and the sheer joy and excitement that we as publishers feel in being a part of the publishing process.

Over the years, we've had the pleasure of publishing some of the finest writing from the subcontinent and around the world, and some of the biggest bestsellers in India's publishing history. Our books and authors have won a phenomenal range of awards, and we ourselves have been named Publisher of the Year the greatest number of times. But nothing has meant more to us than the fact that millions of people have read the books we published, and somewhere, a book of ours might have made a difference.

As we step into our fourth decade, we go back to that one word – a word which has been a driving force for us all these years.

Read.